**W9-AHZ-180**

It is not un_____an elec-
tion or a dec_____d other
fields. Does _____1formed
voters? Or _____hoice of
the decision_____Arrow's
famed theor_____1 proce-
dure is witl_____tya Sen
dashes hope_____ompati-
bility with s

  This high_____ profes-
sionals a ne_____Arrow's
and Sen's t_____ws that
these negat:_____some of
their assum_____e this is
understood,_____d, but a
wide class o_____'hese include inter _____nomics,
statistical p_____xes.

Donald G. _____ics and
Mathematic_____ served
as a full pr_____rsity in
several dep_____ Arthur
and Gladys_____1as held
visiting pos_____zerland,
Spain, and _____ve other
books, including *Basic Geometry of Voting* (1995), and he is the
author of more than 140 publications in leading academic journals. He is currently chief editor of the *Bulletin of the American
Mathematical Society* and associate editor of *Economic Theory,
Social Choice and Welfare, Qualitative Theory of Dynamical Systems*, and *Positivity*. Professor Saari has received a Guggenheim
Fellowship, three honorary doctorates, the Lester R. Ford and
Duncan Black awards, and the Chauvenet Prize.

# DECISIONS AND ELECTIONS
## Explaining the Unexpected

Donald G. Saari
*University of California, Irvine*

CAMBRIDGE
UNIVERSITY PRESS

For **Anneli** and **Katri**
Two absolutely delightful daughters who have made our lives
rich, full, and pleasurable.

PUBLISHED BY THE PRESS SYNDICATE OF THE UNIVERSITY OF CAMBRIDGE
The Pitt Building, Trumpington Street, Cambridge, United Kingdom

CAMBRIDGE UNIVERSITY PRESS
The Edinburgh Building, Cambridge CB2 2RU, UK
40 West 20th Street, New York, NY 10011-4211, USA
10 Stamford Road, Oakleigh, VIC 3166, Australia
Ruiz de Alarcón 13, 28014 Madrid, Spain
Dock House, The Waterfront, Cape Town 8001, South Africa

http://www.cambridge.org

First published 2001

Printed in the United States of America

*Typeface* Computer Modern 9.35/12 pt.    *System* LaTeX  [TB]

*A catalog record for this book is available from the British Library.*

*Library of Congress Cataloging in Publication data*
Saari, D. (Donald)
    Decisions and elections : explaining the unexpected / Donald G. Saari.
        p.   cm.
    Includes bibliographical references and index.
    ISBN 0-521-80816-2 – ISBN 0-521-00404-7 (pc.)
    1. Social choice.   2. Decision making.   3. Elections.    4. Arrow, Kenneth
Joseph, 1921–   5. Sen, Amartya Kumar.   I. Title.
    HB846.8 .S25   2001
    658.4′03 – dc21                                         2001035588

ISBN 0 521 80816 2 hardback
ISBN 0 521 00404 7 paperback

# Preface

I know that you messed up on some decisions. I sure have.

This book is about decisions and elections. It is about decisions in the family, in economics, in engineering, in politics, and in every day life. Decisions are necessary, but even with the best of intentions the outcomes can go astray; they can be dreadfully wrong. Even worse, surprisingly often these "bad outcomes" occur for reasons so subtle that most of us may never realize that a mistake has been made. This can hurt. Realistically, if we fail to recognize that unanticipated, undesired outcomes can occur, we run the risk of inadvertently choosing badly.

In this book, by explaining what can go wrong and why, I describe central difficulties which can infect our decision processes. Examples and new explanations are used to introduce basic results and recent conclusions. The topics are purposely chosen to encourage the reader to further explore why it is so easy for "bad" outcomes to occur in politics, economics, law, engineering, and just about anywhere decisions are made.

This issue of trying to understand what can go right or wrong with decisions is not new; it has been a central concern for centuries if not millennia. Yet, this important topic was not embraced by academics until 1770 when the French mathematician Jean Charles de Borda introduced the issue to the French Academy of Science. Borda did so in a particularly pragmatic and personal manner. He constructed an example to prove to the Academy that their election procedure could cause them to make serious mistakes when selecting new members. Then, in 1785, the French mathematician, philosopher, and politician Marie-Jean-Antoine-Nicolas de Caritat Condorcet provided energy to the study of voting and decisions by criticizing Borda's proposed approach and introducing his own competing method.

Over the last two centuries, this topic has been alternately carefully studied, discussed, debated — and then totally ignored. What ushered in the current interest, a level so intense and extensive that the last half century must be considered the true "Golden Age of Choice Theory," is Kenneth

Arrow's 1951 Ph.D. thesis which identified certain unexpected difficulties which are, according to standard thought, inherent to decision making. His result, which is extensively discussed here, asserts that certain obstacles and complexities haunt any topic involving decisions. Consequently, Arrow's result speaks to, and is relevant for, almost all aspects of daily life. Yet, outside of certain academic disciplines his result is not well known. What a mistake.

Indeed, in spite of the importance of decisions in our daily lives and with all of this research activity, most people have no idea about the perils and difficulties that can plague even common decision procedures. Adding to the problem is that even among those who recognize that something strange can occur, most have no appreciation why or where this might happen and how bad it can be.

How did we get into this sorry state? I expect it is because the deliberation and analysis of decision procedures have remained within the private domain of the "initiated." While deplorable, this status reflects the heavily technical nature of the research in this area. Most results depend upon mathematical equations and logical notation so dense that it will kill the interest of all but the most dedicated. The description and analysis necessary to make advances impose discouraging entry requirements of advanced mathematics. I must confess; I am as guilty as others in writing papers that challenge the patience of even the experts.

But, the central ideas of this area are accessible; they can even be discussed with a flair at a cocktail party. Moreover, the importance of these issues mandates that a better understanding of decision theory must be made available to a wider number of people. This book is my attempt to do so. While I lack the expository skills to make it serious "airplane reading," I hope to at least make certain intriguing developments accessible to a much larger number of readers.

This book is not a survey; several fascinating developments from the last couple of decades are ignored. Instead, and more ambitiously, I emphasize "what can go wrong, and why" without using the traditional deep mathematical analysis and equations. Consequently, most of the book is accessible for almost anyone with an interest in this topic; the formal requirements primarily involve patience and simple addition. All of the technical material is relegated to the final portion of the concluding chapter; this section is included to satisfy the curiosity of the mathematically sophisticated reader who will, correctly, demand more formal support for certain assertions.

I am delighted to acknowledge comments and help because, quite frankly, I would not have attempted this project without encouragement from others.

Probably the first to suggest the need for a book explaining the difficulties and concepts of decision theory, but relatively free from the mathematical obstacles which frustrate the non-expert, was Arthur Pancoe. Art is one of those rare, delightful individuals with an intellectual curiosity in everything. His interests, accompanied with forceful, effective actions which have made a difference, range from ecology, national defense, dangers of nuclear energy, and health, as well as being formally recognized as one of the best on the stock market,[1] to his side interests in celestial mechanics (the mathematics of the dynamics of astronomy), game theory, decision theory, and, most surely, sports. Let me warn you; expect to lose if he challenges you on a ski slope.

Recognition and thanks always must be directed toward Maurice Salles, who, at the Université de Caen, has created an internationally recognized center of decision and voting analysis. Innumerable discussions with Maurice, and with other members of his Center such as Anne Brunel, Vincent Merlin, and Fabrice Valognes, have sharpened my understanding of this field and made me aware of new topics and issues. My frequent visits to Salles's Center always prove to be an intellectual delight where I know that new ideas will be found — and the French wine and excellent food of the Normandy region never are neglected.

To the best of my knowledge, George Hazelrigg is one of the first to recognize that many of the decision issues described here, and Arrow's Theorem in particular, play an important role in engineering and design. George's enthusiasm about the importance of these issues is highly contagious. Indeed, my newly found interests in these directions are completely due to him.

The book owes much to the *Institutet for Framtidsstudier* in Stockholm, Sweden. I thank the institute for providing partial support for the research and writing. In particular, I thank Å. Andersson, the former director who encouraged me to write this book as part of an Institute research theme. Åke is another person with eclectic interests. The many topics in which he has made contributions and the surprisingly wide spectrum of issues which he can discuss with sufficient authority to challenge the best of any expert are matched only by his overflowing enthusiasm to promote creative and effective research. After Åke retired (from the Institute, but never from research), I. Sommestad, the new director, kindly continued the Institute support of this project. Additional research support came from my NSF Grant DMI-9971794 and from my Arthur and Gladys Pancoe Chair of Mathematics

---

[1]Indeed, one professional newsletter had a comment to the effect "Take two Pancoe stocks in the evening and wake up rich in the morning."

which I held while I was on the faculty of the Mathematics Department at Northwestern University.

Technical help came from Miguel Lerma, the computer guru in the Northwestern Mathematics Department, and Louis Narens at my new home at the University of California in Irvine. Teka Swayne, my work-study student at Northwestern, did some library research and typing. My deep thanks to Steve Barney, Don Campbell, Duncan Luce, Louis Narens, Hannu Nurmi, Art Pancoe, Kim Romney, Maurice Salles, Katri Sieberg, John Stackpole, and anonymous referees who offered useful suggestions about ways to improve an earlier draft. My thanks to Scott Parris, the Cambridge University Press editor, who helped get this manuscript in a final form.

As always, my deepest thanks, love, and gratitude goes to my wife, Lillian. Not only has she always put up with the many hours that have been devoted toward my several research and writing projects — this is true even while we supposedly were on vacations! — but she and I have extensively discussed, even debated, these and other issues starting already when we first met as graduate students many years ago. What is impressive about our discussions is that her incisive comments are made about topics that are far removed from her areas of professional interest!

Irvine, California
December, 2000

# Contents

# Chapter 1

# Do We Get What We Expect?

## 1.1 Decisions

At some time today you will make a decision. But, will it be the correct one?

Let me illustrate with an hypothetical example where your book club unanimously decided to drop you from membership because you violated their trust. All of this shame and controversy just because you like pepperoni pizza and have a sincere desire to help others.

To explain, the book club entrusted you to order pizza for their next meeting. Scrupulously checking with everyone, you compiled the following list of their preferences. The first line shows, for instance, that you and two other members are pepperoni lovers. Based on the information

| Number | First Choice | Second Choice | Third Choice |
|:------:|:------------:|:-------------:|:------------:|
| 3 | Pepperoni | Sausage | Anchovy |
| 2 | Sausage | Pepperoni | Anchovy |
| 2 | Anchovy | Sausage | Pepperoni |

the choice is clear; with an election, pepperoni would win with three votes while sausage and anchovy would tie for second place with two votes each. Pepperoni was ordered.

While gagging on a piece of pepperoni and making tenuous comparisons between the writing styles of Hemingway and Joyce, Jack offered his opinion that he really would have preferred sausage. The reaction was immediate; a total of four club members, a majority, voiced their preference of sausage

1

over pepperoni. In response to Mavis's obvious follow-up question, a majority expressed their preference of sausage over anchovy. Since sausage is the club's majority choice, why did you order pepperoni? Such an outrageous abuse of trust!

## 1.1.1 Decisions

Decisions, whether for a group or an individual, play a standard but integral role in our daily lives. The reason is obvious; to avoid chaos, confusion, and, maybe, a good old fashion fist fight, decisions must be made on a continual basis within our social groups, families, organizations, and political and economic units. We vote to decide the kind of pizza to order, what to name a family's new pet dog, where to go for a summer vacation. Over morning coffee, my day starts by searching the sports pages for voting results which determine the weekly ranking of the collegiate basketball teams, or which collegiate football team is the national champ, or who is the MVP (most valuable player) in the Super Bowl football game, or which city will host the next Olympics, or who won a figure skating or gymnastics competition.

Individual and group decisions play a central role in our professional lives. After all, much of what we do involves deciding. We decide who should pass or fail a course, who should be hired — or fired, where money should be invested, who should receive the new contract, what should be the new product and how should it be designed. In a more subtle realm, group and individual economic decisions, based on who wants what, combine in mysterious ways to determine the economic laws of the marketplace.

## 1.1.2 Surf, Snow, or Governor Jesse Ventura?

Our voting procedures are among our most important decision methods. These tools of democracy not only determine that choice of pizza to order ("Let's have a show of hands"), but also the next chair of our social group, our mayors, our legislators, our presidents. In legislative bodies, voting procedures are used to decide among differing alternatives in the development of laws. But, as the book club's pizza altercation suggests, do we really select whom or what we want?

To explore this issue, suppose a marching band one hundred strong is planning a joint winter vacation. Forty of them, who have previously experienced the pleasures of cross-country skiing, want to ski through the frigid but silent hemlock and birch forests found along the beautiful shores of Lake Superior. The other sixty are tired, very tired, of snow and cold; they want to wear nothing more than a very brief swimsuit while swimming, wading, and sunbathing in the warm Caribbean surf. Where? Anywhere! When pushed for a preference, 35 opt for the Bahamas while the remaining 25 suggest Jamaica.

You can finish the story. Even though most of the band members want to enjoy warmth, their vote over the three vacation choices dictates that they better start searching for their long underwear and warm gloves in preparation for their winter trip to the Copper Country of Michigan. (Skiing in Michigan receives 40 votes, Bahama receives 35, and Jamaica receives 25.) Of course, after they arrive and start skiing, these vacationers might agree that Michigan is an excellent choice. But that is not the issue; the point is that the election outcome does not reflect their wishes on election day. While the band story illustrates an unjust outcome, what about actual elections?

While it is difficult to find precise figures, there are reasons to believe that a phenomenon similar to the "band vacation" occurred during the November 1998 election for the governor of the state of Minnesota. To set the stage, Minnesota is an American state which prides itself on good, solid experienced leadership. With its strong Nordic population, a culture where undue public expression tends to be discouraged, Minnesota is hardly known for revolutionary fervor. Entering election season, the candidate for the Democratic party, Hubert "Skip" Humphrey III, was the state's attorney general. Humphrey was expected to win easily thanks to his considerable public support and praise resulting from his sizeable $6 billon victory over the tobacco companies. His Republican opponent, Norm Coleman, was a Humphrey protege. Although an underdog, Coleman was expected to raise at least a reputable challenge based on his strong reputation for efficient public service. Finally, we had Jesse "The Body" Ventura, a 6 foot 4 inch ex-professional wrestler who previously earned his living wearing sequins and a feather boa. This showman, bit-part player in movies, radio shock-jock, and mayor of a small suburb was running on the Reform Party.

Without question, Ventura was a refreshing addition to the political scene. By comparing his charisma with his highly competent, experienced, but somewhat drab opponents, it is not surprising that he pulled thousands upon thousands of new voters to the polls. Press accounts proved that, even though he readily admitted to being a neophyte who didn't really understand all the issues or even the functioning of state government, Ventura's charm and "straight talk" started attracting votes away from Humphrey already in early September.

Let's examine this experience issue. Faced with a legal issue, would you prefer someone fresh out of law school, or an experienced lawyer? Similarly, faced with selecting a new leader to run a complicated state, would you prefer someone with limited experience in a suburb, or a proven person with considerable political experience? While 37% of the Minnesota voters clearly preferred the former, the evidence suggests that around 60% of the voters who voted preferred the warmth of experience in the governor's chair — either Coleman or Humphrey. As with the band illustration, Ventura won the election with 37% of the vote. In fact, the numbers used in the vacation example indicate what happened in Minnesota with percentages that roughly resemble the election outcome.

Immediately after he was elected, Ventura's popularity soared. Quickly it became easy to encounter a debate about whether he is an effective governor or an embarrassment. But, that is not the point. The issue is that on *Election Day* it is strongly arguable that Ventura was *not* the "true" choice of the voters. As with the skiing vacation, Ventura's election appears to manifest an anomaly of our voting procedure. Can elections lead to results which do not reflect the views of the voters? They most surely can.

### 1.1.3   Correct decisions

Making a "correct decision" is an important concern because decision procedures affect all aspects of our lives — from the more mundane concerns of a family, to the viability of the marketplace, to future economic development, and to the direction of our society. Decisions form such a vital part of our lives that, justifiably, considerable effort can and should be expended to ensure "correct decisions." This concern is particularly important for larger organizations, such as businesses or governmental bodies, because once made, strategic choices become exceedingly difficult to reverse.

As examples, imagine the complexities involved in relocating a factory, in introducing new forms of production, or in initiating a different governmental social policy. It is the enormous accompanying costs which tend to chisel strategic decisions into stone. Once made, even a mistake becomes difficult to reverse. Once made, decisions assume a life of their own where subsequent actions tend to modify the original. Faced with this reality, the initial choice must be the "correct" one.

### 1.1.4   Good information to confusion

About now, the reader might complain, "Of course. Nobody wants to screw up; everyone wants to make the right choice." I agree. But then, why is it that we can make very bad decisions?

Our desire to make "good decisions" is manifested by all those good intentions captured by the enormous effort often directed toward analyzing the relevant information. A family planning an annual vacation may spend hours upon hours reviewing maps, brochures, and travel books. A firm considering new product lines or a bank reviewing its investment policies may form research units and employ expensive consultants. A governmental body, with its continual charge to shape the future of a political unit, may consult with professional groups and research institutes for valued input.

This thirst for data is particularly apparent in engineering firms where experiments are conducted to discover information about this or that metal in the construction of an airplane wing, or the value of this computer chip over that one. In politics, this need for information — well, maybe more accurately, the need for an appropriate political "spin" — is continuously on display during an election campaign when political parties can spend obscene amounts of money to get "their message" out to the voters, or to counter an opponent's "lies and damn lies." In the marketplace, information coming from market projections, sale and inventory figures, demand and supply are common inputs into a firm's decision process. This activity reflects the obvious; good decisions require excellent, complete, and current information.

After all this expense, after all this effort to collect correct information, what can be the outcome? Confusion; maybe total confusion reflecting the curse of the multidimensional nature of the acquired information.

Again, we know this can happen. Each of us probably can cite numerous examples where each alternative is "the best choice" with different criteria. On election day, for instance, we might ponder, candidate

- Anni proposes an attractive, strong mental health plan,

- Katri has a great foreign policy,

- Lillian has tremendous ideas about economic growth, but

- Martha has an innovative approach toward our environmental and social concerns,

so who should I vote for?

This confusion is why we need methods to help us decide. After all, whenever the information clearly identifies a unique "best" choice, then, except when mandated by law as in public elections, there is no need for decision procedures. The true purpose of these methods is to help us choose when faced with the uncertainty that all too often can materialize even with complete, reliable information. The purpose of decision procedures, then, is to help sort the informational complexity and conflict. But, which procedure? Is one method better than the others?

To personalize this concern, suppose after you have been subjected to extensive medical tests, your doctor needs to determine the appropriate course of action. She believes that there is a 3/7 likelihood that everything is fine; the symptoms suggest that that tumor is benign, with the second option being that it is serious and an expensive dangerous operation is needed immediately, and the third that it is an anxious situation which needs to be monitored with care. Suppose the doctor's full list of options, with likelihoods, is

| Likelihood | First Option | Second Option | Third Option |
|:---:|:---:|:---:|:---:|
| 3/7 | Benign | Serious | Anxious |
| 2/7 | Serious | Benign | Anxious |
| 2/7 | Anxious | Serious | Benign |

Again, even if the information is as precise as medically possible, the conclusion is in doubt. How should the doctor decide her course of action? The largest likelihood, 3/7, indicates that nothing need be done. On the other hand, if options are compared pairwise, "serious" becomes the diagnosis.

This medical diagnosis illustration should seem familiar; it is just the pizza example where numbers of voters are replaced with "chance," or likelihood, of different possibilities. Rest assured that actual medical decisions involve more sophisticated decision processes comparing a variety of trade-offs with a conservative emphasis. Nevertheless we should worry; will the actual process and procedure yield the correct answer? Rather than a game show where the excitement is centered on whether the big prize is behind door one, two, or three, the reward here is your health and well being.

As this medical example accurately suggests, any discussion about "decision procedures" also addresses the strengths and weaknesses of methods coming from a wide variety of areas. The reason is that decision procedures are just mathematical ways to combine conflicting facts into a convenient, summarized form. Consequently, related procedural cousins are all of those surveys and assessment procedures so commonly used to evaluate success in the classroom, different programs, and — well, often it seems like almost everyone and everything. Other kinds of associated methods are those economic tools such as "supply and demand" and other exotic sounding terms invoked by economists to explain the functioning of the market place.

Even more; by treating decision methods as tools to aggregate information into a simple, convenient form, other "procedural kissing cousins" include those statistical tools which tell us what books we should read, what movies we should see, which TV shows are the "best," how often we should floss our teeth or have sex, or, minutes after the polls close, project the winner of a national election. While not "decision procedures," all of these methods aggregate information into a convenient digestible size; they help rank the information needed to make decisions. And, their conclusions affect us. While the size of an audience watching a particular TV show is, at best, of idle curiosity to most of us, it is a vital input to determine the cost of commercials, or whether the show will survive the season. These statistical tools offer a careful reading of what voters want, what consumers will buy, what books will sell, how attitudes toward central issues of the day, such as entitlement programs, are changing. But, can the outcomes be misleading? Can they lead us astray?

### 1.1.5 Bad outcomes

After all information is gathered, decisions are made. And, what can be the result? *Bad outcomes.*

We know this can happen; most of us have suffered through at least one particularly unpopular election outcome which we might have labelled, perhaps in a loud and boisterous manner, a "mistake." This decision might involve the choice of a new director for a church group, or academic department, or social group, or the senator or governor of a state, or even the President of a country. After a particularly unpopular election outcome, this sense of frustration may be manifested by a flowering of tacky bumper stickers bragging

> *"Don't blame me, I voted for —"*

Maybe. But these bumper stickers blame the awful outcome on others. At times those "others" fully deserve a strong finger-pointing, or even raising, criticism. Quite often, however, this attitude is a mistake because it really wasn't their fault. The basic theme developed here is that maybe, just maybe, a more accurate bumper sticker reads

> *"Don't blame us; we are victims of a lousy election procedure!"*

I am not seeking a new scapegoat to explain away bad conclusions. Instead, this comment is a warning that the choice of the decision method can cause havoc. Unfortunately, even though care can be taken to gather accurate information, surprisingly little attention can be placed on the choice of the decision procedure. There is a sense that the choice of a procedure is not important; it is the information which plays the dominant role. What a major miscalculation. This is a mistake which can cause serious, expensive errors.


## 1.2   What does an outcome mean?

To illustrate that problems can occur, let me start with an example which involved US public sentiment over the possible Congressional impeachment of President Bill Clinton. One of the several times public emotion peaked was during the November 1998 Congressional elections.

From the perspective of the American television networks, this timing provided a particularly propitious opportunity. With public opinion polls perfected to astonishing degrees of accuracy,[1] and with the networks planning to send out armies of questioners to conduct "exit polls" in their competitive race to accurately predict the election outcomes minutes ahead of rivals, both the tools and the resources were in place to accurately sample the sentiment of the American public.

The networks wished to capture the American public's sentiment for the various options that Congress was discussing at the time. These alternatives ranged from impeaching President Clinton, to censuring or fining him a substantial amount of money. For each option and by majorities so large that each conclusion must be treated as "a conclusive opinion of landslide proportions," it was reported that

1. the American public did *not* want President Clinton impeached,

2. the American public did *not* want President Clinton censured, and

3. the American public did *not* want President Clinton fined.

What should we make of this information? What sensible interpretation about the American public opinion emerges from these poll results? It is reasonable to infer that the American public, at least on that November 1998 election day, did not want anything done to President Clinton. Perhaps the public had adopted a charitable "enough is enough; leave him alone!" attitude.

---

[1]The embarrassment suffered by all of the major television networks during the 2000 US presidential election, where they first predicted the state of Florida would be won by Gore, then retracted, then awarded it to Bush, and then retracted, proves that polls are not infallible. Nevertheless, as a predictive tool, this statement is correct.

This analysis sounds reasonable, but as Peter Jennings of ABC News and the other network anchors cautioned, this data does not mean what it seems to mean. Instead, on that November election day, with a similarly large majority,

**4.** the American public *wanted* President Clinton punished in some manner.

This example has less to do with American politics than with the meaning of decision and information gathering procedures. The message is that outcomes of procedures need not mean what we think they do. Even if the outcome appears to provide overwhelming evidence in a particular direction, the true meaning could be something quite different.

But, why? Why can the outcome differ from what was intended? As we explore the source of the difficulties, the answers explain mysteries about a variety of other topics — including why some people seem to be more successful during discussions and debates within an organization.

## 1.3 Which procedure?

To explore why the choice of a procedure is critical in our quest for "correct decisions," separate the role of information from the consequences of a decision procedure. To do so, assume that all information relevant for a decision is gathered, and it is accurate. To promote confidence in this assumption, I try to avoid examples which allow a debate about whether this assumption is true. Consequently, my illustrations involve hypothetical and innocuous settings of, say, an election for the important post of president — but of an unidentified group. Other examples involve simple daily choices such as the selection of the beverage to accompany a meal.

While my vanilla flavor examples purposely avoid threatening liberals, conservatives, or moderates, let me emphasize that these examples most surely have counterparts which illustrate how *your* beliefs probably have been jeopardized or abused. Anywhere on the political spectrum, an example of an actual election probably can be found where "your side" lost unfairly. By "unfairly" I mean that your side lost not because of the voters' beliefs, mischief of election officials, or even ballots not punched hard enough to register a vote, but because of the subtle, hidden inadequacies of an election or decision procedure.

Remember, decision procedures are merely algorithms which count ballots in specified ways — they have no ideological, racial, or gender bias. If a procedure is flawed, it is equally discriminating against all groups. All that is required for a paradoxical, unjust outcome is an appropriate collection of opinions. Because opinions and coalitions shift so often, I can confidently assert that whatever your personal philosophy, examples of actual elections most surely exist where the choice of a procedure — not the information or general desires of the public — frustrated and wronged the goals of your side.

### 1.3.1   Milk, wine, or beer?

To illustrate what can happen, suppose thirteen people are selecting a party beverage. To enjoy the economy of buying in bulk, they agree to choose a common beverage. For notation, suppose four members of this group prefer milk first, water if milk is not available, and then beer. Represent this preference as

$$M\,W\,B$$

where the first letter of each beverage is used. Suppose the preferences of all thirteen party-goers are

| Number | Ranking | Number | Ranking |
|:------:|:-------:|:------:|:-------:|
| 4 | $M\,W\,B$ | 2 | $M\,B\,W$ |
| 2 | $W\,B\,M$ | 4 | $B\,W\,M$ |
| 1 | $B\,M\,W$ |  |  |

(1.1)

Table 1.1 contains all information relevant to make this decision, so which beverage should the group buy? If they use the standard plurality vote, the usual "show of hands" where each voter votes for his or her favorite alternative, the group's outcome is

$$M\,B\,W \quad \text{with the tally} \quad 6:5:2.$$

Without question, the favored alternative is milk.

Is it? Before running off to a beverage store to buy a keg of milk, maybe these party-goers should listen to the complaints of the lonely two "water-lovers." Rather than trying to dampen the proceedings, they argue that with so many alternatives each voter should vote for his or her top *two* choices. This "vote for two" approach, of course, is another commonly used election method. Moreover, since water did so poorly in the plurality election — it received a mere two votes! — it is reasonable to assume that the "water-lovers" are concerned only about electoral fairness.

If the group does "vote for two," rather than just one alternative, *the new outcome is the completely reversed ranking*

$$W\,B\,M \quad \text{with the tally} \quad 10:9:7.$$

With this decision procedure, the new winner is "water" — even though it was the previous "loser." Indeed, with this procedure the former winner, milk, now is relegated to a bottom ranking.

Now what should we do? To resolve the conflict, suppose the group turns to the method which assigns points to alternatives similar to the "four point" grading approach often used in schools. Recall, to determine a student's class standing, specified number of points are assigned to the student's grades, and an average is taken. But instead of the usual 4 points for an A, 3 points for a B, ..., because the beverage example involves three alternatives, assign 2, 1, and 0 points, respectively, to a voter's top, second, and bottom ranked alternatives.

To illustrate this counting procedure by tallying the ballots of the six voters whose preferences are listed on the top row of Table 1.1,

- milk receives $(2 \times 4) = 8$ points from the four voters on the left of this row and $(2 \times 2) = 4$ from the two voters on the right side of the row for a total of 12 points,

- water receives $(1 \times 4) + (0 \times 2) = 4$ points, and

- beer receives $(0 \times 4) + (1 \times 2) = 2$ points.

Although beer does not fare very well with the six voters on the top row, beer wins the election as the outcome for the full group is

$$B\,M\,W \text{ with the tally } 14:13:12.$$

To summarize,

- *milk* wins with the plurality vote,

- *water* wins with the "vote for two candidates" approach, and

- *beer* wins with the method assigning 2, 1, 0 points.

Is the choice of the procedure important? It most surely is. With the same information, *each* of the three alternatives can end up being the "winner" just by using the appropriate voting procedure.

*Rather than reflecting the voters' preferences, the outcome may
more accurately reflect which election procedure was used.*

While this example concerns a hypothetical choice of beverage, concern
should arise by recognizing that this same phenomenon can — and does —
arise in actual elections used to select our leaders. These are decisions which
significantly affect our future. Indeed, it is legitimate to worry whether

*Are we victims of a lousy election procedure?*

## 1.3.2  Another election

The dangers of the choice of a decision procedure can be further illustrated
with a simple ten-voter *profile* (i.e., a listing of all voter's preferences) where
the candidates for the Presidency are Anneli, Barbara, Connie, and Diane.
The voters' preferences are:

| Number | Preference | Number | Preference |
|:------:|:----------:|:------:|:----------:|
| 2 | $A\,B\,C\,D$ | 2 | $C\,B\,D\,A$ |
| 1 | $A\,C\,D\,B$ | 3 | $D\,B\,C\,A$ |
| 2 | $A\,D\,C\,B$ | | |

$$(1.2)$$

The winning candidate for the election is

- Anneli — when the standard plurality vote is used,

- Barbara — (even though she is not the favorite of any voter) when
  each voter votes for two candidates,

- Connie — when each voter votes for three candidates, and

- Diane — where, with four candidates, ballots are tallied by assigning
  3, 2, 1, 0 points, respectively, to a voter's first, second, third, and
  bottom ranked candidate.

This worrisome outcome does not involve weird, unlikely, highly concocted voting methods; each of these procedures are used in actual elections. Yet, each of the four candidates "wins" with an appropriately selected method. Which of these election outcomes is the voters' real choice,
and which is an "error?"

## 1.3.3 For a price, I will ...

The undeniable message of these simple examples is that *the winner of an election may more accurately reflect the choice of a decision procedure rather than the views and preferences of the voters*. Stated in a different manner, if, by chance, we use the "wrong" decision procedure, we can, inadvertently, make a serious error.

To underscore this point, I occasionally joke during lectures that

> *"For a price, I will come to your organization to design your election procedure. You tell me who you want to win. After talking with the members of your organization to ascertain their preferences, I will construct a 'democratic voting procedure' which will ensure the victory of your candidate."*

Rather than bad, boorish humor, this comment is intended as another warning that an election outcome need not mean what we think it does. Surprisingly often this challenge is easy to meet — even when *all voters* view the designated winner as an inferior choice!

To illustrate, suppose a group of thirty is to select from among Angelic, Brandy, Candy, and Despicable. It is arguable that Angelic should be elected — only she is ranked first, second, and third but never bottom ranked. But an undebatable fact emerging from their preferences

| Number | Preferences |
|:------:|:-----------|
| 10 | A D C B |
| 10 | B A D C |
| 10 | C B A D |

is that *everyone* prefers Angelic to Despicable. The challenge, then, is to elect Despicable in a manner so that everyone leaves the election with full confidence that a *fair* choice was made.

For this particular arrangements of preferences, I would compare the alternatives in a carefully designed pairwise manner. The first election is between Brandy and Angelic. Here, Brandy wins with a 67% landslide vote as she receives 20 of the 30 voters. Who can argue with a vote of such magnitude? Similarly, at the next stage, when Brandy is advanced to be compared with Candy, Candy prevails with a 67% landslide vote.

For the final election, compare Candy with Despicable. Here Despicable is the victor — again by the unquestionable landslide 67% vote. Despicable is the final winner! While each voter is unhappy with the outcome, nobody is likely to question an election result which is based on such landslide votes.[2]

These comments form disturbing assertions about our widely used tools for democracies. Again, they underscore the message that the choice of a procedure matters. But, how should a procedure be selected?

## 1.4   Engineering and manufacturing

Modern society can and should be proud of our engineering and manufacturing efficiency and accomplishments. It is a true success story. By discovering new techniques, new approaches, our technical society has created a wealth of imaginative and useful products that are more and more affordable. From the delight of a Swedish Volvo automobile, to the rapidly decreasing costs of highly improved American lap-top and desk-top computers, to the Japanese VCRs and other marvels of electronics, even middle income families can experience the marvels of technology, of the Internet, of convenience beyond the wildest imagination of even the most wealthy a half century ago.

A central part of this success story derives from the recognition that a significant portion of engineering is decision making. The reality of this comment becomes clear by examining any manufactured item within sight — even that can of stale soda still sitting on a desk will suffice. In designing the can, the engineer needed to make compromises between the strength of the material leading to durability, the thickness of the walls, the weight of the can, and the overall cost. Which of many different materials should be used? The tab on top needed to be designed to account for ecological needs (remember the old flip top openers where that little piece of metal littered beaches and cut the bottoms of innumerable feet), ease of use, yet strong enough not to open with an explosion when being transported in the back of a car on a hot day on the way to a picnic. The number of decisions, the number of alternatives that needed to be judged for acceptance or dismissal is staggering. Yes, an important element of engineering is decision making.

The same "decision story" holds on a larger, more imposing and complex scale for manufacturing. Adding to the complication is how decisions made about the construction of an airplane wing must be coordinated with decisions about the size and shape of the body. By recognizing that there is some truth in the long standing joke that "a camel probably is a horse designed by a committee," we can appreciate the importance of a coordina-

---

[2]Although some of my parliamentarian friends might object to this procedure, agendas of this type are not uncommon in meetings.

tion of effort. But coordination introduces a hierarchy and it requires that people be hired to serve as "facilitators;" decisions must be made about the kind of decisions to be made elsewhere.

And, what is the effect of a "bad" decision? I don't mean decisions so bad that they cause catastrophe such as the breakdown of a bridge; I expect that modern reliability techniques can avoid most of these difficulties. Instead, I refer to "bad decisions" where the wrong material, or design, was used to create, say, that new soda can. I refer to those simple but multiple decisions involved in constructing a new airplane, or electronic device. If problems are caught, and most probably are, they will be fixed. But, to do so involves lost time, lost effort, and added costs. In turn, this generates inefficiencies for manufacturing and design. If "bad decisions" are not caught, we end up with a deficient, or overly costly product. Here, the harsh economic realities enforced by an unforgiving marketplace can impose a severe penalty on a corporation.

## 1.4.1 One source of inefficiency

While this commentary suggests there may be an "inefficiency" concern in engineering, the contemporary success story strongly suggests that this is a non-issue. I thought so, therefore I was most surprised to learn from experts around the world about the high levels of "inefficiency."

My first lesson came from a professor at the Swedish Royal Institute of Technology who specializes in engineering. During his comments, he documented his claims about the inefficiencies suffered by even the best corporations around the world. It is not important to provide, or even understand, the numbers and references he supplied; for our purposes it suffices to know that a highly respected scientist and engineer is among many knowledgeable people worried about this problem.

Spurred by our conversations, subsequent discussions with managers and engineers from a variety of corporations proved that this is a wide spread concern. Problems exist; serious problems. Let me hasten to add; engineering remains a success story. But, it is important to understand and correct this lack of effectiveness because solutions provide valued opportunities for greater profits, better products, and a competitive advantage.

While this inefficiency question is a complex issue involving subtle trade-offs and various constraints, for now accept that much of engineering involves decisions. To demonstrate a possible contributor to inefficiency, consider the decision processes of an engineer who needs to use a particular devise — call it a "what-ma-call-it" — in the design and production of a new product.

Three companies, situated in Boston, Washington, and Milwaukee, are known suppliers of what-ma-call-its. To select which product to use, our conscientious engineer evaluates the choices according to thirteen criteria. Some criteria, for instance, may involve cost, strength, reliability, promised delivery time, or appropriateness for the final product.

With each criterion, our objective engineer ranks the three companies according to the merits of their product. Of course, if some characteristics are more important than others, they are given extra weight by treating them as, say, coming from two criteria rather than just one. Suppose the final ranking of the what-ma-call-its is given by Table 1.1 (page 10), reproduced next, where the first letter of the city of the company is used.

| Number | Ranking | Number | Ranking |
|:------:|:-------:|:------:|:-------:|
| 4 | $M\,W\,B$ | 2 | $M\,B\,W$ |
| 2 | $W\,B\,M$ | 4 | $B\,W\,M$ |
| 1 | $B\,M\,W$ | | |

This table provides all of the relevant information, so what should be the decision of our engineer? Remember, a wrong decision can be costly; it can create inefficiencies.

A natural approach, which was embraced by several of the managers with whom I discussed "decision procedures," is to select "the best of the best." Here, the engineer identifies the top-ranked alternative for each criterion and then selects the alternative which is top-ranked most often. As this is equivalent to using the plurality vote where the ranking of each criterion is treated as the preferences of a voter, our engineer's choice is to use the Milwaukee company's what-ma-call-it.

But, suppose our engineer, fully aware of the dangers and costs of using a faulty part in the design of his product, is risk-adverse. His goal is to avoid making a mistake. After all, a "wrong" decision can prove to be costly to the company — and the engineer's job security. As such, this conservative engineer decides to avoid the alternative which is identified as being the worse for each criterion. A way to do so is to assign one point to each alternative if they are either first or second ranked with respect to each criterion. Again, as each criterion plays the role of a voter, it follows from the earlier analysis that this conservative engineer will be ordering the Washington what-ma-call-its.

To complicate the story, in addition to being risk-adverse and striving for excellence, suppose that our engineer is a "middle-of-the road" moderate. This engineer wishes to reward the top-listed and punish the bottom-listed alternative for each criterion. A way to accomplish this goal is to combine — to add together — the above two approaches. Since both the "best-of-the-best" and the "avoid-the worse" approaches assign one point to a top-ranked alternative, our middle of the road engineer assigns two points to a top-ranked alternative. As only the "avoid disaster" approach assigns a point to a second ranked alternative, our middle of the road engineer assigns one point to an alternative whenever it is second ranked. Of course, no points are assigned to an alternative when it is bottom ranked. Again, according to the earlier analysis, this averaged approach, which is equivalent to the method assigning 2, 1, 0 points to alternatives, leads this engineer to order the Boston what-ma-call-its.

Clearly, not all three products are equally as good. Nevertheless, any of the three choices — the Boston, the Milwaukee, or the Washington product — can emerge as the "superior choice." Even after expensive, careful collection of information concerning the merits of the different alternatives over a wide array of criterion, the outcome need not have anything to do with the merits of the different choices. Instead, the final "objective decision" is fully determined by which decision method happened to be employed; the data be damned.

This is a serious concern; the choice of a decision procedure can contribute to inefficiencies which arise within our engineering and manufacturing world. But, do the engineers know about this? Probably not. My favorite illustration involves an experience of George Hazelrigg — probably the first engineer to seriously worry about the effects of these decision issues. When Hazelrigg used an example to illustrate similar concerns about the validity of questionnaires, an editor of a well known engineering education journal probably exposed his complete lack of understanding of the issues by headlining Hazelrigg's example "Voodoo Mathematics at Work." But, rather than being amused by the editor's "Voodoo Mathematics" attitude, perhaps we should worry whether it manifests a fundamental lack of comprehension — a gap which can perpetuate inefficiency and errors.

## 1.5   Economics and other topics

These concerns describing how attempts to determine the "correct decision" can be subverted by the choice of a decision procedure extend into any number of topics. This includes the choice of tools to understand economics and the behavior of the marketplace. In economic policy, however, decisions are made to regulate our economy, to ensure a careful, just distribution of wealth, welfare, and taxes. Here, "bad decisions" have particularly profound effects; they are manifested by inequities, inflation, or "bad times." While certain surprising aspects of basic economic assumptions are described later, right now consider a decision problem involving the location of a new plant.

## 1.5.1   Locating a new plant

With the large amount of money involved, the potential gain or loss of competitive advantages, and the long-term commitment, the task of locating a new plant is an expensive, crucial decision. The process and outcome cannot be taken lightly, so the merits of each location must be carefully evaluated with respect to criteria involving taxes, concessions offered by the candidate cities, the availability and cost of trained labor, the cost of providing needed materials, the proximity to markets, and so forth. This is not a group decision process intended to invoke any semblance of democracy; it a hard-nosed business decision made at the lonely corporate top. Here, the decisions often are made in terms of dollars; it is in terms of something called cost-benefit analysis (a version of which will be discussed later). For now, consider a simple method.

Suppose the candidate cities are Atlanta, Buffalo, Chicago, and Detroit. Suppose after worrying about all tradeoffs, and then after ranking the merits of the three cities based on ten criteria, the resulting information is given by Table 1.2 (page 12). Recall, this table had the preferences

| Number | Preference | Number | Preference |
|:------:|:----------:|:------:|:----------:|
| 2 | $ABCD$ | 2 | $CBDA$ |
| 1 | $ACDB$ | 3 | $DBCA$ |
| 2 | $ADCB$ | | |

I don't need to continue; you know the message. The "best" outcome can be Atlanta, or Buffalo, or Chicago, or Detroit where, rather than capturing the sense of the carefully assembled data, the outcome more accurately reflects which decision method was adopted. The poor deluded Chief Executive Officer may believe the choice was based on a careful, hard-nosed evaluation of the facts. But, this need not be true.

In other words, rather than the corporate decision being made in terms of the merits of the four locales, the final outcome can be totally determined by the choice of a decision procedure. By treating each criterion as a voter, the analysis already is supplied for different multi-criterion decision procedures by the discussion following Table 1.2. All that is needed is an appropriate description justifying each multi-criteria decision approach; this is easy to supply. So, again, the choice of a procedure matters; the choice of a procedure can override the assembled information to dictate the outcome.

## 1.5.2 Law and other areas

The same message continues into most aspects of our life. For instance, decisions are central to our law, to the just distribution of rights. But, there can be difficulties and mistakes. Indeed, it is possible that some lawsuits and litigation manifest the weaknesses of our laws caused by conflicting rules which appear to support each of two different conclusions. Why?

What about individual rights? A measure of democratic societies is that certain actions belong to our individual decision sphere; these are the decisions the individual, and only the individual, can make. But, can these rights be in conflict? As a simple example, when driving my car, it is *my* right, not that of anyone else, to decide what I listen to on my radio. Yet, Duluth, Minnesota, among other communities, has a law regulating how loud I can play my car radio. Anyone who has experienced the painful noise levels of a car driving by, with the radio volume so loud that the car's arrival has been announced blocks in advance, appreciates the value of such ordinances. Is this an unnecessary abridgment of individual rights as opponents (including Governor Ventura of the state of Minnesota[3]) claim? What is the interaction between individual and societal rights?

## 1.6 What goes wrong?

A concern of modern society should be to understand what goes wrong with our decision procedures, and why. But, rather than investigating on a "one-by-one" individual basis these concerns about the inefficiencies and flaws of voting procedures, difficulties in engineering decision procedures, problems of economics and the marketplace, and the delicate interaction between individual and community rights, maybe there is a common source of the difficulties.

This is the theme of the book; it is to identify a common, subtle problem which treads its way through all of these decision concerns. To expose this difficulty, the insight first captured by Kenneth Arrow in his Ph.D. thesis of a half century ago is introduced and examined with several examples. Then, more general insight is extracted from Arrow's conclusion in a nontechnical

---

[3]This comment comes directly from a July 13, 1999, response Governor Ventura made to a question raised by a Duluth listener on a Minnesota Public Radio call-in show.

manner. Once armed with an understanding WHY problems can occur with decision procedures, we are in a better position to recognize when and why they occur, and how to avoid them.

As an overview, Chapter 2 introduces a mysterious difficulty that plagues all decision procedures. The mystery is explained in Chapter 3 in a manner which emphasizes that this difficulty holds for a surprisingly large variety of decision processes whether from economics, law, voting, . . . . These insights are used in Chapters 4 and 5 to describe related problems from a variety of areas. For instance, it is shown how the fundamental difficulty described here plagues us on a regular basis through doubts about statistical tools, about law, about the apportionment of Congressional seats to states based on the census, and even about Adam Smith's "Invisible Hand" story which plays a central role in the development of our economic policies.

Chapters 6 and 7 use these arguments to explore resolutions. Chapter 8 includes a glossary of certain terms, references and notes, and some discussion that is intended primarily for the mathematically sophisticated reader. While I do not expect many readers to venture into this mathematical jungle, I include it because several results reported here are new and, perhaps, controversial, so they must be justified.

# Chapter 2

# Arrow's Theorem

## 2.1  Introduction

Rarely does a result so spectacular and fundamental come along that it forces us to revamp how we view a subject. This happened in 1951 when Kenneth Arrow published his Ph.D. thesis as the book *Social Choice and Individual Values.*

The effect of Arrow's stunning, seminal contribution was to create serious doubt about commonly accepted beliefs concerning decision procedures. This sense of doubt is so pervasive that it affects even the economic and political decision approaches so commonly used in our democratic societies.

Arrow accomplished all of this by listing properties sufficiently basic and natural that it is reasonable to expect them to be satisfied by *all* decision and election methods — particularly those employed by a democracy. Arrow's punch line was that requiring decision procedures to fill these conditions exacts a heavy cost. Once there are three or more alternatives, these requirements can be satisfied only by a dictator.

A *dictator!* What a predicament. By contradicting expectations and common sense, by showing that basic properties mandate a dictator, his conclusion raises serious doubts about fundamental democratic principles. As it is to be expected, Arrow's "dictatorial" assertion has been associated with all sorts of dire Draconian consequences.

More responsible commentary emphasized how Arrow's seminal result speaks to the basics of choosing. In a fundamental sense it addresses the quandary raised in the last chapter about selecting a decision procedure. This is because Arrow's result ensures that *all* non-dictatorial decision procedures are plagued with basic flaws. This is true whether the choice involves economics or politics, or whether it involves election outcomes for a private club, local, state or national elections. It raises questions about the validity of the results when selecting a beverage for a party, the use of statistical tests, or the rankings of collegiate football teams, TV shows, grant proposals, contestants for a prize, or even brands of deodorant. Arrow's assertions hold even for multi-criteria decision procedures, such as in engineering or management, where a single individual is responsible for the outcome. Arrow's conclusion is so essential, so surprising, so counterintuitive, and so troubling that it correctly formed part of his 1972 Nobel Prize in economics.

The shock value of his assertion, and this result is a common thread connecting the concerns described in the previous chapter, is captured by the disbelieving "How can that be!" reaction commonly experienced when someone first encounters this result. After all, how can simple, seemingly innocuous principles — they are introduced and discussed in detail later in this chapter — mandate a dictator? Just from the natural consternation this result continues to generate, it is easy to understand why Arrow's conclusion has spawned a huge and continually growing literature.

As a small sampler of related conclusions, the economist Amartya Sen, the 1998 Nobel winner in economics, found a fascinating variant which suggests a serious conflict between *societal and individual rights*. While a detailed discussion of Sen's result is deferred to the end of this chapter, be assured that the conflict is fundamental; it captures central aspects of that constant tension seeking a balance between the rights of an individual and the needs of society. While Arrow's result suggests the uncomfortable choice between suffering a dictatorship or discarding certain basic democratic principles, Sen's assertion imposes an equally uncomfortable choice where either individuals are restricted from making personal decisions, or society can suffer crippling inaction.

A worrisome theme is emerging; expect unexpected consequences of Arrow's Theorem to identify new kinds of disturbing societal conflicts. Promoting this theme with results from his Ph.D. thesis, Mark Satterthwaite connected Arrow's Theorem to the important Allan Gibbard - Mark Satterthwaite assertion about strategic voting.

To introduce their result, be honest; at times you have not voted sincerely. Such a manipulative attitude often surfaces when our "favored candidate" has little or no chance of winning; so, we justify our strategic behavior with the "not wasting the vote" rationale. consider, for instance, a supporter of the minor party candidate Ralph Nader who might have voted in the 2000 US presidential election for Al Gore as a way to prevent losing his vote in the close election.

Hurt by this phenomenon are those minority candidates and the causes they are promoting. Hurt are those who are attempting to introduce change or to make a political point. Nader wanted to win 5% of the vote in the 2000 election to qualify his party for federal funds in the 2004 election. But, his final tally failed to reflect his true support; because of the close race between Al Gore and George Bush, many of Nader's supporters publicly announced they would vote for one of the two major candidates. When John B. Anderson ran for US president on the Independent Party ticket in 1980, or Jesse Jackson ran in 1984 and 1988 for president on the Democratic Party, or Ross Perot ran on the Reform Party in 1992 and 1996, the persuasive cries of "Don't waste your vote!" most surely eroded the level of their actual support. Anderson, for instance, received about 6.7% of the vote. But, did a large number of voters, who approved of Anderson and this first serious third party candidacy in the US in 32 years, strategically vote for someone else? Remember, election tallies tend to be used for more than just selecting new officials; the strength of support for different parties provide messages about the changing concerns and needs of the voters.

These examples raise an interesting question; is it possible to design an election procedure where it never is in a voter's best interest to vote strategically? The Gibbard-Satterthwaite assertion states that, while admirable, this goal of finding a strategy-proof voting procedure is impossible. Essentially, they independently proved that whatever non-dictatorial procedure is being used with at least three alternatives, situations exist where the procedure can be manipulated. So, no matter what voting or decision method you or your group uses, situations can occur where, by reacting strategically, someone can obtain a better outcome than by responding sincerely.

To make this result more personal and intuitive, recognize that economic interactions are a form of "decisions." Here, the Gibbard-Satterthwaite theme supports what we all have experienced. In our daily economic interactions, there are times when, by being strategic rather than sincere, you can benefit. Recall, for instance, when you bought a car or your home. Even if you were not strategic, your opponent probably was. Consider an auction; your bid most surely was below how you sincerely value the object. In other words, natural extensions of the Gibbard-Satterthwaite notion, which ensure the existence of settings where outcomes can be manipulated, have had profound consequences in economics and other areas. In part, this result coming from Arrow's Theorem has motivated the search for economic and decision theory resolutions, for "incentives" and "strategy-proof" mechanisms, which encourage sincere reactions.

Extensions, explanations, and all sorts of other disturbing consequences of Arrow's result fill hundreds of papers and shelves of books. A half century after its discovery, conference talks still marvel at the mystery of Arrow's Theorem, or they mimic Arrow's basic construction to demonstrate still other unexpected conclusions. Without question, Arrow's Theorem is a major theoretical contribution of the last half century.

## 2.1.1   But, does Arrow's Theorem really matter?

Arrow's lesson appears to be that an "ideal" decision procedure does not exist. We know this; it supports the sense learned as a child on the playground that "nothing is fair." But, although Arrow's theorem is fundamental, we must wonder, who cares; does it really matter? After all, even after accepting his discouraging message, there is no value in throwing up our hands in frustration and quitting. If society, or even a small social group, is to advance, decisions must be made. A natural response, then, is to ignore Arrow's Theorem while continuing to use some favored decision method.

While there is strong pragmatic support for adopting such an attitude, it is unsatisfying if only because it leaves unresolved the fundamental conflict that Arrow identified. We are left with the sense that while we might enjoy the services provided by a decision procedure today, will we still respect it in the morning? Because Arrow warns us that all procedures are flawed, we must wonder; what goes wrong with *our* procedure? What are its limitations and weaknesses? When might *we* become the victim of an inappropriate, "bad" outcome?

To address this conflict, I adopt a different approach. We know *that* Arrow's Theorem is correct, so perhaps we should explore *why* it occurs. I am not suggesting a reexamination of the many technical proofs of his assertion; they just tell us, again, that we cannot fault Arrow's conclusion. Instead, maybe we should try to understand *what causes* Arrow's disturbing outcome. For instance, knowing that my pickup truck won't work is not the same as knowing *why* it won't work; knowing why may lead to a repair.

By adopting this approach, we unexpectedly discover that *Arrow's Theorem does not mean what we have almost universally accepted*. Once Arrow's conditions are carefully analyzed, his theorem admits a surprisingly benign interpretation. Rather than violating common sense, rather than forcing us to confront the dilemma of choosing between a dictator or a flawed procedure, Arrow's result just means that:

- *if a group of rational voters wishes rational outcomes, it must avoid procedures designed for unsophisticated, irrational voters.*

There is no argument here. These kinds of procedures should be avoided whenever possible, so the statement makes good sense. What is not clear is whether and how this message has any relationship to Arrow's Theorem.

The natural converse of this assertion is that

- *for a group to ensure the rationality of its decisions, it must use procedures intended for rational individuals.*

Again, while this claim makes sense, it is not clear how it is related to Arrow's result or even what "procedures intended for rational individuals" means.

Once it is established that Arrow's Theorem can be viewed from this perspective, rather than all of those traditional dire interpretations causing consternation and a sense of futility, Arrow's Theorem firmly joins hands with common sense and expectations. Rather than serving as an obstacle hindering progress in decision analysis and economics, rather than leaving us with the sense that all procedures suffer the original sin of Arrow's blemish, we find guidance about how to create decision procedures. In particular, this information provides insight which allows for partial resolutions of the kinds of problems raised in the previous chapter.

Even more emerges. By understanding the source of Arrow's assertion, extensions become apparent; extensions which speak to a wide class of topics addressing central, important interdisciplinary concerns. Indeed, some of the extensions even provide insight into problems of organizational and industrial design.

## 2.1.2   The real culprit

To understand the approach developed here, suppose, just suppose, that one of Arrow's assumptions has a particularly devastating effect upon another assumption — it annihilates it. If so — and this is what happens — then a central condition we had expected to be in full force is, in fact, either killed off, or seriously injured and just barely limping along with only minimal impact on the decision process. This resembles playing with a deck of cards; by discovering that the aces are missing, we can understand and appreciate the previously unexpected outcomes. Similarly, by discovering that one of Arrow's assumptions negates another one, Arrow's assertion becomes obvious and inevitable.

Of particular importance is that versions of the same assassin assumption arise in other research and decision areas as well as in daily interactions. The danger is that these assumptions are so natural that most of us make

them on a daily basis in various disguised forms. As shown later, these
conditions are the kind which naturally arise in attempts to "decentralize"
or "simplify" organizations, computerized computations, many economic
settings, or politics.

What makes these assumptions so fascinating is that their innocuous appearance and positive intensions mask the ominous fact that they can nullify
other carefully crafted conditions. This killing off of other important properties is accomplished in a subtle, hidden manner remarkably similar to what
happens in Arrow's result. Consequently, the de facto set of assumptions —
the actual properties which determine what will happen with our economic
or political procedures — can differ significantly from the assumptions we
expected and believed to be in full force.

Obviously, whenever the actual conditions defining our decision procedures differ from what we intended, then unexpected conclusions and paradoxes can occur. This point, although obvious, is sufficiently important that
I repeat it often enough to resemble a preacher banging on the pulpit. As we
will discover, this promise to expect the unexpected holds for an impressive
array of concerns coming from law, political science, economics, psychology,
computer science, game theory, and on and on. Many related issues, concerns, and mistaken interpretations are lurking out there — we just need to
learn how to identify them. I indicate how to do this.

As my assertions contradict a half century of acceptance, each step is
described in detail to discover what it does and does not mean. Rather than
assuming familiarity with concepts, all are introduced. As such, this book
serves as an introduction to this portion of choice theory.

## 2.2   Choice Theory

Choice theory is about making choices and decisions. It analyzes the consequences, both positive and negative, of using particular procedures or sets
of rules. Stated more simply, we need to understand what can go right and
what can go wrong when using choice and voting procedures. The ultimate
goal is to identify a reliable approach which captures the true wishes of the
voters.

This seems easy. Why not vote as we always have with the standard
plurality method? For centuries, each voter has cast a ballot for his or her
favorite candidate where the candidate with the most votes wins. If this
"One person, one vote" procedure has served us quite well for hundreds of
years over millions of elections, why mettle? Why not follow the standard

dictum, "If it ain't broke, don't fix it!"

## 2.2.1 Is the plurality vote broke?

While this advice sounds reasonable, maybe we should check whether the plurality vote is, or is not, broken. To do so, consider the following thirty voter example involving candidates Ann, Barb, Candy, and Deanna. To repeat the notation, recall that $ABCD$ represents where a voter prefers Ann, then Barb, next Candy, and finally Deanna; only the first letter of each name is used. The voters' preferences are:

| Number | Ranking | Number | Ranking | |
|--------|---------|--------|---------|---|
| 3 | $\mathbf{A}\,CDB$ | 2 | $\mathbf{C}\,BDA$ | |
| 6 | $\mathbf{A}\,DCB$ | 5 | $\mathbf{C}\,DBA$ | (2.1) |
| 3 | $\mathbf{B}\,CDA$ | 2 | $\mathbf{D}\,BCA$ | |
| 5 | $\mathbf{B}\,DCA$ | 4 | $\mathbf{D}\,CBA$ | |

For convenience, I arranged these preferences to first list the voters who prefer Ann, then those preferring Barb, and so forth. Also, the voters' top-ranked candidate is printed in bold to make it easy to establish that the plurality outcome is $ABCD$ with the 9:8:7:6 tally.

Presumably, Ann is the voters' top-choice. In turn, this outcome suggests that if bottom-ranked Deanna drops out of competition, then nothing changes. After all, if our elections mean what we think they do, the new ranking is $ABC$.

It is not. Check (just reallocate the six votes for the voters who have Deanna top-ranked); without Deanna as a candidate, the election ranking is the *reversed* $CBA$ with the 11:10:9 tally. Similar computations prove that *should any candidate drop out of the competition, the new ranking completely reverses what the original election outcome suggests.* (The $DCB$ outcome is supported by the tally of 12:10:8, the $DCA$ by 11:10:9 and the $DBA$ by 11:10:9.)

Confronted with this conflicting election information, we must wonder, "Who do these voters really want? Who is their favorite candidate?" The four-candidate election outcome promotes Ann, but the highly consistent and contradictory three-candidate election outcomes provide compelling support for Deanna. Obviously, the choice of who wins matters. This is particularly true if the election determines the president of a social group, of an important committee, or of a country.

## 2.2.2   What is wrong?

This example indicates that our widely used plurality election procedure allows outcomes which breach the voters wishes. But, do these difficulties reflect inadequacies of the four-candidate election, or does the problem reside in those four three-candidate elections? For guidance, let's check how these voters rank the candidates in "head-to-head" pairwise comparisons.

The pairwise votes support the notion that the plurality vote is seriously broke. Rather than "top-ranked" Ann prevailing, *all* candidates beat Ann with an overwhelming 21:9 vote. Troubles continue; although Barb easily beats Ann, Barb convincingly loses to the other two candidates. (Both elections have a 10:20 tally.) While Candy beats both Ann and Barb by landslide proportions, Candy loses to Deanna by 13:16. To summarize, the pairwise election rankings are

$$D\,A, \; D\,B, \; D\,C, \; \; C\,B, \; C\,A, \; \; B\,A.$$

Ouch! Directly contradicting the original $A\,B\,C\,D$ election ranking are the troubling, conflicting outcomes for all subsets of candidates. Should *any* subset of candidates be considered — because some candidates dropped out, or a "better election bureau" is making relative comparisons — the new election outcomes embarrassingly support the contention that these voters really prefer the reversed $D\,C\,B\,A$. Now what do we do?

## 2.2.3   Real world examples

While this concocted setting convincingly illustrates that serious problems can exist, why are our actual elections for mayors, or governors, or chairs of departments immune to these perversities? Actually, they are not. Problems exist, but we remain unaware of "real election" difficulties primarily because we do not know how or where to find them. For a quick tutorial, notice that although Ann is bottom-ranked by most voters, a hard core group of her supporters ensures her victory. This suggests that examples can be found by checking actual multi-candidate elections plagued by a similar polarizing effect. They are easy to find; the earlier described Ventura victory in Minnesota is but one of many illustrations.

An interesting example occurred in the early 1996 Republican US presidential primaries which were cluttered with *nine* candidates. Some of the major candidates, Robert Dole, Steve Forbes, Lamar Alexander, and Richard Lugar, had views so similar that minor policy differences were exaggerated and negative campaigning used to try to emerge from the pack. Another candidate, Pat Buchanan, was spared these difficulties.

Buchanan's novel combination of strong populism with extremely conservative social views created a "love him or hate him" atmosphere where he enjoyed a solid 25 – 30% of the vote. News reports along with his polarizing platform, on the other hand, suggest that most of the remaining 70% of the voters did not want Buchanan, and many even feared him. (Compare this division of the voters who prefer someone other than Ann, or the earlier example of voters who did not wish to spend their winter vacation skiing.) In particular, the voters opposing Buchanan sufficiently divided their vote among the eight other candidates to allow Buchanan to win the New Hampshire primary and to do well in other early primaries. But as number counting suggests, Buchanan's fortunes declined as the number of candidates dwindled. Oh, Buchanan still received his hard core support, but the eventual winner for the Republican party, Bob Dole, no longer needed to share and split the majority of the remaining votes with other contenders.

There are excellent reasons to believe that Buchanan, Ann (from the above example), the band enjoying their winter vacation skiing in Michigan, and Governor Ventura from Minnesota enjoyed their success primarily because the voters used our flawed plurality voting procedure. As this method can seriously distort the voters' true wishes, it must be replaced. But, with what?

For another example which may change history, consider the March 2000 presidential elections in Taiwan. These election results are exciting; for the first time a Chinese government changed hands in a democratic manner. But, was the outcome what the voters really wanted on that day?

To set the stage, essentially two candidates represented the Nationalist Party. This is because although James Soong was running as an independent, he was a former Kuomintang official who left the party over a dispute. Lien Chan was the incumbent vice president and KMT nominee. The third candidate from the Democratic Progressive Party and eventual winner, Chen Shui-bian, probably would have lost in a "head-to-head" comparison with either of the other two. (In a record turnout attracting over 80% of the voters, Cheng received 39% of the vote, while Soong received 36% and Chen received 23%; reports suggest that over half of voters had Cheng bottom-ranked.) As true with the Ventura election in Minnesota, it is not important whether you approve or are upset by the election conclusion. The point is that there are reasons to believe that the election conclusion did not represent what the voters from Taiwan wanted on that day.

## 2.3   Shopping for cars — and election procedures

We now know that the plurality vote is "broke," so let's fix it. But how and with what? How can we discover better, improved procedures? Guidance comes from examining the way many of us buy expensive products such as a TV, a new computer, a car, or even a house.

The "impulsive" method is to buy the first item that catches our fancy. While this approach is embraced by many, it is, of course, silly. Guided by personal experience, we understand how such a carefree attitude can quickly degenerate into an expensive course in basic consumer economics. Unfortunately, it is arguable that this cavalier attitude often serves as the de facto way to select voting methods.

Indeed, it is not unusual to find the choices of election procedures restricted between the status quo — the method currently in use — and an opposing "reform procedure" where the supporting arguments have overtones of an "if it looks better than what we got, take it!" philosophy. In the early 1990s, when the city of Evanston, Illinois, changed their election procedure from a straightforward plurality election to a runoff method, all arguments I heard focused on why one procedure is better than the other — there was no discussion about whether an "optimal" method exists. This impulsive reaction, which is hazardous when choosing personal consumer products, is even more dangerous when selecting a voting method. After all, the choice of a decision procedure has a stronger, longer lasting impact on our lives (through its election of a president, congress, and economic policy) than a purchase of a house, car, or refrigerator.

Perhaps when shopping for an election procedure, we should mimic rational ways to purchase an automobile. A reasonable approach is to concentrate on realistic choices; e.g., there is no sense considering a new BMW on a used car income. Thus, a first cut is to consider only those makes of cars which are affordable and reliable. After identifying which brands satisfy personal basic needs, the final choice can be based on personal whim, sex appeal, horsepower, style, or color.

Similarly, to select choice methods, first identify all procedures which satisfy specified basic properties. Maybe, for instance, we should concentrate only on those methods which guarantee essential rights associated with democracy — or at least those methods which promise efficiency or consistency. Once we have identified all approaches which satisfy these fundamental needs, a final choice can be based on personal whim, which method is easier to explain or use, or whatever criteria one wishes to impose. The crucial initial stage is to assemble a list of fundamental properties that our election and choice procedures should satisfy.

Voting and choosing is serious business, so our list of "desired properties" must be constructed with care. Items on this wish list are traditionally called "axioms." Do not confuse them with the "axioms" coming from, say, geometry (see page 213). Instead, they are the "basic properties" we want satisfied by election methods. What are they? To provide insight about the first assumptions, I invite you to join me in a little wagering game.

## 2.3.1 A little game

*"Step a little closer. I will give you a chance to become rich by playing my little dice game. The rules are simple. We each choose a die and roll it — high score wins. Before choosing one of the three dice, you can roll each of them, examine them, do whatever you want. In fact, you even have the first choice. Only after you select a die will I choose one of the remaining two. Indeed, I am such a nice guy that after we have played for a while, if you want a different die — even mine — no problem. Change to whatever die you want; I will just select a different one."*

To add variety to the action, instead of using the standard dice found in a common board game, each die is identified with three numbers where each is repeated twice. The markings are

$$
\begin{array}{cccc}
\textbf{Die} & & & \\
A & \boxed{8} & \boxed{1} & \boxed{6} \\
B & \boxed{3} & \boxed{5} & \boxed{7} \\
C & \boxed{4} & \boxed{9} & \boxed{2}
\end{array}
\tag{2.2}
$$

What simplifies the analysis is that any two dice define nine combinations. To illustrate, the nine possible $\{A, B\}$ outcomes are

$$
\begin{array}{ccc}
(8,3), & (8,5), & (8,7), \\
(1,3), & (1,5), & (1,7), \\
(6,3), & (6,5), & (6,7)
\end{array}
\tag{2.3}
$$

where the first and second terms in each pairing are, respectively, the $A$ and $B$ values.

These dice are fair in the sense that each face of a die is equally likely to occur. In practical terms, this means that each of the nine Table 2.3 outcomes is equally likely to occur. But with nine possibilities where ties are impossible, one die must win over half of the possible outcomes. Clearly, the die that wins more often is the better choice. As die $A$ wins everything in the top row of Table 2.3 and the first two in the last, $A$ wins five out of the nine possible arrangements. Consequently, $A > B$ (meaning "$A$ is better than $B$"). A similar analysis shows that $B > C$. (Both 5 and 8 beat 4 and 2 while 3 beats 2.) Knowing that $A > B$ and $B > C$, which die do you want?

The natural tendency, given this information, is to choose $A$. But, if you do, you will make me a rich man because $C > A$. (Here, 9 beats everything and both 4 and 2 beat 1.) Namely, these dice generate the

$$A > B, \quad B > C, \text{ but } C > A$$

cycle of Figure 2.1 making it impossible to choose the "best one." (The arrows point from the "better" to the "poorer" alternative.) Whatever your choice, I will choose the die from the cycle which beats you. If you want my die, fine; I can easily select another one to keep bleeding your wallet dry.[1]

**Figure 2.1.** Cycles

Cycles, then, prohibit an optimal choice from existing. This is true whether the cycle involves alternatives in an amusing dice game or, more troubling and central to our concerns, in a societal decision problem. Cycles subvert the societal goal of being able to make optimal decisions. Therefore, the following is a key requirement for choice procedures.

**Assumption 1** *The outcomes of a choice procedure do not admit cycles.*

## 2.3.2    Garbage in, garbage out

To develop understanding about societal cycles, suppose fifteen people debate whether to adopt a specified proposal $\mathcal{P}$. If ten voters favor $\mathcal{P}$ while the last five are directly opposed, then $\mathcal{P}$ is the voters' clear choice as manifested by the 67% landslide vote of 10:5.

---

[1]This Table 2.2 arrangement is called a "perfect square" because the sum of the entries of each column, each row, and each of the two diagonals is 15. To construct a different dice example, define the markings on the three dice from the columns, rather than the rows. To construct an example with more dice, use larger perfect squares; they can be found in books on recreational mathematics.

This argument holds for any proposal $\mathcal{P}$; even for the proposal

$$\mathcal{P} = \{A\,B,\ B\,C,\ C\,A\}$$

where the first ten voters have *irrational cyclic preferences*, and the five opposition voters have the opposite cyclic preferences

$$\{A\,C,\ C\,B,\ B\,A\}.$$

To attach meaning to these abstract symbols, suppose the alternatives are apple pie, blueberry pie, and cherry pie. The first ten voters, then, prefer apple to blueberry (A B), blueberry to cherry (B C), and, to create a cycle, cherry to apple (C A). The remaining five voters are equally as cyclic about the choice of pies, but just in the opposite direction.

Our "fairness criterion" (as tacitly determined by using the pairwise vote) requires the outcome to be the cyclic $\mathcal{P} = \{A\,B,\ B\,C,\ C\,A\}$. The outcome is as it should be. This is because, as represented in Figure 2.1, the debate is about the direction the three alternatives should cycle; should it be in a clockwise or counterclockwise direction?

It is interesting to note that should these voters use the pairwise vote to determine each pairwise ranking, the outcome is, again, the cyclic proposal $\mathcal{P}$. This is because for each pair the preferences of the first ten voters always prevail forcing their choice with a 10:5 victory.

This computation proves that the pairwise voting procedure can generate the cyclic outcomes that we have just learned to fear. But, this cycle is neither disturbing nor even interesting; it merely manifests the familiar

*"Garbage in, garbage out!"*

adage. By admitting voters with cyclic preferences (garbage in), we must anticipate cyclic outcomes (garbage out).

Obviously, we wish to avoid this effect where cyclic inputs generate a cyclic output. A natural way to do so is to prevent the "garbage in" phenomenon; voters with cyclic preferences are prohibited.

**Assumption 2** *Voters cannot have cyclic preferences; they must have rational preferences.*

Please do not interpret this assumption as implying the absence of irrational voters. They exist; indeed, many of us have acquaintances, colleagues, and most surely relatives whom we strongly suspect as being closet cyclic thinkers. Rather than denying the reality of irrationality, this assumption is imposed primarily as a means to identify which procedures work as desired — at least when used by rational voters. After all, what good is a procedure if it fails to be rational with rational voters?

### 2.3.3   Transitive preferences and points along a line

But, what is a "rational voter"? Rather than evaluating the merits of arguments and beliefs, the standard definition merely emphasizes "consistency" of opinions. A weakness of this definition is how it even allows an acknowledged village idiot to be labeled "rational" as long as his views are consistent. The strength of this approach is that the definition introduces a powerful tool of analysis which is separate from personal value judgements; after all, maybe that "idiot" is a genus or prophet. The notion of consistency needed for this definition of rationality borrows from the orderly properties of points on a line as displayed in Figure 2.2.

**Figure 2.2.** Points along a line

To understand the approach, select any two numbers, or points on a line; give them the unimaginative names of $x$ and $y$. When comparing points, the options are limited; if $x$ and $y$ are not the same, then one is larger than the other. If $x$ is larger than $y$, the usual notation is $x > y$; if $y$ is larger than $x$ we have $y > x$.

Preferences are more complicated to understand than the ordering of points on the line. This is true if only because preferences need not be comparable. Do I, for instance, prefer a Faulkner novel to a snowy afternoon? Answers probably do not exist for this "apple–orange" setting where comparisons are not realistic nor possible. *But*, when alternatives can be compared, follow the lead of comparing points on the line by saying that either the alternatives are essentially the same where no difference is perceived — they are tied or "indifferent" — or one is preferred to the other. To be more formal, when comparing alternatives, we say that

- preferences are *complete* if for any two alternatives either $A = B$ (i.e., the voter is *indifferent* between $A$ and $B$), or one is *strictly preferred* to the other. If $A$ is preferred to $B$, denote this as $A \succ B$; if $B$ is preferred to $A$, denoted this as $B \succ A$.

The "$\succ$" notation is intended to suggest the "$>$ *means 'greater than'* " notation used to compare numbers or points on the line. However, I use this notation only when there is a need to emphasize the ranking or when the $A B$ notation can be confusing.

Continuing to transfer the ordering properties of points on the line to preferences, notice from Figure 2.2 that if $x$ is bigger than $y$ and $y$ is bigger than $z$ than $x$ must be bigger than $z$. Using the ">" notation, this becomes

if $x > y$ and $y > z$, then it must be that $x > z$.

Adopting this ordering to describe preferences, we say that

- preferences are *transitive* if $A \succ B$ and $B \succ C$ imply that $A \succ C$.

This transitivity condition is what excludes a voter with cyclic preferences. It captures the notion that should a person prefer apples to blueberries, and blueberries to cherries, then we should expect that person to prefer apples to cherries.

Remember, this is an *imposed condition*. These comments do not mean that reasonable people always respond in a "transitive" manner. Instead, research carried out by several prominent psychologists, such as Amos Tversky, suggest that, at times, the preferences of quite reasonable people may fail to be transitive. After all, a wine connoisseur, after conducting the usual sniff, taste, and color testings — samplings carried out over several dimensions — might prefer a merlot to a burgundy, a burgundy to a chardonnay, and the chardonnay to the merlot. Of course, this person might make the rankings transitive if confronted with the cycle, but the original choices remain. Also, be assured, not all preference rankings are transitive. Sue, for instance, might love Chet, and Chet loves Mavis, but Sue need not love Mavis.

While "strict" preferences can describe the consistency of our rational voter, a bit more is required to describe transitive election outcomes. To complete the definition of transitivity, it remains to describe what happens with a tie, or indifference, between a pair of alternatives. Again, the needed conditions are seized from the ordering properties of points on the line. For instance, if Figure 2.2 had positioned point $y$ on top of $x$, then $x = y$. If, in addition, $y$ is larger than $z$, then, trivially, $x$ also is larger than $z$. Using the ">" notation, this becomes

- if $x = y$ and $y > z$, then $x > z$.

Transferring this ordering relationship to preferences, transitivity goes on to require conditions such as

- if $A = B$ and $B \succ C$, then $A \succ C$;
- if $A = B$ and $B = C$, then $A = C$.

A basic assumption is the following.

**Assumption 3** *Voters have complete, strict, transitive preferences.*

Why *strict* preferences? This assumption seems to violate reality. All of us have experienced indifference between, say, whether apple or cherry pie is served; we all have stood in the voting booth liking one candidate but indifferent about the rest of them.

We assume strict preferences primarily to simplify the analysis. After all, searching for explanations of voting difficulties has proved to be as difficult as searching for that proverbial needle in the haystack. Allowing voters to have all possible preferences is akin to complicating the needle search by dropping another load of hay on the pile. Rather than adding to the disarray, let's first understand what happens when voters have strict, transitive preferences.

The next condition captures the sense that voters should be allowed to rank the candidates in any desired strict manner. Ann's supporters (from the introductory example on page 27), for instance, could correctly argue that freedom fails to exist if nobody is permitted to rank Ann as their favorite candidate. A standard way to capture this "freedom of belief" is to impose the condition of *Unrestricted Domain.*

**Definition 1** Unrestricted Domain *requires each voter to have a strict, complete, transitive ranking of the candidates. There are no other restrictions on the choice of the ranking.*

This unrestricted domain condition completes our modeling of the rational voter. A voter without rational preferences is traditionally called *irrational.* As this term is somewhat harsh, occasionally I use more gentle terms of calling such a voter *cyclic* or *unsophisticated.*[2]

**Definition 2** *A* profile *is a listing of all voters' preferences.*

For instance, all of the examples given so far list the number of voters who have each ranking of the candidates; these are the profiles.

### 2.3.4    Procedures

Now that a rational voter is defined, it is time to specify basic and obvious properties that the procedures should satisfy. Most of my discussion

---

[2]Although "unsophisticated" often is used to describe a voter who is *not* strategic, I prefer an alternative choice of calling a non-strategic voter "sincere."

addresses procedures, like our elections, which rank the candidates. To provide a name, such a procedure is called a *social welfare function*. Examples include standard elections, the rules for judging figure skating, and any other group decision procedure (based on voters' preferences) where it is possible to state whether a particular candidate is ranked above, below, or equal to another candidate. In other words, a social welfare function assembles a societal ranking of the candidates. This is accomplished by using the beliefs of the voters as represented by the profile.

Simpler than ranking the candidates is to choose somebody; i.e., "Melanie is the winner!" Maybe the goal is to identify a subset of candidates. This kind of procedure is called a *social choice function*.

Presumably, the candidates selected by a choice function are the "best ones" as determined by the profile. But, why concentrate just on the best? Maybe we want to know who is "second best," who is the worse, or any other specified subset of candidates. To be polite, for instance, I may select the second best piece of meat during a dinner party. Or, the faculty of a department occasionally needs to select who will *not* receive tenure — they are interested in determining who they find to be the worst. Nevertheless, a typical social choice function is not concerned with who is in, say, sixth or seventh place, but rather who is the winner, or who are the top two candidates. A natural way to create a social choice function from a social welfare function is to choose the top-ranked candidates.

What follows are natural conditions these decision and choice procedures should satisfy.

### Pareto

The first condition to be imposed on decision procedures comes from the work of Vilfredo Pareto (1848-1923). Pareto, an Italian trained in mathematics and physics, worked for 23 years as an engineer before he was appointed to a chair in political economy at the University of Lausanne in Switzerland. Thanks to his extensive training in mathematics, he was one of the first in the world to analyze economic and sociological problems by use of mathematical tools. For instance, his sense of a societal equilibrium — a sense where all mutual advantage has been extracted from society because any change to improve the economic or social standing of one person comes at the cost of hurting someone else — most surely was influenced by notions of balancing forces that were used in his engineering thesis "The Fundamental Principles of Equilibrium in Solid Bodies."

Think of Pareto's concept in terms of one of those sales where garments are tossed in a bin and the doors are opened to admit a crowd of customers. Now imagine several competing hands grabbing and pulling at the same indestructible shirt. From the perspective of physics, that shirt remains in an equilibrium position — it stays in the same physical location — only if all forces (all people pulling on the garment) are balanced. But, if someone pulls harder, then the balanced position is broken at the disadvantage of the others. Similarly, Pareto's sense of a societal or economic equilibrium is a position of balance where any change to the advantage of one person comes at the expense of another.

To introduce the very special portion of Pareto's sense of an "optimal point" which is used in voting theory, suppose without exception that all voters prefer Ann to Barb. In face of such unanimity, it is silly — no, worse, it invites an outright revolt — for the societal outcome to rank Barb above Ann. The Pareto condition imposes a sense of "fairness" by prohibiting this pathology.

**Definition 3** *For any pair of candidates* $\{A, B\}$, *if all voters prefer* $A\,B$ *(respectively, if all prefer* $B\,A$), *then the* Pareto Condition *requires this unanimity ranking to be the societal ranking of this pair*

While this condition seems so obvious that we might assume it always is satisfied, this is not the case. For instance, recall my challenge (page 13) where I claimed that I could design a voting procedure to elect a designated candidate. When this challenge can be met in extreme cases, such as with my illustration where I showed how to elect "Despicable" even though all voters preferred Angelic to Despicable, the selected procedure must violate the Pareto condition.

### Binary independence

It is worth carrying this Pareto argument a step further. Instead of just respecting unanimity, it seems reasonable to base the relative ranking of any two candidates strictly upon their relative merits. To be more specific, when determining the societal relative ranking of a particular pair, what do the other candidates have to do with this ranking? Surely, the virtues or faults of these other candidates are totally irrelevant for this comparison.

To illustrate this point, suppose that a prize committee announces their Sue $\succ$ Mary $\succ$ Ellen outcome. Mary's supporters would be justifiably upset should the committee members confess that they would have ranked Mary above Sue if more voters had had a better opinion of Ellen. *"What does*

*Ellen have to do with the Sue - Mary comparison?"* The Sue-Mary ranking should be based strictly on what the voters think about Sue and Mary; all opinions about Ellen are irrelevant for this particular decision.

Arrow avoids this annoying problem by imposing his condition of *binary independence*; a condition which often is called *Independence from Irrelevant Alternatives* (IIA). While a formal definition of binary independence is given next, an informal description is that binary independence requires the group's relative ranking of any two candidates to depend only on what the voters think about these two candidates; information about other candidates is irrelevant. Again, this makes sense. To capture this intent, Arrow states that if two profiles agree in how each voter ranks a particular pair, both profiles should define the same societal ranking of that particular pair. Differences in how the two profiles rank other alternatives should be irrelevant.

**Definition 4** *A social welfare procedure $F$ — that is, a decision procedure which ranks the alternatives — satisfies* Binary Independence *if and only if the following conditions hold. Let $A$ and $B$ be any two social states or alternatives. Suppose $\mathbf{p}_1$ and $\mathbf{p}_2$ are any two profiles where each voter's $\{A, B\}$ ranking in $\mathbf{p}_1$ agrees with the voter's $\{A, B\}$ ranking in $\mathbf{p}_2$. The group's $\{A, B\}$ ranking for $F(\mathbf{p}_1)$ and $F(\mathbf{p}_2)$ agree.*

### Voting paradoxes and binary independence

To explain the subtleties of this somewhat abstract concept, I use two examples to illustrate what binary independence is, and what it is not. A natural choice is the earlier Ann, Barb, Candy, and Deanna election of the Equation 2.1 profile (page 27). The attraction of this example is that although the plurality outcome ranks Ann above Barb, the election outcomes for all subsets of candidates rank Barb higher. But, while informative, this example has nothing to do with binary independence. Instead, the argument casts doubt on the plurality vote by showing how its outcome is directly contradicted by the outcomes of a large class of unspecified procedures.

Wait; what methods? No other procedures are mentioned in the example. Yet, the extreme conformity of the election outcomes for the triplets conveys the strong sense that *any reasonable method* using the rankings of triplets must rank Barb above Ann. Similarly, the total agreement and consistency of the six pairwise election outcomes dictate that the outcomes of any reasonable procedure using these rankings — say an agenda that compares alternatives in pairs, or a tournament — reverses the plurality ranking.

Even more; reasonable procedures involving the rankings of the triples and pairs would contradict how the plurality method treats this profile.

So, this election example proves that when a large parade of procedures are applied to the Equation 2.1 profile, only the plurality method is out of step — and badly. But, while useful, this information has absolutely nothing to do with binary independence. The intent of binary independence is to analyze a *specified* procedure with *specified* candidates and voters; this concept has nothing to do with comparison with other methods.

### Figure skating and binary independence

An event dramatically capturing the meaning of binary independence was observed by millions of people across the world during the 1995 Women's World Figure Skating Championships in Birmingham, England. To set the scene, recall how in 1994 figure skating suddenly attracted wide international attention with the knee-bashing of Nancy Kerrigan by a competitor's associates just prior to the Olympic games — a lowly act which, ironically, elevated figure skating into unprecedented heights of popularity. Adding to the 1995 drama was the young, pretty American skater Nicole Bobek who, in the weeks prior to the Birmingham event, bravely endured intense news exposure reportedly revealing her own troubled past.

All of this world-wide publicity guaranteed considerable international interest attached to the TV commentator's announcement that, with only one contestant left to skate, Nicole Bobek was in second place ranked above France's Surya Bonaly. Bobek's silver medal seemed ensured because the earlier performance of the remaining skater in the "short program" made it impossible for the American Michelle Kwan to place in the top three.

Kwan skated a far more posed, artistic, and technically precise performance than a 14-year-old has any right to expect. It was exciting. Her superb performance was justly greeted with the only standing ovation of the afternoon. Ms. Kwan was rewarded with an unexpected fourth place finish. What makes her skating of particular interest for choice theory is a secondary consequence of her display of excellence; it *dropped Bobek to third place and elevated Bonaly to second.* Had Kwan not done as well, Bobek would have received the second place silver medal and Bonaly the bronze.

Let's be honest; isn't this ridiculous? Although delightful, what did Michelle Kwan have to do with the relative merits of Nicole Bobek and Surya Bonaly? Both skated earlier than Kwan, and the judges publicly expressed their evaluations of the two skaters' relative merits with irrevocable scores that were immediately flashed on TV sets across the world. What did Kwan's performance have to do with Bobek's and Bonaly's?

It did; in fact, Bonaly even thanked Kwan for her strong performance because it catapulted *Bonaly* into second place. Clearly, something is wrong with the procedure used to rank skaters. Of equal surprise is that while the news media widely reported this twist of fates, the press, the public, and the skaters meekly dismissed this peculiarity as just another of the inexplainable mysteries of figure skating judging.[3]

### Comparison

To review the major difference in the two examples, the one involving Ann and Barb has nothing to do with binary independence because it compares outcomes from different procedures. The skating example, on the other hand, involves the same candidates (skaters), the same voters (judges), the same procedure (the ranking rules), and the same comparison (the skating competition in Birmingham). Here, there is no debate; Kwan's performance radically altered the final ranking between Bobek and Bonaly. Binary independence is intended to prevent this more subtle failing of choice procedures.

Binary independence captures this meaning that the relative ranking of two candidates should depend only on the voters' relative rankings of these candidates by comparing the *same* procedure's outcomes with different profiles. If in each profile each voter's relative ranking of two candidates is the same, binary independence requires society's relative ranking of these candidates to remain fixed. In the figure skating example, one of the profiles, $p_1$, is what history recorded; it is where Kwan turned in a beautiful skate. Let the other profile, $p_2$, be the hypothetical but expected one where Kwan succumbed to the enormous pressure of an internationally televised performance and performed poorly. The only difference in the two profiles is the ranking of Kwan. If figure skating had used a judging procedure which satisfied binary independence, the final relative ranking of Bobek and Bonaly would not have been affected by anything Kwan did or how the judge ranked her.

---

[3]These scoring peculiarities hold no surprise for skating wizards. After a crowd pleasing performance in the 1997 US Women's Nationals in Memphis, Tennessee, Bobek was ranked first. Although the next skater, Tonia Kwiatkowski, did not have one of her better nights, the judges' scores ranked Kwiatkowski *above* Bobek. Reacting to the audience's loud expressions of displeasure, the highly regarded TV commentator, a former Olympic champion, counseled patience by noting that the complicated nature of the scoring rules could cause this relative ranking to change quickly. It did; after the very next skater Bobek was ranked above Kwiatkowski.

## 2.4   Arrow's Theorem

While only a few natural conditions have been identified, it is reasonable to
pause at this point to determine which procedures satisfy this partial list.
The purpose is to examine the strengths and weaknesses of those procedures
which are acceptable with our partial list in order to develop a sense about
what more refined requirements should be imposed next.

This is the plan, but it collapses into failure. This is because Arrow's
Theorem asserts that with three or more candidates, these minimal conditions already require the procedure to be equivalent to a dictatorship.
Before stating the theorem, let me be more specific about what is meant by
a "dictator."

**Definition 5** *A social welfare function is* equivalent to a dictator *if there is
one agent where the societal outcome always agrees with this agent's preferences independent of the preferences of the other voters.*

The "equivalent" modifier is intended to emphasize that dictatorial behavior extends far beyond settings of dark, damp torture chambers with
emaciated souls in tattered clothes hanging in chains from a wall with dry
crusts of bread scattered on the floor. Instead, modern society supports
all sorts of dictatorships — dictatorships that even occur in envied, widely
applauded institutions where the approved attire is a three-piece business
suit and "power lunches" are the norm.

To explain, suppose fifty of us are to rank three candidates by using
the tallying procedure which assigns, respectively, two and one points to a
voter's top- and second-ranked candidate. The candidates are then ranked
according to the number of points they receive. This approach seems to
be democratic — until you discover that I have 100 ballots while each of
the other voters has only one. No matter what the other voters want, my
preferences strictly determine the outcome — I am the dictator.

The point of this story is that whenever one person manages to accrue
sufficient power, a de facto dictatorship prevails. It now is easy to find other
examples; e.g., a political machine which carefully ensures the continued
voting rights of the dead can define a de facto dictatorship. More common
examples occur in companies or law firms where the weight of a voter's vote
depends upon how much stock she owns — a voter with a majority holding
is equivalent to a dictator.

With this added appreciation of what all of the terms mean, we now can
formally state Arrow's Theorem.

**Theorem 1** *(Arrow) Consider any social welfare function which always has transitive outcomes for the three or more candidates. Assume that the strictly transitive preferences of the voters, where there are at least two of them, satisfy the Universal domain condition. If this procedure satisfies binary independence and Pareto, then it is equivalent to a dictator.*

## 2.4.1   Examples

How could this assertion possibly be true! Surely there are many counter-examples disproving it. What is wrong, for instance, with the plurality vote, or with the earlier 2, 1, 0 point system but where everyone has a single ballot?

These natural questions identify why Arrow's assertion continues to be particularly bothersome. Namely, rather than deriving a negative result based on esoteric, debatable conditions — a conclusion which would allow us to play the usual intellectual game of dismissing personally uncomfortable or repugnant arguments as being "irrelevant" — Arrow's assertion relies upon properties which are so simple and basic that they are commonly assumed to always hold. But, they do not. Instead, Arrow's result proves that these basic properties are in conflict. From a pragmatic perspective, this means that unless your favorite procedure is a dictatorship, then your pet decision procedure must violate at least one of Arrow's properties. But, which ones?

### Borda Count

A way to appreciate Arrow's Theorem is to determine why different procedures fail the grade according to Arrow's criteria. To start, I use a method which plays a central role in this story about decision procedures.

This is the procedure introduced to the French Academy of Sciences back in 1770 by the French mathematician, engineer, astronomer, and naval hero Jean Charles de Borda. Among Borda's many contributions, which even include his military service supporting the American side in the American War for Independence and his scientific and political efforts contributing to the development of the metric system which is so widely used around the world, Borda developed a voting approach. The method, called the Borda Count and designated by BC, closely resembles the grading procedure so often used to rank students in schools. In our schools with the five grades A, B, C, D, F, four points are assigned to an A, three to a B, and so forth down to zero points for an F. Generalizations of this method are obvious;

with three alternatives, the starting value is two points, and the second-ranked choice receives one point, so this becomes the earlier 2, 1, 0 system. With, say, ten alternatives, 9 points are assigned to the top candidate, 8 to the second, ... , and zero to the bottom ranked candidate.

The following table computes the BC tally (where two and one points are assigned, respectively, to a voter's top- and second-ranked candidate) for a highly restricted eleven-voter profile which involves only two preferences. The Borda Count outcome is $BAC$.

| Number | Ranking | $A$ | $B$ | $C$ |
|--------|---------|-----|-----|-----|
| 5 | $ABC$ | $5 \times 2 = 10$ | $5 \times 1 = 5$ | 0 |
| 6 | $BAC$ | $6 \times 1 = 6$ | $6 \times 2 = 12$ | 0 |
| | **BC Totals** | 16 | 17 | 0 |

$$(2.4)$$

To check the BC with Arrow's conditions, note that:

- (*Transitive outcomes.*) The candidates are ranked according to their assigned BC tallies, so the BC ranking mimics the ordering properties of points on the line — the BC societal ranking always is transitive.

- (*Unrestricted domain.*) The BC can be used by any voter who has strictly transitive preferences.

- (*Pareto.*) If everyone prefers $A$ to $B$, then $A$ is BC ranked higher because she receives more points than $B$; Pareto is satisfied.

- (*No dictator.*) As the BC satisfies anonymity (i.e., the procedure does not favor the wishes of any particular voters), it is not a dictatorship.

It remains to check binary independence. But Arrow's Theorem requires the Borda Count to violate one of his properties, and binary independence is the only remaining candidate. This means that examples of profiles can be found where the Borda Count violates binary independence.

Actually, these examples are easy to discover. For instance, let the Table 2.4 example define $\mathbf{p}_1$. Next, modify this example to create a new profile, $\mathbf{p}_2$; to do so, let the first five voters suddenly gain a better opinion of $C$ with their new $ACB$ ranking. As shown in the table

| Number | Ranking | $A$ | $B$ | $C$ |
|--------|---------|-----|-----|-----|
| 5 | $ACB$ | $5 \times 2 = 10$ | 0 | $5 \times 1 = 5$ |
| 6 | $BAC$ | $6 \times 1 = 6$ | $6 \times 2 = 12$ | 0 |
| | **BC Totals** | 16 | 12 | 5 |

this new profile $\mathbf{p}_2$ changes the Borda Count ranking from the original $B\,A\,C$ to $A\,B\,C$ with a 16:12:5 tally. The important point to notice for our purposes is that even though *all voters*, including the changeable five, have the same $\{A, B\}$ relative ranking in each profile, the BC relative ranking for $\{A, B\}$ reverses with the two profiles to violate binary independence.

As an amusing but intriguing aside, notice the consequences of the five voters' improved attitude toward $C$; rather than rewarding $C$, it punished $B$. This curiosity might cause cynics to wonder; did these five voters really develop a new appreciation for $C$, or were they trying to manipulate the election outcome to ensure that their first choice candidate $A$ would win? This commentary suggests, and it is true, that strategic behavior is intimately related to the violation of binary independence.

### Other procedures

Other commonly used non-dictatorial procedures, such as the plurality vote, also define transitive rankings. As these methods work quite well with rational voters, they must violate Pareto and/or binary independence. Either violation is troublesome because a procedure violating Pareto ignores unanimous sentiment, while if the method ignores binary independence, it encounters the problems illustrated by figure skating. What can we do?

## 2.5 Consequences of Arrow's Theorem

With a little imagination and armed with Arrow's statement, we now can explain some of the earlier voting paradoxes, re-examine and then revise earlier comments, and explore unexpected extensions. Somewhat surprisingly, I even relate Arrow's result to certain fairly successful strategies which can help you win your way during a group discussion and debate.

Toward this end, I use Arrow's result

- to explain why, rather than a surprise, we must anticipate voting peculiarities of the type illustrated by the Ann, Barb, Candy, and Deanna example (Table 2.1, page 27) where the plurality election outcome conflicts with the pairwise election rankings,

- to relax the earlier restriction that Arrow's Theorem emphasizes the properties of a specified procedure; I now show how it also can be used to compare procedures,

- to show how Arrow's Theorem has implications for activities far out-side of voting — his result applies even to statistical analysis, sport events, class rankings of students, and

- to suggest how Arrow's result offers insight into those efficiency issues coming from manufacturing and engineering.

## 2.5.1   Comparisons with pairwise elections

What makes the Table 2.1 election (page 27) involving Ann, Barb, Candy, and Deanna troubling is that the plurality outcome, a procedure we use so often, is in dramatic conflict with the same voters' pairwise ranking of these candidates.  But, the plurality vote is not the only discordant procedure; this same disturbing behavior plagues *all* procedures.  To make this comment personal; consider the method you use, or wish to use, in your office, home, or social group.  Whatever this method — the Borda Count, the plurality vote, "vote for two candidates," or whatever procedure you wish — an example always can be created displaying a conflict between the rankings of the procedure and the pairwise comparisons.  I now show how Arrow's Theorem ensures this negative conclusion.

While this guarantee of conflict with pairwise rankings is a consequence of Arrow's result, it is not an immediate, direct one.  After all, earlier I carefully emphasized that Arrow's binary independence has nothing to do comparing pairwise votes and various procedures.  Instead, binary independence is a property directed toward the merits of a particular procedure.  To underscore this point, I offer another example.

### Eva, Florence, and Gloria

If a damning flaw of the plurality vote, from Arrow's perspective, is that it violates binary independence, then two profiles can be constructed for the candidates {Eva, Florence, Gloria} which have the following properties:

- In both profiles, each voter has the same relative ranking of Eva and Florence.

- These two profiles give different relative societal rankings for Eva and Florence.

The design of the illustrating profiles follows the lead of the example (page 44) constructed for the BC.  To create a story, suppose Eva, Florence

and Gloria are candidates to be the new chair of the mathematics department.  On the day before the election, suppose the voters' preferences —
this defines the first profile $\mathbf{p}_1$ — are

- 6 voters prefer Eva $\succ$ Florence $\succ$ Gloria,

- 7 voters prefer Gloria $\succ$ Florence $\succ$ Eva.

If the election were held at that time, Gloria would win as the plurality
outcome would be

Gloria $\succ$ Eva $\succ$ Florence with the tally $7 : 6 : 0$.

Suppose, however, that during the departmental tea the afternoon before
the election, Gloria made a monumental error.  Unintentionally she let it
slip that she really *wants* to be the new chair.  Using the standard academic
rationale that if someone wants to be the chair, then there is something
seriously wrong with her, the seven voters who previously preferred Gloria
immediately dropped her to second place.  The second and final profile $\mathbf{p}_2$,
then, is

- 6 voters still prefer Eva $\succ$ Florence $\succ$ Gloria,

- 7 voters now prefer Florence $\succ$ Gloria $\succ$ Eva.

The actual election outcome has Florence as the winner because the plurality
election outcome is

Florence $\succ$ Eva $\succ$ Gloria with the tally $7 : 6 : 0$.

The point of this example is that in both profiles, each voter has the
same relative ranking of Eva and Florence.  The societal outcomes for the
two profiles, however, reverse the relative rankings of these two candidates.
As this example proves, the plurality vote fails binary independence.

For comparison with what follows, notice how the pairwise majority
votes have absolutely nothing to do with the binary independence of the plurality vote.  The challenge is to introduce ways to establish this connection.

### If the moon were purple

A way to use Arrow's Theorem to compare pairwise and plurality rankings
is to argue by contradiction.  To illustrate this means of reasoning, let me
tell a story about one of my daughters.  When she was about four years

old, she enjoyed exploring notions such as, "If the moon were purple, then rain would fall upwards." A well meaning, busy-body neighbor, probably in constant fear of the adverse effects that academic parents would have on their children, tried to correct our daughter's faulty reasoning by carefully explaining, "But dear, the moon is not purple." That poor woman; she was met with a barrage possible only from an indignant, young girl. "I *didn't* say the moon was purple, I said *'If!' 'If!' 'If!'* Anyway, rain doesn't go up so the moon can't be purple."

So, to argue by contradiction, first make an assumption. For my daughter, the starting assumption was "if the moon were purple." Next, a consequence of this assumption is derived. If the logical connection between the assumption and consequence is valid,[4] and if the consequence is false, then the starting assumption must also be false.

There are times when logical terminology can confuse the issue. However, once this formal approach is stripped from the trappings of a formal description, we can recognize this "arguing by contradiction" as a commonly used, powerful method. We all have used it; sometimes it is described with the adage "the proof is in the pudding." For a common illustration, "Everything else being the same, if the food is carefully prepared, it will be tasty. The food in this restaurant is particularly horrible, so the original assumption, that it was carefully prepared, is false."

Following this approach and my daughter's reasoning, I now use Arrow's Theorem to show that silly conclusions result *if* the plurality and pairwise vote always agree. The game plan is as follows: *If* these two procedures always agree, then it does not matter which approach is used to compute the common election outcome; the initial assumption makes these two procedures alternative computational approaches.

What should we compute? Well, how about verifying Arrow's list of properties? By carefully using one or the other of these computational approaches, it turns out that Arrow's conditions are satisfied; but only *if* the two procedure always agree.

Whenever Arrow's assumptions are satisfied, Arrow's conclusion must follow. In particular, Arrow's claim that the procedure is dictatorial provides a "rain always falls upward" assertion — that is, Arrow's Theorem helps identify an obviously false consequence of our "plurality equals pairwise" assumption by claiming that these procedures are dictatorial. (Clearly, neither the plurality or pairwise vote is dictatorial.) By establishing a false conclu-

---

[4]Here, any logical relationship between "purple moons" and "rain falling upwards" is restricted to the imaginative mind of a four-year-old.

sion, we now know that the initial assumption — if you prefer, the starting "pretend statement" — must also be false. Consequently, this means that pairwise and plurality rankings do *not always agree*.

**Plurality "purple moon" analysis**

To start the analysis, *if* the plurality and pairwise votes always gave the same ranking, then we have the following properties. (Remember, in verifying the following statements, the "IF" assumption allows these assertions to be checked by using either the plurality or pairwise vote; the trick is to use the approach which makes each particular statement correct.)

1. *Transitive societal outcomes.* To show that the societal outcomes are transitive, compute them with the plurality vote. Because the plurality outcome is determined by the number of points each candidate receives, and because numbers on the line satisfy the ordering property used to define transitivity, it follows that the plurality election rankings always are transitive.

2. *Unrestricted domain.* Neither approaches imposes restrictions on the voters' rational preferences.

3. *Pareto.* To check the Pareto condition, carry out the computations with the pairwise vote. If for any pair, say $\{A, B\}$, all voters prefer $A$ to $B$, then $A$ beats $B$ in the pairwise vote. According to our "assumption" that the plurality and pairwise rankings always agree, it follows that this procedure satisfies the Pareto condition.

4. *Binary Independence.* To check the binary independence condition, use the pairwise vote. I make this choice because the pairwise vote always satisfies binary independence. After all, when two candidates are compared in a pairwise vote, only the voters' relative preferences of these two candidates are involved. So, according to our "assumption" that the pairwise and plurality rankings always agree, it follows that the plurality vote satisfies binary independence.

The above listing proves that *if* the pairwise and plurality outcomes always agree, then the plurality vote satisfies all of Arrow's conditions. According to his theorem, the plurality vote must be a dictatorship. Now, whatever negative thoughts we might harbor about the plurality vote, it most surely is *not* a dictatorship. Consequently, we have derived the sought after "rains always falls upwards" statement. By this I mean that since the "plurality vote is a dictatorship" conclusion obviously is false, the initial "the plurality and pairwise votes always give the same ranking" assumption must also be false. Just as the discovering that a restaurant's food is horrible negates any assumption about the food being carefully prepared, this voting contradiction means that

> *once there are three or more candidates, there exist profiles exhibiting a conflict between the plurality and pairwise rankings.*

### Borda Count and other procedures

To be more adventurous, notice that there is nothing special about the plurality vote. Instead, all aspects of my argument revolve around the "purple moon" construction that *if* the rankings of a given procedure and the pairwise majority vote always agree, then the properties of this joint procedure can be computed from either the procedure or the pairwise vote. This assumption and the subsequent construction *converts the pairwise vote into the procedure's de facto binary independence condition.*

The "rain always falls upward" assertion needed for our analysis is a direct gift of Arrow's Theorem because his theorem states that the procedure must be a dictatorship. Clearly, neither the pairwise vote nor the plurality vote, or BC, or other standard voting methods, define a dictatorship. Thus, this contradiction proves that the initial "purple moon" assumption is false; it proves that the rankings of the procedure cannot always agree with those of the pairwise vote.

**Theorem 2** *Consider any non-dictatorial procedure for three or more alternatives. Suppose the procedure can be used by any group of transitive voters and that it always provides transitive societal rankings of the alternatives. There exist profiles where the rankings of the procedure and of the pairwise vote are in conflict.*

This use of Arrow's Theorem proves that profiles always can be found where

- the ranking of the Borda Count does not agree with the rankings of pairwise majority vote,

- the ranking of the method where voters vote for their two top ranked candidate does not agree with the pairwise, majority vote.

- the transitive ranking of *any non-dictatorial method,* whatever method you may design, need not agree with the majority pairwise vote.

Since every procedure can be "bad" relative to the pairwise rankings, the next natural question is "How bad can it be?" While I don't explore this issue here, the answer is that the plurality vote, or the method where we vote for two candidates, or three candidates, or four candidates, or ... always are among the worse offenders in creating conflict with the pairwise vote. The unique standard voting method enjoying the strongest compatibility with the pairwise vote is the Borda Count.

To partially explain, during the late 1980s, I showed that for any non-Borda Count way to tally ballots by assigning other choices of points to the candidates, the Table 2.1 (page 27) phenomenon persists. By this I mean that profiles can be created where the method's ranking directly opposes that of the pairwise vote. Only the rankings of the Borda Count always are related to the pairwise rankings. Among its several positive properties, the BC ranking, for instance, can never directly oppose that of the pairwise rankings.

## 2.5.2 More general comparisons

Even though I emphasized how Arrow's binary independence condition concerns only *a specified procedure,* we have just seen how a purple moon, or "the proof is in the pudding," argument allows Arrow's conclusion to be used to compare the pairwise vote with the plurality, BC, or any other method. The same approach guarantees conflict with *any* imaginable way to compute pairwise rankings.

The idea is as follows. Although the plurality and pairwise rankings need not agree, maybe someday a highly imaginative person will invent a clever pairwise method which does allow compatibility. While this is an interesting conjecture, Arrow's result trashes all hope. By using Arrow's result in the "purple moon" manner, we discover that this wishful thinking is, well, wishful thinking.

To explain, suppose through incredible ingenuity, you did develop a new procedure; a procedure where its rankings always agree with the rankings coming from a specified way to rank pairs. *If* this compatibility condition were always true, then, again, the societal rankings and the properties of these procedures can be computed by using either computational approach.

The main difference from the earlier purple moon analysis is that the pairwise majority vote is replaced with new, imaginative ways to determine pairwise outcomes. The new pairwise procedures, for instance, may allow George to determine the {Helena, Irene} ranking. Maybe the {Irene, Judy} ranking are decided by asserting that Judy wins unless all voters prefer

Irene.  The {Helena, Judy} outcome might be determined by a majority vote of those voters whose last name starts with "S."

**Theorem 3** *(Compatibility Comparisons) For three or more alternatives, suppose we have procedures to determine the societal ranking of each pair. All we require about each pairwise ranking procedure is that their outcomes depend only on the voters' relative ranking of the indicated alternatives, and if all voters have the same ranking, then that is the pair's societal ranking.*

*For any nondictatorial procedure which is defined over all rational profiles and which always provides a transitive ranking of the alternatives, there exist profiles where procedure's ranking of the alternatives disagrees with the rankings of the pairwise procedures.*

The supporting "purple moon" argument is essentially the same as above. By *assuming* that the nondictatorial procedure and the specified pairwise procedures always agree, these different methods become different ways to compute the same outcome.  To verify Arrow's conditions, use the non-dictatorial procedure to verify that the societal ranking is transitive and use the pairwise procedures to verify the Pareto and binary independence conditions. Arrow's result now asserts that the non-dictatorial procedure must be a dictatorship.  Thus the compatibility assumption — which generated this false assumption — must be wrong.  This is the assertion.

Going beyond the majority vote, no matter what pairwise ranking procedure is proposed, profiles always can be found where

- the plurality ranking does not agree with the rankings of the pairs,

- the Borda Count ranking does not agree with the rankings of the pairs,

- the ranking of the method where voters vote for their two top ranked candidate does not agree with the rankings of the pairs,

- the transitive ranking of any non-dictatorial method does not agree with the rankings of the pairs.

In a later chapter, I show how to construct examples illustrating all of this behavior.

## 2.5.3  Don't expect compatibility

This modification of Arrow's Theorem teaches us to be leery of different decision procedures because they can result in conflicting outcomes.  To discover other consequences of the Compatibility Theorem, return to the Chapter 1 mystery surrounding the opinion polls about President Clinton impeachment. This poll involves the four alternatives

1. impeach President Clinton,

2. censure President Clinton,

3. fine President Clinton, or

4. do nothing.

Polling is not a "decision procedure," but these methods rank the alternatives. Moreover, all of these polling methods satisfy the basic properties described in the Compatibility Theorem. Because each posed question captures what people thought about each of two choices — yes or no to each question — binary independence is immediately satisfied. If the voters were unanimous in their answers for any question, then that sentiment most surely would be reflected in the statistical outcome. Thus, Pareto is satisfied.

Polling techniques fall under the purview of the Compatibility Theorem. Therefore, we have the surprising conclusion that it is not possible to assemble the conclusions from each question in a meaningful manner which always accurately captures what the people truly mean. This negative observation is, of course, compatible with what the television networks cautioned concerning the interpretation of the impeachment polling results; it may explain some of the embarrassment suffered by the networks during the 2000 Presidential elections.

Even more can go wrong. To explain, suppose a statistical polling approach ranks all of the alternatives in a transitive manner. It follows from the above discussion and Compatibility Theorem that this transitive ranking need not always be compatible with pairwise polling conclusions.

## 2.5.4 Further Implications

These consequences of Arrow's Theorem extend far beyond voting and statistical approaches to include concerns coming from, for instance, engineering, finance, sports, and even the class rankings of students. To suggest how to generate other suspects in this much wider class of examples, just be imaginative about the meaning of the word "voter."

The manner in which this flexibility is achieved is indicated in the introductory chapter. By replacing "voters" with "criteria," we immediately transferred paradoxical voting examples into equivalent and equally disturbing examples about multi-criteria decision making. In multi-criteria decision processes, a single person makes the decision based on how the alternatives fare with respect to several criteria.

This connection between "voters" and "criteria" means, then, that all of the concerns coming from Arrow's result also hold for the poor, struggling engineer, designer, entrepreneur, and manager who are attempting to make "correct" decisions. Whatever decision process these individuals adopt it is subject to the dictates of the Compatibility Theorem and Arrow's insight. In other words, whatever approach decision makers adopt, there are settings where the conclusion conflicts with pairwise comparisons.

### Engineering

To offer a slightly different thrust while previewing comments that will be made later, consider an engineering firm that is developing a new product. Important for this discussion is the recognition that the design of even a simple product can be surprisingly intricate. This complexity is amply manifested by advice in professional journals (such as the *Journal of Manufacturing Design*) about the need to decompose problems into simpler parts. This decomposition captures the nature of that widely used solution to correct all ills — decentralization.

To consider the effects of decentralization, imagine an overly simplified setting whereby pairs of alternatives, which are involved in a particular engineering design, are farmed out to different units within the firm. Maybe the goal is to construct a new phone where one unit has to worry about which cord should be used, another unit specializes in the choice of the ringer, and so forth. In this decentralized way to achieve excellence, each unit has the responsibility to do whatever it is that they do to rank the assigned alternatives based on standard, company-determined, criteria.

Notice how this decentralized, organizational structure already has created the basic elements of the Compatibility Theorem. The Pareto conditions is satisfied because should one of the alternatives assigned to the unit always be better than another over all criteria (remember, the rankings over criteria replace the rankings of the voters), then this alternative will be ranked superior. Binary independence is satisfied simply because in ranking the pair of assigned alternatives, the engineering unit is concerned with this, and only this, assigned pair of alternatives.

While the needed decomposition of an organization into units provides one class of decision procedures, we should assume that management's more

global way to rank alternatives involves the general good and financial success of the firm. What we now know from the Compatibility Theorem is
that management's general ranking can be in conflict with the advice from
the different units. *This conflict can arise even if each unit finds the optimal solution for its part of the puzzle.* One has to wonder; is this conflict
— which Arrow's Theorem identifies as being fundamental — related, in
any manner, with the reported inefficiencies in manufacturing? Even more
surprising, this assertion claims that "doing the best" at each part need not
lead to a superior product.

**Sports and class ranking**

It is difficult to find anything more enjoyable than spending a sunny Saturday afternoon at a track meet where the boasts of athletes from Houghton,
Onekama, and Baraga high schools finally can be measured on the field.

What does this have to do with Arrow's Theorem? Very simple. The
"three alternatives" are the three high schools. Replacing each "voter" is
an athletic event. The question is to determine whether the ranking of the
three schools from this joint meeting is compatible with their rankings from
dual meets. Of course, this analysis is complicated by how the athletes
would perform on different days. So, avoid this complexity by assuming
away the "We would have done much better if Lauri didn't have such a bad
day" excuses. Assume that each athlete's performance — how high each
can jump, how fast each can run, how far each can throw — is precisely the
same on any day during any meet.

To see how the Compatibility Theorem is applicable, notice that in a dual
meet between Houghton and Onekama, the ranking is totally independent of
how well the athletes from Baraga would perform — the jocks from Baraga
are not there, so who cares? Any such comparison is irrelevant. Thus, the
outcomes of each dual meet only depends upon what two teams are involved
— this means that the binary independence condition is satisfied. To verify
"unanimity" or "Pareto," notice that if, say, Houghton beats Onekama in
each and every event, Houghton would win the dual meet. But, as all
Compatibility Theorem conditions are satisfied, we now know there will be
situations where the ranking of the combined track meet is not compatible
with what would happen in all dual track meets.

Similarly, consider the class standing of students. Here, each student
is the "alternative," each course is the "voter." The same Compatibility
Theorem reasoning shows that while it is arguable that Darlene is a better
student than Winnie because Darlene did better in more courses, Winnie

has the higher class standing.

Probably the easiest way to summarize all of these varied, widespread implications is to caution

> *For rankings from any source, do not expect compatibility to exist between the ranking of the whole, and rankings of the pairs.*

The introductory pizza example, where book club pairwise comparisons differed from the full appraisal, is only a special case of a widespread phenomenon. Arrow's result, and its many extensions, invades all aspects of our lives.

## 2.6   Sen's Theorem

Arrow identified a serious issue, but the problem gets worse. To explain, start with the obvious fact that probably only a dictator wants to live in a dictatorship — the rest of us want to avoid it. But, Arrow's result suggests that the only way to prevent a dictator is to dismiss or weaken one of his axioms. Given a choice, it is reasonable to retain the unanimity of Pareto over binary independence. This suggests replacing binary independence with a related but sufficiently relaxed assumption.

To illustrate a particular choice, who decided what shoes you wore today? Surely you did as it is nobody else's business; such decisions are within each of our personal spheres of decision. So, let's follow Amartya Sen's lead by investigating the consequences of granting at least some of the voters these limited rights.

**Definition 6** *A social welfare procedure satisfies the Minimal Liberalism (ML) condition if each of at least two voters are decisive over a specified pair of alternatives. Namely, the decisive voter's ranking of an assigned pair determines the pair's relative societal ranking.*

The purpose of ML is to model the rights of an individual; this is the condition Sen imposes as a way to capture the sense that you, and only you, have the right to determine what shoes or sweater to wear. While the condition seems most reasonable, Sen shows that it creates the feared societal cycles frustrating any attempt to identify the "best choice."

**Theorem 4** *(Sen) Assume there are three or more alternatives and that there is a social welfare function for the two or more voters. Suppose the Unrestricted Domain condition is satisfied. If procedure satisfies Minimal*

*Liberalism and Pareto, then there are profiles where procedure has cyclic outcomes.*

This statement admits the far-fetched "for the want of which shoes to wear, society was lost" scenario where you, by selecting which shoes to wear (ML), created a situation where society cannot decide on some monumental condition.  OK, this ridiculous illustration is almost as irresponsible as a popular myth suggesting that the flapping of a butterfly's wings in Africa can affect Chicago's weather.  More responsible examples are offered below.

## 2.6.1   Three alternatives

The proof of Sen's troubling assertion is immediate with three alternatives. For candidates $\{A, B, C\}$, let Adrian and Bob be decisive, respectively, over the pairs $\{A, B\}$ and $\{A, C\}$.  Maybe these alternatives are the makes of a car they are to share where the choices are an *A*udi, a *B*uick, and a *C*hevy.  If Adrian's preferences are $A\,B\,C$ while all other voters prefer $B\,C\,A$, then the following table identifies all of the information needed by a ML procedure. The blanks in the table identify those particular pieces of information which are irrelevant for the process because the societal outcome for this pair is decided by a decisive voter.

| Voter | $\{A,B\}$ | $\{B,C\}$ | $\{A,C\}$ | |
|---|---|---|---|---|
| Adrian | $A\,B$ | $B\,C$ | — | |
| Bob | — | $B\,C$ | $C\,A$ | (2.5) |
| Others | — | $B\,C$ | — | |
| **Outcome** | $A\,B$ | $B\,C$ | $C\,A$ | |

To show why the outcome is the indicated cycle (as listed in the bottom outcome row of Table 2.5), note that the $A\,B$ outcome is determined by the preferences of decisive Adrian, the $B\,C$ ranking is due to unanimity, and $C\,A$ is due to preferences of decisive Bob.  As this example demonstrates, a procedure satisfying ML and Pareto can suffer the pain of cyclic outcomes.

### College roommates

By treating Table 2.5 as a template, it becomes easy to construct illustrating examples of Sen's assertion by modeling conflicts which occur on an almost daily basis.  This includes even two contentious college roommates who constantly argue over the use of the TV.  Define the alternatives $A$, $B$, $C$ to be as follows.

- "A" is the option of watching a TV channel known for its loud shows which feature the latest rock music.

- "B" is the option of turning the TV off.

- "C" is the option of watching the evening news.

One of the students, Adrian, fully enjoys the social aspects of college life as manifested by his $A\,B\,C$ preferences. His studious roommate Bob, on the other hand, reflects a more serious side of the collegiate experience with his $B\,C\,A$ preferences. If an attempt to resolve the conflict allows Adrian to be decisive over $\{A, B\}$ while Bob is decisive over $\{A, C\}$, then Table 2.5 applies and the resulting cycle ensures a stalemate with continued turmoil.

**Lascivious books**

Sen provides a spicier example (at least for the time when it was published) involving censorship. His scenario imagines a debate between a prudish and a lascivious reader over the rights to read the book *"Lady Chatterley's Lover."* Their alternatives follow.

- "A" is the censorship option where nobody can read the book.

- "B" is where the prude reads the book.

- "C" is where the lascivious reader reads it.

Reflecting an "If someone has to do it, it might as well be me" attitude, prude's preferences are $A\,B\,C$. But our lascivious crusader, hoping to convert the prude, to turn him on to a freer way of thinking, prefers $B\,C\,A$. For decisive sets, a natural choice is to have the prude and the lascivious reader decisive, respectively, over $\{A, B\}$ and $\{A, C\}$. Their common agreement of the $B\,C$ ranking combined with their conflicting opinions about the common alternative $A$ in their respective decisive sets dooms the outcome to be the cycle $A\,B$, $B\,C$, $C\,A$ which destroys any hope of literary harmony.

## 2.6.2   More alternatives

A natural criticism of this proof of Sen's Theorem is that both decisive voters can make binding judgments about the same alternative $A$. Indeed, in each scenario the conflict arises when one decisive voter selects, while the other dismisses $A$. (In Sen's censorship example, for instance, both make decisive but conflicting judgments whether the book should be read by anyone.) This suggests that maybe Sen's difficulty is artificial; maybe it can be avoided with four or more alternatives if the decisive voters make their choices over disjoint pairs of options. No; the basic problems continue.

To illustrate with the $n = 4$ alternatives $\{A, B, C, D\}$. To devise a story, maybe these four alternatives are four different stocks that a stock-club is considering whether to buy. Because of their expertise over certain stocks, let Art and Neal be decisive, respectively, over $\{A, B\}$ and $\{C, D\}$. When Art prefers $D\,A\,B\,C$ and all other voters prefer $B\,C\,D\,A$, the ML informational table is

| Voter | $\{A, B\}$ | $\{B, C\}$ | $\{C, D\}$ | $\{A, D\}$ |
|---|---|---|---|---|
| Art | $A\,B$ | $B\,C$ | — | $D\,A$ |
| Neal | — | $B\,C$ | $C\,D$ | $D\,A$ |
| Others | — | $B\,C$ | — | $D\,A$ |
| **Outcome** | $A\,B$ | $B\,C$ | $C\,D$ | $D\,A$ |

(2.6)

Two of the entries in the outcome row are decided by decisive voters, the other two by unanimous consent. Again, the combination of Pareto and decisiveness dictates the $A\,B$, $B\,C$, $C\,D$, $D\,A$ cycle. I leave to the reader the pleasure of creating other examples by assigning a property or action to each of these four alternatives. By being sufficiently creative, both amusing and disturbing illustrations result.

From a theoretical perspective, the real mystery is to understand how these two natural properties, "Pareto" and "Minimal Liberalism," allow "garbage out" conclusions. After all, Sen tried to prevent this difficulty by prohibiting "garbage in" preferences. To do so, he explicitly requires rational voters. What went wrong?

## 2.6.3  Libertarians

According to the philosopher Allan Gibbard, "The libertarian claim is that each person has a right to determine certain features of the world." This modest request seems acceptable, but Sen's result dampens our expectations about whether it ever is possible to attain without causing collateral damage to society. But, maybe we just need to try harder. Maybe it is possible to discover inventive ways to circumvent the difficulties identified by Sen. This has been tried, and the attempts have created a large literature demonstrating the uncomfortable, negative conclusions. (Jerry Kelly's web site "www.maxwell.syr.edu/maxpages/faculty/jskelly/biblioho.htm" offers an extensive listing of the literature.) A small sample is offered next.

Perhaps the libertarian's goal can be rescued by imposing stronger conditions as to *when* an agent can be decisive. For instance, maybe part of Sen's problem results from the Pareto condition. This was the insightful direction pursued by the political scientist David Austen-Smith who wondered whether a resolution can be obtained by deciding which is more important, decisiveness or Pareto? He proposed a hierarchy between the two concepts. While Austen-Smith has an interesting conclusion, we will discover that the basic problem remains.

A related approach, explored by Gibbard is to wonder whether an agent should be allowed to be decisive only when his actions affect *his interests, and only his interests.* To explore this thought, Gibbard restricted attention to settings where a person's decision has no affect on any other person. To illustrate with one of his examples, suppose an anticonformist and a conformist are deciding whether to wear red or blue tee shirts.

For notation, represent their differing options with a pair, such as $(R, B)$, where the first entry indicates the anticonformist's choice. So, $(R, B)$ means that the anticonformist prefers to wear a red tee shirt while the conformist wishes to wear a blue tee shirt. To illustrate Gibbard's condition, the situation

$$(B, B) \text{ or } (R, B),$$

affects only the color of shirt worn by anticonformist; in either setting, the Conformist still has a blue tee shirt. For this particular setting, then, Gibbard would argue that it is the anticonformist's and only the anticonformist's right to select between them. After all, to permit the conformist to have a voice in deciding between these options allows the conformist to interfere and determine what the anticonformist must wear. Stated in another manner, as this setting involves a choice between two options where the final outcome only affects which shirt the anticonformist wears, the decision is in anticonformist's sphere of influence.

The following definition extends this concept to a wider setting which involves tee shirts, dresses worn to a dance, grilling in a back yard, and any other social state. In this definition, $\mathbf{a} = (a_1, a_2, \ldots, a_n)$ defines the social state for each of the $n$ agents. In the tee shirt example, $n = 2$ as only two people are involved, and $a_i$ is either R or B indicating whether a red or blue shirt is to be worn by the $i^{\text{th}}$ person. In another problem, $a_3$ and $b_3$ might represent, say, that the third person wants to grill hot dogs or hamburgers on Sunday night. In other words, this abstract notation allows considerable flexibility to capture all sorts of settings.

**Definition 7** *(Gibbard) For n people, consider two social states defined by*

$\mathbf{a} = (a_1, \ldots, a_n)$ and $\mathbf{b} = (b_1, \ldots, b_n)$. *The components $a_i$ and $b_i$ define what the $i^{th}$ agent does, so they are said to be in the $i^{th}$ agent's private domain. An individual is Gibbard Decisive for "$\mathbf{a}$ over $\mathbf{b}$" if and only if $\mathbf{a}$ and $\mathbf{b}$ differ only in this individual's sphere of influence. (So $a_k = b_k$ for $k \neq i$.) The societal outcome honors the choice of the decisive agent.*

To explain this abstract notation in words, the definition just states that when confronted with two options where the only difference between them affects you, and only you, you can make the decision. If, for instance, when ordering ice cream on a hot day your choice between vanilla or chocolate has no effect on anyone else — you are not using the last scoop, you are not requiring anyone else to change their choice — then that is your decision.

Who can complain about something as innocuous as this? If my choice has absolutely no effect on what anyone else must do, then surely I should be allowed to make the selection. This condition allows a person to unilaterally make decisions only when the outcome imposes absolutely no change upon anyone else. Surely, Gibbard's setting allows acceptable conclusions. But, this is not the case.

**Theorem 5** *With two or more people, there does not exist a decision approach which avoids cyclic outcomes and which satisfies the Gibbard decisiveness condition.*

It is worth examining the proof of this assertion because it compares a very real conflict between what a person *must* do with what the person *wants* to have happen. It is this added dimension of what we *want to occur* which permits the cycle. To be contemporary, consider the conflict between conservative parents and rebellious teenagers about the importance of fashion statements made by the latest body puncture or a large red rose tattoo fully decorating the left shoulder. But then, if only to avoid family controversy, maybe we should stay with the tee shirt example.

In the tee shirt problem, the anticonformist's choices between $(B, B)$ or $(R, B)$ keeps the conformist dressed in blue. But, should the anticonformist make the $(R, B)$ choice, it will cause discomfort to the conformist who *wants* to wear the same color shirt. Of course, once the conformist changes shirts, it is the anticonformist who becomes uncomfortable. The formal proof evokes amusing images of the anticonformist and conformist rapidly changing shirts in a futile, never ending attempt to achieve their conflicting goals.

*Proof:* The simple proof captures the conflict between what the anticonformist and conformist want to wear. The anticonformist wants to wear something different; the conformist wants to wear the same color Tee shirt. Of the four possibilities presented by whether each person wears a R or B shirt, the anticonformist has the preference ranking

$$(B, R) \succ (R, B) \succ (B, B) \succ (R, R),$$

while the conformist has the preferences

$$(B, B) \succ (R, R) \succ (R, B) \succ (B, R).$$

To set up the information table, because $(B, B), (R, B)$ and $(B, R), (R, R)$ differ only with respect to what the anticonformist decides to wear, the anticonformist is decisive over these two pairs. Similarly, the conformist is decisive over $(B, B), (B, R)$ and over $(R, B), (R, R)$. The information table, now divided into two parts, becomes

| Agent | $\{(B, B), (B, R)\}$ | $\{(B, R), (R, R)\}$ |
|---|---|---|
| Anticonformist | — | $(B, R) \succ (R, R)$ |
| Conformist | $(B, B) \succ (B, R)$ | — |
| **Outcome** | $(B, B) \succ (B, R)$ | $(B, R) \succ (R, R)$ |

| Agent | $\{(R, R), (R, B)\}$ | $\{(R, B), (B, B)\}$ |
|---|---|---|
| Anticonformist | — | $(R, B) \succ (B, B)$ |
| Conformist | $(R, R) \succ (R, B)$ | — |
| **Outcome** | $(R, R) \succ (R, B)$ | $(R, B) \succ (B, B)$ |

As the bottom row with the societal outcome defines a cycle, this completes the proof. Notice, the Pareto condition does not appear anywhere. This absence suggests that Sen's difficulty is more subtle than Austen-Smith's worries about establishing a hierarchy between Pareto and decisiveness.

The cycle arises in this example because, while each agent can decide what he or she does, *what each agent wants to occur* is determined by the actions of others. Be honest; this is not a rare situation. It is not unusual for our preferences to be determined by what others do, so this slightly abstract statement models real problems. After all, not only does this result capture the "parent-rebellious teenager" setting between what each wants the other to do, but it even includes those worries over which dress different women choose to wear to a party. This is not a hypothetical academic concern — this is the kind of conflict which can arise on a continual basis.

## 2.6.4 Prisoner's Dilemma

Not only can natural examples be created to illustrate how Sen's structures allow cycles to emerge among the four or more alternatives, but these illustrations extend to connect the Sen phenomenon to disturbing behavior found in the social sciences and our daily lives. More specifically, the *Prisoner's Dilemma* from game theory has been successfully applied to explain a wide variety of issues ranging from crime and punishment to business dealings and even problems of nuclear disarmament.

One reason this particular game theory model enjoys such wide applicability is that, as in the Sen type examples, it captures a fundamental sense of conflict between an individual's concern for self-interest and the community. To illustrate this discord, suppose that two prisoners, Bob and Zeke, are suspects for a crime. Unfortunately, the supporting evidence is highly questionable. As anyone who has watched a TV detective show knows, the strategy adopted by the police is to separate the prisoners and to try to get each of them to testify against the other. If both remain silent, both may be released[5] or serve a minimal sentence. If one suspect confesses, he may obtain a better deal while the other person faces a long sentence. If both confess, both end up with a bad deal of serving prison time.

To model this game, suppose there is enough evidence to convict both offenders only of a minor crime leading to a year prison sentence. However, if one squeals on the other, then this criminal receives probation while the other prisoner will be sentenced to ten years. If both confess, each will serve a five year sentence.

An advantage of the formalities of game theory as advanced by John Nash, a mathematician who won the 1994 Nobel Prize in economics, is that they avoid all of those "if she, than he" type of arguments. One way to do this is to catalogue all options and their consequences in a single table. A way to envision the following table, then, is that it is a variant of the truism "A picture is worth more than a thousand words." A Chicago version of this phrase reportedly replaces "picture" with "fist in the face," while this game theory variation replaces "picture" with "game table."

To illustrate the use of the table by using the notation where the first and second entry of any tuple determine, respectively, Bob's and Zeke's outcome

---

[5]While there seems to be no credible evidence, there are some who suspect this "silence strategy" was adopted by the parents of a six-year old child who was murdered in a highly publicized crime.

— time served in prison — the game and its options are captured by

$$
\begin{array}{c|cc}
 & Cooperate & Defect \\
\hline
Cooperate & (1,1) & (10,0) \\
Defect & (0,10) & (5,5)
\end{array}
\tag{2.7}
$$

Here, "cooperate" means that each player "cooperates" *not* with the police, but with his partner in crime — the other prisoner — by remaining silent. In this game, Bob's decision controls which row is used to determine the outcome; he does this by deciding whether to cooperate (with his fellow suspect) or defect (by admitting the crime and implicating his partner). Similarly, Zeke's actions control the choice of the column.

To illustrate what happens, if the players adopt the strategies (Defect, Cooperate) (so Bob defects from their vow of silence and squeals on Zeke while Zeke "cooperates" with the criminal code of remaining silent), the outcome is in the second row and first column. This $(0,10)$ outcome rewards Bob with probation while Zeke loses by serving ten years of jail time.

To simplify the notation, use the letters $E$, $F$, $G$, $H$ to represent the four possible strategies.

| Strategy | $E$ | $F$ | $G$ | $H$ |
|---|---|---|---|---|
|  | $(D,C)$ | $(C,C)$ | $(D,D)$ | $(C,D)$ |
| Bob's Prison Time | 0 | 1 | 5 | 10 |
| Zeke's Prison Time | 10 | 1 | 5 | 0 |

$$\tag{2.8}$$

To assist in the analysis, the last two rows specify what happens to each criminal when each strategy is played. For instance, $H$, which represents (Cooperate, Defect) (as indicated by the shorthand $(C,D)$ in the table), is where Bob cooperates by remaining silent, and receives a 10 year sentence, while Zeke defects and stays out of jail.

The ranking each player assigns to these strategic alternatives is determined by what happens to them. For instance, Bob prefers $E \succ F$ because option $E$, where Bob defects and Zeke cooperates, keeps Bob out of jail while option $F$ mandates a year of jail time. In this manner, just by comparing possible prison time, it follows that Bob's and Zeke's preferences are

**Bob:** $EFGH$,  **Zeke:** $HFGE$.

A way to determine who is decisive over which alternatives also comes from the repetitious plots of those TV shows. As Bob is sitting alone in a separate room, he has the right to decide whether to cooperate or defect from his pact of silence with Zeke; this right is independent of what Zeke does. In fact, this is precisely why the police shuttled Bob off to a separate room. As such, Bob is decisive over sets $\{E, F\}$ and $\{G, H\}$. Similarly, Zeke is decisive over sets $\{E, G\}$ and $\{F, H\}$.

Compiling all of this information into a ML informational table, we find that

| Player | $\{E, F\}$ | $\{G, H\}$ | $\{E, G\}$ | $\{F, H\}$ | $\{F, G\}$ |
|---|---|---|---|---|---|
| Bob | $E \succ F$ | $G \succ H$ | – | – | $F \succ G$ |
| Zeke | – | – | $G \succ E$ | $H\,F$ | $F \succ G$ |
| Outcome | $E \succ F$ | $G \succ H$ | $G \succ E$ | $H \succ F$ | $F \succ G$ |

$$(2.9)$$

where the Outcome line proves that this game defines the two cycles

$$E \succ F,\ F \succ G,\ G \succ E \text{ and } H \succ F\ F \succ G,\ G \succ H.$$

To appreciate the consequences of these cycles, recall how the earlier dice game (page 31) demonstrated how cycles create difficulties which can be exploited by outsiders. In the dice game, I used these cycles to relieve my opponents of their money. With the cycles of the Prisoner's Dilemma and by appealing to each criminal's self-interest, the outsider — the police — exploits the situation to extract a confession from at least one of the criminals.

A valued aspect of the Prisoner's Dilemma is that, via the above identification of the game with individual preferences, it introduces a wealth of societal examples which experience the Sen type conflict. In fact, you most surely have been intimately involved in several such settings — either as a person creating the problem (by defecting from intended behavior) or as the victim. A commonly experienced example involves driving on a highway during construction season. The sign clearly states that the two lanes will merge into one just a mile ahead. If all drivers start moving into one lane, all will move along smoothly. But there always are those impatient drivers who "defect" from the community goal by waiting until the last instant to merge. By doing so, they save time while contributing to the resulting bottle neck and traffic jam which inconveniences those who "cooperate."

As another example, rather than prisoners, suppose the players are two communities trying to cope with the homeless problem. A compassionate solution is for both communities to provide housing, food, and education to help these folks. To see the potential Prisoner's Dilemma, if both communities "cooperate" by carrying out this program, then both spend tax money. However, suppose one of the communities "defects" by ignoring the homeless issue while the other community "cooperates." It is clear what will happen (and, it is easy to document with actual cases); the homeless will move from the "defecting" community which offers no services to overload the streets and resources of the "cooperating" community which is attempting to do what is needed. This version of Sen's Theorem supports the "No good deed goes unpunished" warning. If both communities "defect," the tragic conclusion is that nothing is done for the homeless; the problem continues.

As a final example which goes to the heart of the conflict between individual and societal rights, consider China's "one-child" policy. When viewed strictly in terms of individual rights, there is no debate; a family should be permitted to have as many children as desired; this is an intimate, family decision. But, if this individual freedom causes a societal population overload, then the problem begs for resolution. Quite realistically, should a country neglect to impose population reforms, then we must anticipate that their subsequent "solutions" for the resulting hunger and need of resources will require, for instance, an expansion of territory. This is called war. It is easy to model this conflict in either Sen's or the game theory formulation. Both approaches indicate that these are the kinds of problems which dictate a serious conflict between individual rights and societal needs.

## 2.6.5   Relationship between Sen and Arrow

The Compatibility Theorem (page 52) provides a partial link between Sen's and Arrow's result. To see this, consider the introductory setting (page 57) involving the three alternatives of cars labelled $\{A, B, C\}$. Here, Adrian was decisive over the pair $\{A, B\}$, Bob was decisive over the pair $\{A, C\}$. As in the Compatibility Theorem, these outcomes are decided in a pairwise manner (so the binary independence condition is satisfied) and the Pareto condition also is satisfied. All we know about the decision procedure for the pair $\{B, C\}$ is that it satisfies the Pareto condition. If, in addition, this ranking is determined by using the information only from one voter's ranking of this pair, then it follows from the compatibility theorem that it is impossible to assemble this pairwise information in a manner that always provides a transitive ranking.

Where Sen's result differs is that when unanimity is not achieved over the pair $\{B, C\}$, the procedure might use information other than each voter's relative ranking of this pair; it could emphasize Adrian's opinion if Bob happens to select $C$ from his assigned pair; it could select a $\{B, C\}$ ranking to make the full societal ranking transitive (so, it would have to incorporate Adrian's and Bob's choices over their assigned pairs), and so forth. Also,

Sen does not require transitivity of the societal outcome; he only wants the outcome to avoid that pernicious cycle. In very real ways, then, Sen's result differs from that of Arrow's.

## 2.6.6   What else?

As one might anticipate, Arrow's and Sen's assertions have been extended in many different directions. Some results allow elite ruling groups to make decisions, others provide a hierarchy of dictators. In a subsequent chapter, some of these conclusions are explained. But, the explanation for Sen's and Arrow's results extends to all of these other conclusions as well as to a wide variety of other topics. We now turn to this common explanation.

# Chapter 3

# Explanations And Examples

## 3.1   Are all methods unfair?

How frustrating. Sen's and Arrow's results appear to establish the discouraging conclusion that "no method is fair." To explain, both of these theorems use assumptions so fundamental that, presumably, all acceptable decision procedures should satisfy them. The theorems of Arrow and Sen, however, prove that this never can happen. Consequently, any procedure — no matter whether it is intended to assist in economics, voting, or ordinary daily decisions, and no matter how carefully it may have been designed — is condemned to abuse at least one of these basic conditions.

These theorems appear to force us into an uncomfortable situation. Either we must accept and use flawed election and decision methods fully aware that that the outcome may violate the group's true intent, or we must embrace a dictator. This does not offer much of an encouraging choice.

Although this dismal and gloomy "paradox or dictator" interpretation is almost universally accepted, I emphatically disagree with it. As I show, what spares us from this uncomfortable dilemma is that, when the various axioms are combined with one another, they need not mean what we commonly thought they did. What we encounter is an effect somewhat similar to what parents quickly learn about their charming four year old child. Individually, each little darling can be attractive and predictable; the parents can rightfully brag about how their child plays quietly in a productive manner. But, bringing all of these little angels together into a large, loosely supervised play group, or set free on a playground, well, now we have a real example of "chaos." Forget all predictions based on each child's individual behavior; no knowledgeable person would even dare guess what the group will do. While the collective outcome would never approximate "The Lord of the Flies," William Golding understood how, when combined, the properties of individual parts can be misleading.

Similarly, by uncovering the true implications of the defining properties of decision procedures — not individually, but how they actually behave when they interact with one another — we discover that rather than being a surprise or concern, Arrow's and Sen's conclusions are to be expected. Even more; rather than forcing us to suffer because "all procedures are inadequate," once we understand what goes wrong with decision procedures and why, it becomes possible to create acceptable and realistic alternatives.

Of equal importance, by identifying what goes wrong with these fundamental theorems, we learn why the difficulties suffered by all sorts of decision procedures occur. The first lesson is to be skeptical about the meaning of individual properties when they are combined — no matter where this occurs. The whole can radically differ from the sum of the parts.

## 3.2   Sen's Theorem

In developing his theorem, Sen requires the voters to have rational preferences. A purpose of this assumption is clear. It eliminates those annoying "garbage in" effects which cause easily anticipated but uninteresting societal cycles. To illustrate this comment, assume that Sen's assumption is *not* in effect and then examine the consequences.

Namely, rather than Sen's rationality condition, consider what happens if irrational voters of any type are welcomed to participate. Start with the extreme case where *all* voters are irrational because they all have the same

$$\{A\,B, \quad B\,C, \quad C\,A\}$$

cyclic preferences. Here, each and every person prefers, say, apples to bananas, bananas to cherries, and cherries to apples. Although irrational, since this group unanimously agrees about how to rank each pair of alternatives, the Pareto condition mandates the cycle as the societal ranking. This commentary just argues that when everyone wants the cycle, then let the cycle be the societal outcome. Rather than a surprise, this conclusion merely illustrates the "garbage in, garbage out" phenomenon.

To complete the "garbage in, garbage out" analysis, compute the associated informational table for a procedure respecting Minimal Liberalism when two of these cyclic voters, Adrian and Bob, are decisive, respectively, over $\{A, B\}$ and $\{A, C\}$.

| Voters | $\{A, B\}$ | $\{B, C\}$ | $\{A, C\}$ | |
|---|---|---|---|---|
| Adrian | $A\,B$ | $B\,C$ | — | |
| Bob | — | $B\,C$ | $C\,A$ | (3.1) |
| Others | — | $B\,C$ | — | |
| **Outcome** | $A\,B$ | $B\,C$ | $C\,A$ | |

Notice anything familiar? You will once you compare this table with Table 2.5 (page 57); they are identical. But there is a major difference; the above table represents information from *the cyclic preferences of irrational voters* while the earlier Table 2.5 uses the *transitive preferences of rational voters*. To appreciate what this means, notice that both tables list all information a ML procedure (recall, ML represents Minimal Liberalism as defined on page 56) is permitted to use. Therefore, the agreement of both tables raises the worrisome notion that, for some reason, *by respecting even a minimal level of liberalism, procedures become incapable of distinguishing between voters with rational or with cyclic preferences.*

## 3.2.1 Lost information

The thrust of this observation is that, in some mysterious manner, Sen's properties combine in a way to drop the crucial assumption that the voters are rational. Remember; even though Sen explicitly assumes the individual rationality of voters, all that truly matters when a procedure computes outcomes is the information the procedure actually uses. All other information is superfluous — not to us, but to the algorithmic processing of the procedure.

On reflection, this argument that problems can be caused when information is ignored agrees with common sense. For a roughly related example, consider all those times a person is judged in terms of isolated, separated impressions — but the conclusion can be wrong. Is that bearded, disheveled person, slowly shuffling along the sidewalk, head down, and distracted a homeless person lost in despair? Maybe. But maybe he is a university professor lost in thought about his new book. Prejudices reflect opinions determined while ignoring available, crucial information.

Suppose that this speculation is correct. Suppose the inherent prejudices of a procedure so severely limit what available information is actually used that the procedure cannot distinguish between rational or irrational voters. If true, then Sen's result just manifests the regrettable inability of procedures to value and use crucial assumption about the rational nature of the voters.

If this speculation is true, it suggests how to avoid Sen's mystery. After all, if bothersome problems occur when crucial but available information is not used, then find ways to use it; search for approaches which reincorporate the data into the decision process.

As analogy, consider a hotel which serves a complimentary breakfast for lodgers. If the dining room has access to the street, how do we know whether "free loaders" are not walking in for a free meal? If the overworked waiter cannot distinguish the hotel guests from others, he cannot determine who to serve. The solution for this real problem is obvious; if the current procedure admits unintended people, then change it to include distinguishing information. A standard approach is to require the lodgers to show their room key. "No room key? Please leave."

Sen's result forms a mystery primarily because we expect the voters' individual rationality to play a central role. Remember, this assumption is an explicit attempt to restrict who can participate; it is intended to exclude cyclic voters with "garbage in" effects. But if Minimal Liberalism allows the unintended, we must discover ways to distinguish the rational from the cyclic voter. We need a "No rationality? Please leave!" condition.

To advance this program, I also explore certain surprising consequences. For instance, I explain why "deciding by consensus" can saddle us with horrible outcomes. All of this depends on explaining why Sen's liberalism can lose information about the individual rationality of the voters when society is sufficiently heterogeneous.

Please note; this confusion does not require an outrageously complex, highly heterogeneous society filled with conflict caused by individuals coming from different cultures with highly diverse interests and beliefs. Instead, as underscored by Table 2.5 where *only one voter disagrees with the unanimity beliefs of the others,* a single person can generate disarray for ML procedures. Moreover, for similar reasons of lost information, many other procedures experience related problems of undesired outcomes. In particular, we should worry whether, in our professional and daily lives, problems arise because in a subtle manner crucial but available information is not being used. As indicated starting in the next chapter, this can be the case.

## 3.2.2   Loss of transitivity

The central argument is that, contrary to expectations and intentions, admitting even a token level of liberalism requires *all* ML procedures to vitiate the basic assumption that the voters have rational preferences. To illustrate the basic idea, suppose Sue, ordering her breakfast at a restaurant, is confronted with the three alternatives of {apple juice, blueberry juice, cranberry juice}. Suppose the waiter learns that her preferences are $AC$ and $CB$ (where each juice is represented by its first letter). Are Sue's preferences rational?

Without more information, we cannot answer this question. After all, transitivity is a particular sequencing property which compares the rankings of all three pairs. To check whether Sue has rational beliefs, the waiter also must know Sue's $\{A, B\}$ ranking; if she prefers apple juice to blueberry, Sue is rational. If not, well, .... The main point is that without knowing Sue's $\{A, B\}$ preferences, it is impossible to determine Sue's rationality.

With the Sue story in mind, review the limitations forced upon a ML procedure with our three candidates examples of Tables 3.1 and 2.5. Staying with the apple, blueberry, and cherry alternatives, because the Minimal Liberalism procedure *must ignore* how everyone except Adrian ranks the $\{A, B\}$ pair, it can use only the information about Bob's $\{B, C\}$ and $\{A, C\}$ rankings; it cannot even peek at Bob's $\{A, B\}$ choice.[1] As with Sue, the limited information — caused by Minimal Liberalism — is insufficient to determine whether Bob's preferences are, or are not, transitive.

This is the key point; Sen's problem arises because when ML dismisses information about the sequencing of a voter's preferences, the procedure becomes indifferent about how the third pair is ranked. In particular, the ML procedure is indifferent whether the missing ranking identifies the voter as rational or irrational. It is interesting how (as we will see) a similar effect creates problems in law, economics, voting, engineering, and other settings.

To further illustrate this point, let Erik and Fred be decisive, respectively, over $\{A, B\}$ and $\{A, C\}$. This assumption means that nothing needs to be listed in the Table 3.2 positions designated by "None;" any entry is irrelevant for the decision process as the societal ranking for the pair is solely determined by the decisive voter's preferences over this pair.

| Voter | $\{A, B\}$ | $\{B, C\}$ | $\{A, C\}$ | |
|:---:|:---:|:---:|:---:|---|
| Erik | — | — | None | |
| Fred | None | — | — | (3.2) |
| Others | None | — | None | |

Thus, the decisiveness of Minimal Liberalism — the excluding effect of the "this is my decision; it is none of your business" property — causes the problems. A voter's actual preferences in the "None" locations have no effect

---

[1] Either it cannot use this information, or it is equivalent to such a procedure.

on the final outcome. But, as with Sue, this missing information determines whether the voter is, or is not, rational. As the missing terms can be chosen to make each voter's full ranking transitive or cyclic, Minimal Liberalism emasculates the rational voter assumption. Indeed, a ML procedure can be used with equal ease with rational or with cyclic voters.

Is this criticism fair? Maybe it is impossible to design procedures which require rational voters. This is not the case; there are an infinite number of them. To see why the Borda Count is one choice, notice that to tally a voter's BC ballot the voter *must* specify which candidate is top-ranked, which one is second ranked, and so forth; namely, to mark the ballot, the voter must have transitive preferences. For instance, how would a BC ballot be tallied for a voter with $A B$, $B C$, $C A$ cyclic preferences? Who should get two, or one, or zero points?

Translating a voter's transitive ranking into distinct point values enables the Borda Count and most other ways to assign weights to candidates — these are called *positional methods* — to monitor and demand the individual rationality of voters.[2] Of equal importance, this assertion has the following surprising consequence.

> *If a procedure can be used only by rational voters — such as the positional methods — then the procedure* must *violate the Minimal Liberalism axiom.*

This observation returns us to the introductory comment of Chapter 2 — if we want to have rational societal outcomes, we should avoid procedures that can be used by irrational voters.

### 3.2.3   Costs of Minimal Liberalism

The flexibility of a procedure to service both rational and cyclic voters may appear to be an attractive feature — until the accompanying costs are inventoried. These costs become particularly apparent when Minimal Liberalism is combined with the Pareto condition.

Pareto is intended to be a "good condition;" it provides a sense of "fairness" where unanimity over a pair identifies the societal choice. But the Pareto condition contributes to the problem because, it, too, worries only

---

[2]To explain the "most" qualifier, notice that the plurality vote provides one point for a voter's top-ranked candidate and zero to all others. By ignoring how a voter ranks the other candidates, the plurality vote admits an irrational voter who has a top ranked candidate and cyclic views about the others. This fact is one reason the plurality vote has so many flaws.

about how the voters rank *pairs*. By emphasizing what happens with a *pair*, Pareto ignores the information needed to determine the rationality of voters. The fact that Pareto can be used by voters with irrational preferences was illustrated earlier when the Pareto criterion dictated the cyclic Table 3.1 outcome for the irrational voters who unanimously embraced cyclic preferences.

So, both Minimal Liberalism and Pareto ignore the precise type of information needed to established the rationality of voters. The problem is worse; in some settings the Pareto condition *requires* a ML procedure to misinterpret the data as coming from cyclic voters.

To explain, I use Table 3.1 (page 71) where, presumably, the reader accepted the cyclic outcome based on the unanimous consent of cyclic voters as "fair." (If not, then the reader rejects the Pareto condition.) As this Pareto fairness condition is not disrupted by Minimal Liberalism, the cycle must be treated as the only "fair" outcome for *any profile* which generates the same information table. The problem for us (not the procedure) occurs when this same table arises with rational profiles. Here, Pareto requires the procedure to treat the information table data as coming from anything other than a unanimity cyclic world. The cyclic societal outcome is "natural" whether or not the actual voter preferences are, or are not, cyclic.

The difficulties with Sen's model now are easier to understand. Minimal Liberalism severs all connections among the rational voters' binary rankings of the alternatives. The remaining sterile collection of the disjoint parts can be assembled to define many different wholes; the data could constitute the desires of cyclic voters, or of a mixed society where some voters are rational while others are not, or the intended rational society.

Remember, a procedure is agnostic; it is merely an algorithm carrying out designed, rather than intended, responsibilities. Think of it as a highly limited employee. Our intentions and the reality of what can be accomplished with this intellectually challenged employee can disagree. In an highly homogeneous rational society[3] the ML condition causes no problems. But with a sufficiently heterogeneous society, the information ignored by a procedure satisfying Minimal Liberalism renders it incapable of determining whether it is trying to minister to rational or unsophisticated voters.

To explain with an analogy, suppose we are providing transportation for a technologically unsophisticated society. While a Porsche always catches my fancy, it is useless for this culture; a donkey and cart might be more

---

[3]Here, a society with rational voters which ML cannot identify with an unsophisticated society.

welcomed. But adopting a "one size fits all" approach imposes limitations. Even a highly sophisticated driver carefully attired in sun glasses, driving gloves, with a scarf casually tossed over the shoulder cannot extract a flashy performance out of an ass. The simple reality is that performance is constrained by the limitations of a vehicle.

The same argument applies to voting. Even if all voters are sophisticated, there are limits as to what can be expected when they use an election decision vehicle so crude that it also can be used by the irrational. If certain conditions, such as Minimal Liberalism, require us to use an "donkey-and-cart" decision procedure, then do not anticipate flashy conclusions such as transitive outcomes. Again, this explains the introductory comment that *if a group wants rational outcomes, it cannot use the crude procedures designed for irrational voters.*

### 3.2.4   More examples

Armed with the knowledge that certain irrational and rational profiles are indistinguishable for ML procedures, it becomes trivial to construct many as many new "paradoxical" examples as desired.

First, specify a desired societal cyclic outcome, say $AB$, $BC$, $CD$, $DA$. To create an example exhibiting this pathological behavior, start with *irrational* voters whose cyclic preferences unanimously agree with the specified societal outcome. Because all voters have the same preferences, the Pareto condition forces this common cycle to be the societal outcome. Next, select the decisive voters and their assigned pairs of alternatives; for instance, let Alfred and Carl be decisive, respectively, over $\{A, B\}$ and $\{C, D\}$. The resulting table of ML information is

| Voter | $\{A, B\}$ | $\{B, C\}$ | $\{C, D\}$ | $\{A, D\}$ |
|---------|------------|------------|------------|------------|
| Alfred  | $AB$       | $BC$       | —          | $DA$       |
| Carl    | —          | $BC$       | $CD$       | $DA$       |
| Others  | —          | $BC$       | —          | $DA$       |
| **Outcome** | $AB$   | $BC$       | $CD$       | $DA$       |

$$(3.3)$$

It remains to construct a transitive profile which defines the same information table. But, this already is done because Table 3.3 agrees with the Table 2.6 (page 59) — a table defined by voters with transitive rankings. Again, this agreement between tables demonstrates the inability of a ML procedure to distinguish between rationality and irrationality.

## 3.2.5   Salles' example

By identifying and then amending a bothersome aspect of Sen's censorship example (starting on page 56), Maurice Salles, an expert in this area who is the founder both of the research journal *Social Choice & Welfare* and of a recognized research center of decision analysis at the Université de Caen in France, escalated the complexity of the issue by creating the troubling situation where the same transitive profile generates *two* cycles for our lascivious and prudish readers.

From a technical perspective and with what we have just learned about Sen's Theorem, it now is easy to construct other cycles similar to those generated by Salles. As above, start with an irrational society where all voters have the same non-transitive preferences

$$A\,B,\,C\,A,\,D\,B,\,C\,D,\,B\,C$$

which correspond to the desired outcome. As above, Pareto and this unanimity setting require the societal rankings to include the two cycles

$$A \succ B,\ B \succ C,\ C \succ A \text{ and } B \succ C,\ C \succ D,\ D \succ B.$$

To compute the associated ML Table 3.4, let Dana be decisive over $\{A, B\}$ and $\{C, D\}$, and Lauri be decisive over $\{A, C\}$ and $\{B, D\}$.

| Voter | $\{A,B\}$ | $\{A,C\}$ | $\{C,D\}$ | $\{B,D\}$ | $\{B,C\}$ | |
|---|---|---|---|---|---|---|
| Dana | $A\,B$ | — | $C\,D$ | — | $B\,C$ | (3.4) |
| Lauri | — | $C\,A$ | — | $D\,B$ | $B\,C$ | |

Next, exploit the inability of ML procedures to distinguish between rational and irrational profiles. Namely, take advantage of the empty slots in the columns (created by decisive voters) to convert the cyclic profile into a transitive profile which generates the same ML table. Notice how the rankings can be immediately read off of Table 3.4; one choice is where Dana and Lauri have, respectively, preferences $A\,B\,C\,D$ and $D\,B\,C\,A$.

Again, the Sen-type problems illustrated by this example arise because the crucial transitivity assumption is dismissed when "natural conditions" admit indistinguishable non-transitive voters. Transitivity cannot be squeezed out of a procedure satisfying Minimal Liberalism; instead, these methods reflect the simpler life of the unsophisticated, cyclic voters.

## 3.2.6   Designing examples as complex as desired

Now that we understand the basic principle behind the Sen-type conclusions, we can design examples which are as complex and convoluted as desired. The only fact to remember is that ML disrupts the gathering of the sequencing information needed to monitor transitivity, so all examples must reflect this trait. A quick way to design examples is as follows.

- Specify a desired societal outcome; it can have as many cycles and be as convoluted and complicated as desired.

- Start with the unanimity profile of irrational voters where each voter's preferences is the desired societal outcome.

- To replace the non-transitive preferences with transitive ones, information about at least one pairwise ranking from each cycle for *each* voter must be irrelevant for the ML table. So, assign these pairs of alternatives to decisive voters in an appropriate manner. This choice — which disrupts the sequencing information — allows each voter's pairwise rankings from the resulting information table to be completed either as cycles or as transitive preferences.

- Select a transitive preference for each voter that is consistent with the information table.

- The fun part is to concoct a wild but convincing story which justifies why the specified agents are decisive over the indicated sets and why they should have the assigned transitive preferences.

To further illustrate, suppose we wish to construct an example resulting in the two cycles

$$\{AB,\ BC,\ CD,\ DA\} \text{ and } \{AB,\ BC, CF,\ FA\}.$$

Start with the unanimity profile of irrational voters where each ranking is the intended societal outcome. This defines the ML information table

| Voter | $\{A,B\}$ | $\{B,C\}$ | $\{C,D\}$ | $\{A,D\}$ | $\{C,F\}$ | $\{A,F\}$ |
|---|---|---|---|---|---|---|
| Rob | $AB$ | $BC$ | $CD$ | $DA$ | $CF$ | $FA$ |
| Lance | $AB$ | $BC$ | $CD$ | $DA$ | $CF$ | $FA$ |
| **Outcome** | $AB$ | $BC$ | $CD$ | $DA$ | $CF$ | $FA$ |

To design transitive preferences with the same outcomes, use ML to disrupt the sequencing information which distinguishes between transitive and irrational preferences. Namely, for each cycle, assign the decisive sets to agents so that each voter's ranking of at least one pair is irrelevant. One choice is to let Rob be decisive over $\{A, D\}$ and $\{C, F\}$ while Lance is decisive over $\{C, D\}$ and $\{A, F\}$ to create the table

| Voter | $\{A, B\}$ | $\{B, C\}$ | $\{C, D\}$ | $\{A, D\}$ | $\{C, F\}$ | $\{A, F\}$ |
|---|---|---|---|---|---|---|
| Rob | $A\,B$ | $B\,C$ | — | $D\,A$ | $C\,F$ | — |
| Lance | $A\,B$ | $B\,C$ | $C\,D$ | — | — | $F\,A$ |
| **Outcome** | $A\,B$ | $B\,C$ | $C\,D$ | $D\,A$ | $C\,F$ | $F\,A$ |

The outcomes stay fixed, so all that remains is to find transitive preferences for the two voters. This is simple; choices can be read directly off of the last table. For instance, a choice for Rob is $D\,A\,B\,C\,F$ while a choice for Lance is $F\,A\,B\,C\,D$.

Alternatively, use four voters where each is decisive over one pair.

| Voter | $\{A, B\}$ | $\{B, C\}$ | $\{C, D\}$ | $\{A, D\}$ | $\{C, F\}$ | $\{A, F\}$ |
|---|---|---|---|---|---|---|
| Don | $A\,B$ | $B\,C$ | — | $D\,A$ | — | — |
| Ed | $A\,B$ | $B\,C$ | — | — | — | $F\,A$ |
| Frank | $A\,B$ | $B\,C$ | — | — | $C\,F$ | — |
| Grant | $A\,B$ | $B\,C$ | $C\,D$ | — | —— | — |
| **Outcome** | $A\,B$ | $B\,C$ | $C\,D$ | $D\,A$ | $C\,F$ | $F\,A$ |

In this table, Don, Ed, Frank, and Grant are decisive, respectively, over $\{A, D\}$, $\{A, F\}$, $\{C, F\}$, and $\{C, D\}$. There are many choices for the transitive rankings of the four voters.

Other examples involving more complicated arrangement of multiple and interconnecting cycles now are easy to construct. This totally explains the technical requirements for such examples. The fun part is the design of stories to justify why particular voters are decisive over the specified pairs.

### 3.2.7 A converse

This approach captures more than *some* of the examples which illustrate Sen's Theorem, it characterizes how to construct *all possible illustrating examples.*

**Theorem 6** *With at least three alternatives, suppose an example involving rational voters is constructed which illustrates Sen's Theorem because the portion of the outcome determined by the preferences of the decisive voters and the Pareto condition has cycles. There exists a unanimity profile of irrational voters over these pairs where the outcome is a natural one (due to unanimity) and which has an identical ML information table.*

Stated in other terms, the above explanation of Sen's Theorem which uses the Pareto condition and the confusion of the data from an unanimity profile of irrational voters explains all possible illustrations of Sen's result.

*Proof:* The proof is simple. In designing the cyclic preferences from the given transitive ones, it may, or may not, be necessary to change a voter's ranking for a particular pair. If the pair's societal outcome is determined by the Pareto condition, then leave each voter's ranking unchanged. If the pair's societal outcome is determined by a decisive agent, then make each of the other voters ranking of the pair agree with the pair's societal ranking. This change has no affect on the ML table because only the decisive agent's ranking is listed in the table.

By construction, the common ranking assigned to each voter agrees with the societal ranking. As the societal ranking involves cycles, each voter's ranking is not transitive. So, we have constructed an unanimity profile involving irrational preferences which has an identical ML information table as the actual data coming from transitive preferences. Since the cyclic outcome of the table agrees with each irrational voter's preferences, the outcome is a "natural" one. This completes the proof.

## 3.2.8   Gibbard's cycles

This same "lost information" description explains why Gibbard's approach (page 59) fails to prevent Sen's problem. Recall, Gibbard's result addresses, among other examples, conflict between conservative parents and adventurous teenagers. The illustrating example involved the anticonformist and conformist worrying about which color tee shirt to wear. To construct a Gibbard type example, follow the above formula by starting with irrational agents where both have the same

$$(B, B) \succ (B, R), \ (B, R) \succ (R, R), \ (R, R) \succ (R, B), \ (R, B) \succ (B, B)$$

cyclic preferences. These preferences define an informational table identical to the one on page 62 defined by transitive preferences.

This construction provides insight about the difficulties of the clever, natural arguments and approaches which have been put forth as ways to avoid Sen's Theorem. If they allow the disruption of the sequencing information needed for transitivity, they will not provide a satisfactory solution. Instead, we need arguments to counter the loss of the crucial and available information that the voters are, indeed, rational.

## 3.3 Arrow

An almost identical "lost information" argument explains Arrow's Theorem. Again, the key theme is to explain why Arrow's "binary independence" divorces all connections among the binary rankings of the rational voters. Doing so establishes that binary independence emasculates the central assumption that the voters have transitive preferences. As with Sen's result, the problem arises because the disjoint parts of the pairwise rankings define too many wholes. It is not clear to the algorithmic properties of the procedure which society — a rational or a cyclic one — the parts represent. Again, without an effective rational voter assumption, we return to a de facto "garbage in" environment; an environment which, with the Pareto condition, dictates that Arrow's conclusion must be anticipated.

It is easy to understand why Arrow's binary independence condition dismisses the assumption of individual rationality. To illustrate with the Anneli, Barbara, Connie, and Diane example from Chapter 1 (page 12), suppose we learn that a new voter prefers Connie to Anneli. Does this voter have transitive preferences? This question, of course, is impossible to answer until additional information is provided; transitivity requires comparing how this voter ranks each pair from each triplet.

Similar to the new voter problem, binary independence explicitly prohibits its admissible procedures from comparing how the candidates from a particular pair under consideration fare when compared with any other candidate. In this manner binary independence dismisses all information concerning the rationality of voters. The point is that if a procedure does not value this crucial information as an input, then it is difficult to conceive how the procedure can, mysteriously, impose rationality on the outcomes. This limitation becomes particularly true should a society be sufficiently heterogeneous.

### 3.3.1 Too many parts

In the introductory comments of Chapter 2, I claimed that Arrow's Theorem includes a "killer" assumption which nullifies another crucial condition. The assassin, as we now understand, is binary independence; the victim is the individual rationality assumption. The actual mayhem comes about because binary independence separates the relevant information about the voter's rational preferences into seemingly unrelated parts. With apologies to the cliche that "the sum of the parts is greater than the whole," the difficulty created by binary independence is that "the sum of the parts defines far too many wholes;" there is no natural way to determine which society is the correct one.

Why can't a procedure be designed to reassemble the parts in an intended way? To indicate the complexity of such a project, imagine the purchase of a new word processor that does not live up to its advertisements. Adopting a processor, or an axiom for voting procedures, carries several tacit assumptions. It is natural, for instance, to assume that the processor can deal with the integrated parts of a sentence. But, as anyone who has purchased software knows, assumptions about the merits need not always hold. To invent a particular horror story, suppose on a particular machine that the word processor has the disastrous flaw of divorcing letters from the way they are connected. This might, for instance, force us to deal with the set of letters

$$
\begin{array}{llllllll}
7 \text{ a's} & 6 \text{ c's} & 4 \text{ d's} & 14 \text{ e's} & 2 \text{ f's} & 1 \text{ g} & 5 \text{ h's} & 8 \text{ i's} \\
1 \text{ j} & 2 \text{ l's} & 3 \text{ m's} & 5 \text{ n's} & 11 \text{ o's} & 5 \text{ p's} & 6 \text{ r's} & 8 \text{ s's} \quad (3.5) \\
13 \text{ t's} & 3 \text{ u's} & 2 \text{ v's} & 2 \text{ w's} & 1 \text{ x} & 1 \text{ y}
\end{array}
$$

rather than an expected integrated whole: e.g., a sentence. I challenge the reader to figure what this set of parts — this collection of separated letters — means, where it came from, and how to reassemble it into its original formulation.

This set of letters mimics the kind of problems created by binary independence. Instead of integrated units of pairwise rankings defining rational beliefs, binary independence starts with a given picture of rationality, cuts it into separate pieces of binary parts where connections among them represent speculation rather than fact, and leaves us with a puzzle. Further complicating the issue is that a procedure satisfying binary independence only reacts to the available inputs about *that* pair, it cannot examine other binary information. To further illustrate this complexity, reach into your closet to get that 2000 piece puzzle and then try this approach of using only isolated information, of only examining individual puzzle pieces *without* checking how they might relate to one another, to put the puzzle together.

Incidentally, Table 3.5 lists the letters of the second sentence of the paragraph which ends in the table. The point is made; once the parts are separately cataloged, it is difficult to even speculate about the correct connection. Any *scrabble* expert probably would discover many different sentences that could be constructed from these parts, but probably not the intended one. We now know the intended construction, but once the connections are removed almost anything can apply. For Table 3.5, the correct connection is the one particular sentence; for binary pairs it is the appropriate rational society. As shown later, by being separated, the binary parts pose an even more complex difficulty.

## 3.3.2 A beer party and the free rider problem

To develop intuition as a way to anticipate related kinds of binary independence consequences where the "parts" take precedence over the "whole," recall the standard arrangements for a college beer party. Before going to the local beverage store to buy a keg, a hat is passed around where each person is encouraged to contribute an amount of money commensurate with the intended level of consumption. After the keg is bought, the party begins.

It is clear what can happen; some participants will take a "free ride" by contributing little but drinking much. To understand the binary independence relevance of this example, notice that although the intent is to closely coordinate the collection of money with the use of the product — this is the rational interpretation — the two acts are separated. But, and this is central to the argument, there is nothing built into the procedure to connect an individual's actions between the parts. Indeed, the procedure is perfectly capable of dealing with irrational individuals who sincerely believe that a minimal cash contribution and maximum level of drinking are compatible. Our free rider, of course, does not suffer any such misconception; this cheap skate just exploits the procedure's emphasis on "parts" by assuming the characteristics of the unsophisticated, misguided individual.

Remember, procedures are agnostic; by being algorithmic devices designed merely to "compute," they are indifferent about who to serve, or how to adjust the outcome in order to carry out *our* intention. To expand upon this beer party story, *our intent* is for the procedure to integrate and coordinate the parts — we intend the collection of funds to be related to each person's use of the provided service. But the adopted procedure fails to meet our intended wishes primarily because, instead of collecting coordinated information, it separates the information into divorced parts; it ignores the connecting information. The method's emphasis on parts, then, makes it perfectly capable of handling individuals whose personal preferences of the parts are any combination of desire to contribute and wish to use. Unintentionally, the resulting procedure can accommodate the irrational. The manipulative actions of others merely reflect an individual who strategically adopts one of these unintentionally admitted preferences. The societal cost is that if enough people do not contribute, the service is impossible.

Rather than novel, this insight has long been recognized and even systematically exploited. A natural example comes from the so-called "Right to Work" laws  still found in some American states.  These are the laws which specify that a worker need not join a labor union and be required to pay supporting dues, nor even contribute toward bargaining expenses, in order to enjoy the full benefits and higher wages of a labor contract.

To encourage workers to exploit these, more accurately called "Right to be a Free Rider" laws, the rhetoric attempts to justify what I called "irrational" behavior for the beer party. It does so by claiming that many workers do not wish to be affiliated with labor unions for personal or philosophical reasons. This may be true. But whatever the merits of these claims, it is arguable that the true intent is to weaken and destroy the unions by depriving them of needed operating funds through free-riding. Of primary interest for our discussion, this goal is accomplished by mandating a binary independence type of procedure which separates the collection of needed funds to provide a service from an individual's right to enjoy the benefits.

### 3.3.3   Pairwise vote

Let me illustrate this source of Arrow's disquieting assertion by turning to the widely used pairwise vote. As shown next, pairwise voting comes remarkably close to satisfying all of Arrow's conditions.

- (*Unrestricted domain.*)  As there are no restriction on how the voters rank the candidates, the pairwise vote satisfies the Unrestricted Domain condition.

- (*Pareto.*)  For each pair of alternatives $\{A, B\}$, if everyone prefers $A$ to $B$, then that is society's ranking. The pairwise vote satisfies the Pareto condition.

- (*Binary independence.*)  When determining the ranking for each pair of alternatives, say $\{A, B\}$, information about how the voters rank another alternative $C$ is irrelevant. The pairwise vote satisfies binary independence.[4]

- (*No dictator.*)  The pairwise vote satisfies anonymity where the outcome is determined by a majority vote. Consequently, the pairwise outcome is not determined by a dictator.

---

[4]It is interesting how "binary independence" and "independence of irrelevant alternatives" are misinterpreted. For instance, one internet discussion group on voting procedures condemn this property because it leads to Arrow's Theorem; it is, in their words, "undemocratic." But, to find more "democratic" procedures, they emphasize pairwise voting and other procedures which satisfy the precise property they condemn.

It appears that all of Arrow's conditions are satisfied for this non-dictatorial procedure. So, where is the guaranteed conflict?

**Condorcet triplet**

It remains to check whether outcomes of the pairwise vote always are transitive. They are not. The proof of this assertion underscores the importance of the following profile, discovered by Condorcet in the 1780s, displayed in Table 3.6 with its separated binary parts.

| Ranking | $\{A, B\}$ | $\{B, C\}$ | $\{A, C\}$ |
|---------|------------|------------|------------|
| $A\,B\,C$ | $A\,B$ | $B\,C$ | $A\,C$ |
| $B\,C\,A$ | $B\,A$ | $B\,C$ | $C\,A$ |
| $C\,A\,B$ | $A\,B$ | $C\,B$ | $C\,A$ |
| **Outcome** | $A\,B$ | $B\,C$ | $C\,A$ |

$$(3.6)$$

By counting who is preferred in each column, the pairwise elections define the familiar $A\,B$, $B\,C$, $C\,A$ cycle where each election is decided by a 2:1 vote. In other words, the only reason the pairwise vote fails to contradict Arrow's Theorem is that even without a "garbage in" problem (i.e., even with transitive preferences), it suffers "garbage out" conclusions (i.e., nontransitive outcomes).

It is useful to think of this voting method as a dutiful, honest servant capable only of tallying ballots. The important point is that there is nothing built into the algorithmic duties of this procedure which allows it to check whether the voters are, or are not, rational. As far as the pairwise vote is concerned, as long as the voters can rank each pair, as indicated by an ability to mark the ballots, the ballots can be tallied. This certifies the pairwise vote as a procedure that can be adopted by unsophisticated voters who cannot transitively sequence binary rankings. More bluntly, pairwise voting is a "donkey-and-cart" decision procedure. But, we know this; earlier (page 33) the pairwise vote was used to determine the outcome for the confused voters who embraced a proposition $\mathcal{P}$ of cyclic rankings.

It is interesting to learn how, thanks to binary independence, the disassembled binary parts of a Condorcet's profile can be reconstructed to define five different societies. By this I mean that there are five different profiles that the pairwise vote finds indistinguishable. Four of them involve irrational voters where it is arguable that the "correct" societal conclusion is a cycle; the last is the Condorcet profile. If this assertion is true; then it is only natural for the procedure to select the cyclic outcome as the appropriate conclusion for any profile with these particular "parts." Treat the procedure as playing the odds by trying to successfully serve "most" possibilities.

### Mix-and-Match

To find all profiles that are indistinguishable from Condorcet's choice, interchange, in all possible ways, the rankings in each column. For instance, in the last column of Table 3.6 interchange the first two rankings, and in the next to the last column interchange the last two rankings. By satisfying binary independence, the pairwise vote is indifferent as to whether the voters casting ballots have the original transitive rankings of Equation 3.6, or the rankings defined by the rows of

$$
\begin{array}{l|ccc}
\textbf{Voter type} & \{A, B\} & \{B, C\} & \{A, C\} \\
\hline
\text{Cyclic} & A\,B & B\,C & C\,A \\
\text{Reversed Cyclic} & B\,A & C\,B & A\,C \\
\text{Cyclic} & A\,B & B\,C & A\,C \\
\end{array}
\tag{3.7}
$$

   This inability of the pairwise vote to distinguish whether the voters are from Table 3.7 or Table 3.6 requires the outcome for both tables to be the same cycle. But this cyclic societal conclusion is natural and expected for Table 3.7. This is because the rows define a cyclic profile where two voters support $\mathcal{P} = \{A\,B, B\,C, C\,A\}$ and the third has opposing cyclic rankings. In Chapter 2 (page 33) we decided with an earlier version of this profile that the only fair societal outcome is the cycle $\mathcal{P}$.

   In a real sense, then, the cyclic outcome for Condorcet's profile merely manifests the "fair" conclusion[5] attached to an indistinguishable cyclic profile. Because the procedure cannot distinguish between rational and irrational voters from a sufficiently heterogeneous society as captured by Condorcet's profile, the procedure administers to the needs of the non-existent but indistinguishable cyclic voters rather than the actual rational voters. The confusion — and cycles — reflect the lost but available information about the actual profile.

   By continuing to "mix-and-match" the binary rankings of Table 3.6 in all possible ways, we discover all possible profiles — either of the rational or irrational type — that the pairwise vote finds indistinguishable from the Condorcet profile. For instance, interchanging only the bottom two ranking of the $\{A, B\}$ column of Equation 3.6 leads to the profile

---

[5] "Fair" is tacitly defined by the adoption of the procedure; here, "fair" means the majority preference.

| Voter type | $\{A, B\}$ | $\{B, C\}$ | $\{A, C\}$ |
|:---:|:---:|:---:|:---:|
| $A\,B\,C$ | $A\,B$ | $B\,C$ | $A\,C$ |
| Cyclic | $A\,B$ | $B\,C$ | $C\,A$ |
| $C\,B\,A$ | $B\,A$ | $C\,B$ | $C\,A$ |

$$(3.8)$$

As the first and third rows represent transitive voters with directly opposing views, they cancel each other's vote in each of the three pairwise elections; this creates a complete tie. Thus the remaining voter's preferences (row two) must break the tie by defining a societal outcome which reflects this voter's views. It does; both the remaining voter's preferences of the second row and the outcome are cyclic. Again for this profile, the pairwise outcome is the correct one.

By mixing-and-matching binary rankings, five kinds of profiles emerge.

- For three profiles, two voters have directly opposing transitive preferences which cancel each other's vote in each pairwise election. (To find these rankings, start with any strict transitive ranking and then include its reversal.) The fair outcome, then, reflects the preferences of the remaining voter who breaks the tie; this voter always has the cyclic rankings $A\,B$, $B\,C$, $C\,A$.

- All voters have cyclic preferences where two have the $A\,B$, $B\,C$, $C\,A$ rankings and one has the reversed ranking. As already analyzed, the cycle is the only fair outcome.

- The last choice is the Condorcet profile where all voters have transitive rankings and each candidate is listed in first, second, and third place once; no candidate has an advantage. Based on this information about how the pairwise rankings are similarly sequenced, it is arguable that the only fair outcome is the $A = B = C$ tie.

As far as an binary independence procedure is concerned, then, the pairwise information from the pairs of Equation 3.6 could come from five different types of profiles. For 80% of them, the fair outcome is the cycle; the remaining Condorcet case suggests an indecisive tie. Thus, it is arguable that the "correct" outcome is the cycle.

## 3.3.4 Ranking disk

The problems created by the Condorcet triplet significantly escalate with the number of alternatives. To show this, I first introduce an easy way to construct an $n$-candidate version of this Condorcet profile; it uses what I call a *ranking disk*.

Attach a freely moving disk at its center to a fixed surface; say, a wall. Evenly spaced, place on this disk the numbers $1, 2, \ldots, n$. Next, do something you secretly wanted to do ever since your artistic career was sharply halted at the age of three for "artistically painting" the dining room walls. On the wall, write each candidate's name next to her ranking number. For instance, in the following Figure 3.1, A is ranked first, so her name is placed over the number 1, D is ranked fourth, so her name is over the number 4. The ranking disk of Figure 3.1 displays the rankings for

$$r = A \succ B \succ C \succ D \succ E \succ F \succ G \succ H.$$

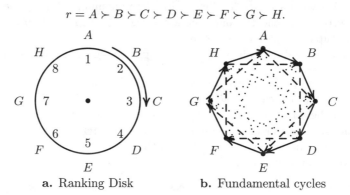

a. Ranking Disk          b. Fundamental cycles

**Figure 3.1.** Ranking disk and Condorcet tuple

Next, rotate the ranking disk in a clockwise manner so that ranking number "1" now is under the name of the next candidate. In Figure 3.1, the ranking number "1" now is beneath $B$ while the ranking number "2" is under $C$. This new position of the ranking disk defines a second transitive ranking for our Condorcet $n$-tuple. For the above choice of $r$, this second ranking is

$$B \succ C \succ D \succ E \succ F \succ G \succ H \succ A.$$

Continue until $n$-distinct rankings are defined. This construction defines what I call the *Condorcet $n$-tuple*. With the Figure 3.1 example, eight distinct rankings occur; it is an useful exercise to compute all of them.

**Many, too many cycles**

An important aspect of the Condorcet $n$-tuple is that it defines several pairwise voting cycles. There is a surprisingly simple way to extract all of them by using what I call the *fundamental cycles*. To do so, remove the disk and use the names permanently marked on the wall. First, connect adjacently listed candidates with solid lines (see Figure 3.1b). This connection defines what I call the *primary cycle*; it involves all $n$ candidates. For Figure 3.1b, this primary cycle is $A \succ B, B \succ C, \ldots, H \succ A$.

Next, draw a line connecting *every other candidate*; this defines a *secondary* cycle. If $n$ is odd, this new cycle involves all $n$ candidates; if $n$ is even, then (as in Figure 3.1b) this construction identifies two different secondary cycles where each cycle involves half of the candidates. To be precise, these two new Figure 3.1b secondary cycles are $A \succ C, C \succ E, E \succ G, G \succ A$ and $B \succ D, D \succ F, F \succ H, H \succ B$.

Continue this process. Thus, the next step is to draw a line connecting every third candidate to create another set of secondary cycles. In Figure 3.1, this becomes $A \succ D, D \succ G, G \succ B, B \succ E, E \succ H, H \succ C, C \succ F, F \succ A$. Then, do the same every fourth for another set. Continue creating these secondary cycles until you have used up just less than half of the candidates. So, for eight candidates, there are $3 < 8/2 = 4$ sets of cycles. For 15 candidates, this construction defines seven (as $7 < 15/2$) sets of cycles.

In Figure 3.1b, the solid arrows indicate the primary cycle while the dashed lines determine two secondary cycles involving every other candidate, and the dotted lines determine still another secondary cycle involving every third candidate. These cycles move in a clockwise direction where an arrow points from a preferred to a less preferred candidate. That is, when computing the pairwise tallies of this Condorcet $n$-tuple, the pairwise rankings follow the arrows.

This construction already identifies many different voting cycles defined by the Condorcet profile — and there are still others. To find all possible cycles defined by this profile, start at some candidate, say $A$, and follow one of the outgoing arrows. As it doesn't matter which one, choose the one in Figure 3.1b going to $D$. Now, choose one of the $D$ outgoing arrows to another candidate, say, to $E$. Continue this process until returning to $A$. For instance, one cycle constructed in this manner is $A \succ D, D \succ E, E \succ H, H \succ C, C \succ F, F \succ G, G \succ A$. This cycle, of course, is just one of many which are admitted by the Condorcet profile.[6] As indicated next, these cycles complicate our decision processes. We already know that they cause Arrow's conclusion.

---

[6]Adding more Condorcet profiles makes the pairwise mess messier.

### Rational vs. irrational

How many profiles can be constructed from the "binary parts" of a Condorcet $n$-tuple as allowed by binary independence? As the numbers are so amazing that they belong to the "Gee whiz!" category, let me turn technical for a couple of paragraphs to indicate how to compute them. Those readers not interested in the computations might be satisfied to accept the conclusion that, while millions of different societies can be constructed from the parts, *the Condorcet n-tuple is the only rational profile among them.* (Verification is left to the highly adventurous reader with a strong understanding of mathematics.)

To construct the other possible profiles allowed by these parts — in these profiles some of the voters will have cyclic preferences — first use the binary parts to define profiles where $(n-2)$ of the voters have preferences identical to the primary cycle, while the last two voters have transitive preferences. These transitive preferences can be anything, but these two voters must have directly opposing views. Actually, these directly opposing views can be any ranking defined by the pairs.

Readers comfortable with combinatorics will recognize that this construction generates at least $2^{[n(n-1)/2]-1}$ profiles. (There are many more profiles due to the ways rankings from the secondary cycles can be assigned to the voters.) For readers not familiar with this notation, it means that with only eight voters, there are $2^{27}$ profiles — this is 2 multiplied by itself 27 times — for a total of at least 134,217,728 different ways to compute different and indistinguishable (for the pairwise vote) profiles. For each such profile, the preferences of the two opposing voters cancel, so the tie is broken by the remaining cyclic voters. Thus, for almost all profiles exhibiting this data, the cyclic outcome is the only natural choice — for the pairwise vote.

To illustrate with eight candidates, how can we argue that the cycle is the wrong outcome when it is the correct one for more than a 134 million of the possible interpretations of the data, but maybe the wrong one for just one interpretation? Using numbers, the cycle is the "correct" societal outcome for than $2^{27}/[2^{27}+1]$ of all possible societies submitting the same information about these pairwise parts. Stated in another manner, the cycle is the correct conclusion for more than 99.999999% of the profiles — all indistinguishable — that can be constructed from these binary parts. From the perspective of the pairwise vote, then, the transitive preferences (even though they are the intended preferences) are, by far, the highly unlikely choice defined by these parts. Consequently, the cycle is the natural conclusion for most profiles serviced by this procedure.

### The hidden power of a chair

To take a slight but needed break from this somewhat technical description, I digress to show how this ranking disk generates all sorts of troubling election conclusions. In fact, whenever a problem, or a surprising paradox, occurs with a procedure based on pairwise comparisons, be assured that the root cause is that the group's preferences contain at least a portion of a Condorcet tuple. This is not speculation; recently I proved this result. Indeed, the power of these Condorcet terms to cause problems is so enormous that decision paradoxes of all sorts can arise even when only a couple of the terms from this "ranking disk" construction are used.

To demonstrate this subtle but enormous effect, start with the ranking $r = N \succ M \succ T \succ S \succ R \succ Q \succ P \succ O$ where each letter, arranged in a reverse order from the alphabet, is the first letter of a name. After subjecting $r$ to the ranking disk where, instead of generating the full eight rankings (mathematicians call this "the $Z_8$ orbit of the original ranking"), keep only the first three to generate the three-voter profile

1. $N \succ M \succ$ **T** $\succ S \succ R \succ Q \succ P \succ$ **O**,

2. $M \succ$ **T** $\succ S \succ R \succ Q \succ P \succ$ **O** $\succ N$

3. **T** $\succ S \succ R \succ Q \succ P \succ$ **O** $\succ N \succ M$

The nice structure of this profile leads to several immediate conclusions. First, notice the highly favored status of $T$, Teka; she enjoys the honor of being ranked in first, second, or third place. As no other candidate is so highly favored by these voters, it is arguable that Teka should wear the title of being the group's favored candidate.

For symmetric reasons, $O$, Olivia, appears to be the group's least favored candidate; Olivia always is ranked near the bottom. In fact, the only other candidates to suffer similar poor respect by a voter are Neena and Matilda; but at least Neena and Matilda can point to their top-ranking by one voter. This listing strongly suggests the societal ranking should rank the four discussed candidates as

Teka $\succ$ Matilda $\succ$ Neena $\succ$ Olivia.

To find the societal ranking for the remaining candidates, notice that, without exception, *each voter* prefers Teka $\succ$ Sue $\succ$ Robin $\succ$ Queeny $\succ$ Priscilla $\succ$ Olivia. That each voter prefers the same five candidates to Olivia adds further evidence to the claim that Olivia should be relegated to the unfortunate status as being the societal bottom ranked candidate.

Now that we have established the superiority of Teka along with the inferior status of Olivia, consider the powers of being a chair of an organization. Quite frankly, thanks to *Robert's Rules of Order* and other accepted democratic principles intended to protect the rights of the voters, a chair's role is limited. For instance, usually a chair can vote only in those highly unlikely setting where there is a tie. Even more limiting, the chair cannot even join in the debate. In practice, a chair's role often is merely a "discussion traffic-cop" trying to maintain order by ensuring the voters speak in some correct order. Other than that, the chair's responsibilities entail house-keeping, such as ensuring there is plenty of coffee, the meeting room is available, and carrying out much of the busy-work such as duplicating copies of documents members want distributed, preparing the agenda, and making sure the meeting starts on time. Not much glamor or power here.

Or, is there? Suppose our chair just happens to preside over an organization consisting of these three voters who despise Olivia. To add insult to his duties of chairing the meeting, only our chair favors Olivia — and the chair's responsibilities prevent him from arguing why she is the best candidate. In addition to providing coffee, our chair has to design an agenda for the meeting. This is a source of enormous power. Against seemingly impossible opposition, this "task" enables our chair to ensure the election of Olivia — without even having to speak or vote. In fact, the following explanation of the hidden source of this power helps explain my earlier boast (page 13) that, "For a price, I will ... "

To see how to do this, notice that with the full Condorcet eight-cycle, the primary cycle is Neena $\succ$ Matilda, Matilda $\succ$ Teka, ... , Olivia $\succ$ Neena. But, this primary pairwise cycle already occurs with only the above three voters. So, to ensure Olivia's election *in spite of the preferences of the members which are stacked against her,* our chair puts forth a majority vote, pairwise comparison agenda. While some parliamentarians may object, this is a standard, widely used procedure; at each stage, the majority winner advances to be compared with the next listed candidate.

To design the "manipulative" agenda, work backwards from where Olivia can win. The *only* candidate Olivia can beat in a majority vote is Neena. Therefore, the *last* pairwise vote should be between Neena and Olivia. But, to ensure that Neena is a candidate at the last stage, the stage before should be between Neena and someone she can beat — Matilda. By working backwards through the cycle, we obtain the Figure 3.2 agenda. Here, the winning alternative at each stage is determined by her location in the primary cycle. So, the winner of the {Queeny, Priscilla} election is Queeny; the winner of the next {Robin, Queeny} election is Robin, and so forth. This strategically

designed agenda ensures the election of Olivia where, at each step, the outcome is determined with either two-thirds or unanimous votes. Olivia is the
"overwhelming" winner — even though no voter really likes her.

The point of this example is to illustrate the damage caused by these
Condorcet $n$-tuple profiles; with the pairwise vote, the order of comparison
matters. An important conclusion, which I described and proved elsewhere,
is that *these Condorcet profiles are the sole source of the many, many different
difficulties experienced by pairwise voting procedures.* In any setting where
the order of comparison matters, it is due to the Condorcet term; if there is
a paradox, it is due to the Condorcet term. The intuition is clear; as shown,
the combination of these profiles with the pairwise vote dismisses the crucial
assumption that the voters are rational.

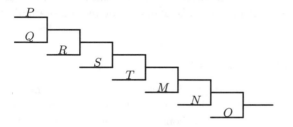
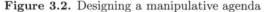

**Figure 3.2.** Designing a manipulative agenda

To underscore this "loss of rationality" argument, by using only pairwise
comparisons at each stage, the agenda severs all information about transitivity. Thus, the procedure cannot distinguish the actual profile from the
cyclic profile where two voters have the preferences

$$N \succ M, M \succ T, \dots, P \succ O, O \succ N$$

while the last voter has the slightly altered cyclic preferences

$$O \succ N, N \succ M, M \succ T, \dots, P \succ O.$$

### 3.3.5 Winning against unanimity

Return to my earlier comment (page 13) how it is possible to go into an
organization and find ways to elect a specified candidate. I can imagine the
reader searching for qualifications in this claim. For instance, clearly such
a despicable feat never could occur if the voters are unanimous about how
to rank the candidates. Most surely, it is impossible to strategically select
a procedure in this extreme setting.

Or, is it? Start with an unanimity situation where not only does everyone love Teka, but they share the unanimous ranking

$$T \succ S \succ R \succ Q \succ P \succ O.$$

Look familiar? It should; it is the core part of the above profile leading to Olivia's selection. In other words, in addition to selecting a procedure, the strategic approach I would advocate is to introduce a couple more alternatives — $M$ and $N$ — in a manner which splits the voters. More work? Of course. But extra effort must be expected as it takes more work to counter the impossible.

Again, this illustration is no hypothetical, academic exercise. While I am unaware of any real example involving so many candidates which are so nicely lined up, realistic examples can be found involving a more limited number of alternatives.

### 3.3.6   How to win your way

I can imagine certain readers smugly pushing away the book in a firm belief that his or her congenial organization is immune to all of these shenanigans. "My group cooperates; we always rule by consensus." Think again; you may discover that you and your group have been victimized by this phenomena. In fact, a mediocre or inferior decision may have been made without anyone realizing what happened.

**Problems caused by consensus**

The point is, this worrisome voting phenomena can arise in full force during the debate and discussion prior to a vote. As an illustration, think back to a recent meeting where someone suggested adopting the just published art history book by Priscilla only to have it compared with that written by Queeny. As everyone prefers the introduction in Queeny's book, Pricilla's book is dismissed without a vote. But Robin's book did receive a better book review than Queeny's, so, by consensus, attention now is focussed on Robin's book. The debate — covering a variety of aspects — continues by emphasizing different details and issues: Sue's book has a more solid description of Rodin than Robin's, Teka's book handles Renoir in a more sensitive manner than Sue's. The debate goes around the cycle. The result? Olivia's inferior text is selected with a strong two-thirds "consensus."

The disturbing point is that all of these societal nightmares and inefficiencies are not restricted to actual elections. Instead, the problem of choosing poorly can be inherent in the dynamics of the discussion; it can be an unfortunate consequence of the coveted goal of deciding by consensus. The sad fact is that the organization may suspect they made an inferior choice, but they may never recognize why.

### Manipulative opportunities

On the other hand, this description provides tempting opportunities and a manipulative guideline for an aspiring Machiavelli to have his way. In fact, the above argument outlines techniques our Machiavelli should use to snooker the group into selecting his preferred alternative.

The strategy follows the above outline. Govern the dynamics of the discussion — find issues and details to compare the stronger competitors at an early stage so they are eliminated. But, wait, always wait during the discussion to introduce your personally desired alternative until the very end. This is not hypothetical advice; many people have learned from experience that waiting till the end of a discussion to raise a preferred course of action provides uncommon success.

### Seeding for tennis, or a basketball tournament

An agenda is a particular version of a tournament used to determine who plays whom in sports. Every spring in the US, for example, everyone from self proclaimed "athletic supporters" to the true collegiate basketball fanatics carefully examine the sports news to determine which teams are invited to the national (NCAA) basketball tournament. But more than who will be playing, morning discussions among those who know, most surely will argue about the significance of which teams are in which "bracket."

Much like a tennis tournament, at the first stage the teams are matched into pairs where the winner from each pair moves on to play the winner from another specified pair. This procedure continues until only one team wins — the National Champs!

Does it matter who plays whom at each tournament stage? Most tournament seedings start by matching a weak team with a strong team giving the weak team little chance to survive even the first game. But for the ultimate goal of selecting the national champ, won't the "best" team always persevere to end up the ultimate victor no matter how the tournament is structured? Quite frankly, no.

To see why this is the case, instead of a sports tournament, consider a "voting" tournament where, at each stage, the outcome is determined by a majority vote. Our example requires devising a new set of voter preferences where the construction sheds more light on decision process. The goal is to find a way to elect Olivia. But, for Olivia to win, she needs to beat more than one candidate. The reason is clear; to win a tournament, a team must win at each stage. So, for Olivia to be victorious among the eight candidates, she has to survive the first stage of the tournament which reduces the number of candidates from eight to four. Then, Olivia needs to survive the second cut which reduces the remaining candidates from four to two. Finally, she must win the finals. In total, then, Olivia has to beat at least three candidates. On the other hand, two of the three candidates Olivia beats also must win enough to advance to the intended tournament level.

To create an example, start by specifying who should beat whom. In Figure 3.3, for instance, I have Olivia capable of beating only the three indicated candidates. As one of these candidates must beat someone to advance to the second stage, I require Matilda to beat Sue. Finally, another candidate, I selected Teka, must beat two others to make it to the finals.

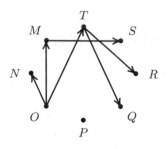

**Figure 3.3.** Who has to beat whom

To create a profile satisfying these cyclic conditions, examine the fundamental cycles of Figure 3.1b. By doing so, one solution to this design problem is

**1.** $M \succ T \succ S \succ R \succ Q \succ P \succ O \succ N$,

**2.** $S \succ R \succ Q \succ P \succ O \succ N \succ M \succ T$, and

**3.** $P \succ O \succ N \succ M \succ T \succ S \succ R \succ Q$.

Again, this profile suggests that Olivia is the distinctly minor candidate; she beats only Neena, Matilda, and Teka, while Sue, Robin, Queeny and Priscilla can beat her. Yet, thanks to the cyclic nature of the pairwise outcome, a tournament seeding can be designed which ensures that Olivia will be the national champ. Figure 3.4 gives one choice.

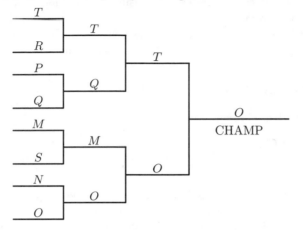

**Figure 3.4.** Designing a manipulative tournament

As with the agenda example, there are many cyclic profiles which share the same election outcomes for the above seven comparisons. Even more; these phantom cyclic preferences can justify the tournament outcome as a reasonable one. It is this inability of pairwise procedures to distinguish among the potential profiles which allows the phantom irrational profiles to crown Olivia as the procedure's natural winner.

In the introductory chapter, I stressed the importance of compiling reliable information. However, to be useful, the information must be used. As we are learning, suspect outcomes can occur should the decision procedure ignore portions of the available information — as true with the tournament example. On the other hand, us sport fans not only suspect this phenomenon, but we derive immense, continued pleasure from it. It is this doubt caused by the inadequacies of the pairwise comparison procedure which permits us to wallow in extended post mortems after every tournament putting forth all our "if only" arguments to explain why our favorite team failed to win.

I leave it to the reader to use the Condorcet tuples and the ranking disk construction to create "paradoxes" for other procedures dependent upon the pairwise vote. Again, the explanation for these paradoxes remains much the same; since the procedure is incapable of distinguishing between cyclic and transitive voters, the outcome could be the correct one — for those profiles with irrational voters.

**The Clinton poll — creating examples**

Even more mysteries can be resolved by using the ranking disk. For an illustration coming from statistics, return to the public opinion polls trying to capture the American sentiment about the possible impeachment of President Clinton (page 8). In describing this poll, label the four alternatives as

**A:** impeach President Clinton,

**B:** censure President Clinton,

**C:** fine President Clinton, or

**D:** do nothing.

The mystery is to understand how, for each proposed punishment, a vast majority of the American public could be against it even though a vast majority wanted President Clinton to be punished in some manner. To explain, use the ranking wheel — not with all four alternatives, but with only three of them — as displayed in Figure 3.5.

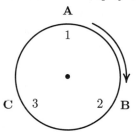

**Figure 3.5.** Creating paradoxical examples

By spinning the wheel, the three preferences define the standard Condorcet triplet

$$\mathbf{A\,B\,C}, \quad \mathbf{B\,C\,A}, \quad \mathbf{C\,A\,B}.$$

To convert this setting into preferences over the four alternatives, in each ranking insert **D** as the second choice. Instead of assuming only one voter of each type, assume that of the thousands upon thousands of people who were interviewed, one-third of them had each of the following beliefs

$$\mathbf{A\,D\,B\,C}, \quad \mathbf{B\,D\,C\,A}, \quad \mathbf{C\,D\,A\,B}.$$

An interesting aspect of this concocted setting is that rather than the percentage of respondents wishing for some sort of penalty hovering in the sixty percent range, this example has the paradoxical behavior whereby *all voters believe a punishment of some sort is appropriate*. Yet, whatever the proposed approach, a full two-thirds of the voters are against it!

So, by use of the spinning ranking disk — and the resulting loss of the integrity of the pairwise outcomes as manifested by the actual poll — we can create all sorts of examples illustrating a host of disturbing phenomena. Can or should we trust pairwise comparisons? I think not.

### Creating paradoxes

Let me carry this analysis one step further. Earlier, when describing the consequences of the Compatibility Theorem (page 52), I claimed that examples can be created displaying the conflict between standard election procedures and the pairwise ranking. A quick way to accomplish this is to use the ranking disk. After all, we know that the preferences which emerge from a full swing of the ranking disk have no effect upon the outcomes of the usual positional methods.

To illustrate this construction, start with a setting involving just two members of a cinema group. As for their preferences of favored actress, both prefer

$$\text{Bobbie} \succ \text{Alice} \succ \text{Candy}.$$

There is no debate; as far as this cinema group is concerned, Bobbie is favored. This is the election outcome provided by all of the usual positional methods; it is the pairwise election outcome.

To put a spin on this situation, turn the ranking disc of Figure 3.4 three full circles to create the preferences for the nine new members of the cinema group. Because the preferences of these nine voters should cancel — each actress is in first, second, and third position three times — the tied outcome should be determined by the first two members. In other words, the favored candidate still should be Bobbie. This is the election outcome of any positional methods which assign points to candidates.

Now consider what happens to the pairwise vote. Here, the original two members' rankings are

$$B \succ A, \quad B \succ C, \quad A \succ C,$$

where each ranking is supported by the unanimous 2:0 tally. But, because the preferences for the new nine come from a ranking wheel, the pairwise vote loses the information that they are rational individuals.  Instead, it confuses their preferences with those of a group of irrational voters with cyclic preferences. This is manifested by the cyclic nature of their election ranking

$$A \succ B, \quad B \succ C, \quad C \succ A,$$

where each ranking is supported by the tally 6:3.

In total, then, even though it is arguable that Bobbie remains the group's favored candidate, the outcome is

- Alice beats Bobbie by a 6:5 vote,

- Alice beats Candy by a 6 to 5 vote, and

- Bobbie beats Candy by a 8 to 3 vote.

The point is that the Condorcet triplet — with it concomitant loss of information about the rationality of voters — is the source of the difficulties of Sen's and Arrow's results. Faced with this information, we should expect that illustrating examples are constructed in this manner. As shown, this is the case; this is one of the sources of the assertions of the Compatibility Theorem (page 52).

### 3.3.7   Arrow's dictator

So far, I have taken you on a side excursion exploring consequences caused by losing the crucial "rationality of the voters" assumption. To repeat the main point, the binary independence requirement emasculates the crucial assumption that voters are rational.  The voters *are rational* (by explicit assumption), but, because binary independence forces the sequencing information about pairs to be ignored, the separated binary parts can define a wide range of radically different societies; societies where many of them differ significantly from the intended one.  Because binary independence procedures can be used with cyclic and other kinds of irrational voters, the new purpose of the *Unrestricted Domain* condition is to sift through the binary independence admitted methods to determine whether any admitted procedure allows rational outcomes in the special case when the voters are rational. The only such procedure is a *dictator*.

To understand why a dictatorship is the only possible choice, recall that, by definition, a dictator's ranking of each pair becomes society's ranking of that pair.  If a dictator happens to have transitive preferences, then this one person's pairwise rankings can be reconstructed in only one manner —

the same transitive ranking is returned. But, once more than one voter can influence the outcome, the transitivity of preferences is lost. Namely, the information dismissed by binary independence is so extensive and central that even a two-voter society can become "sufficiently heterogeneous" to prevent an binary independence procedure from recognizing that it is not dealing with an irrational culture.

## 3.3.8   Avoiding Arrow's dictator

As we now understand, procedures which satisfy "binary independence" should be viewed as designed for the unsophisticated voter. Quite frankly, as far as these procedures are concerned, the rationality issue is irrelevant. No wonder Arrow's conclusion holds.

Indeed, binary independence makes the data from Condorcet profiles appear to be coming from irrational voters. This raises a question; what would happen if we could cleanse the data of all Condorcet terms? (Positional methods do this; they force such terms to cancel into a tie.) The surprising answer is that Arrow's Dictator can be replaced with almost all procedures based on the pairwise vote. This includes the Borda Count, any agenda, the pairwise vote itself, and on and on.

As shown in a later chapter, by repairing the binary independence condition so that the new condition must use the information about the voters' rationality, Arrow's dictator is replaced by an assortment of reasonable procedures. This returns us to the introductory comments; *by requiring procedures designed for rational voters, rational outcomes can emerge; by using binary independent methods, which can be viewed as being designed for irrational voters, problems arise.*

# Chapter 4

# What Else Can Go Wrong?

## 4.1 Some assembly required

What do games of chance, analyzing the spread of AIDS, gambling on football games, hedging on the market, appointment of congressional seats to states, and even strategic behavior have to do with this part-whole conflict?

I already explained why an array of important assertions — Arrow's Theorem, Sen's Theorem, as well as the difficulties experienced by pairwise voting, agendas, tournaments, conflicting comparisons, and even the search for consensus — reflect the loss of central, readily available information. Simply stated, by not using crucial information, the integrity of the outcomes cannot be ensured. Problems must be expected whenever information about the disconnected parts fails to characterize the connected whole.

The situation resembles those three feared words which can accompany a new purchase — *some assembly required*. Panic rushes in. Where is the instruction sheet? Without instructions explicitly explaining how the parts are related, without a guide to clarify how to put them together, the purchase can become an expensive pile of junk — a useless collection of parts collecting dust rather than meeting an intended goal. Similarly, as described in the last chapter, whenever a voting or decision procedure concentrates on the parts, it can unintentionally ignore the assumption that the voters have rational preferences. Lost is the instruction sheet describing how the parts — how each voter's ranking of the pairs — should be assembled. Since the properties of a procedure reflect its inability to use "connecting" information, we must anticipate results such as those of Arrow, Sen, and the free rider.

## 4.1.1   Expect the unexpected

This "part - whole" information loss extends far beyond voting and decision analysis; indeed, almost all aspects of our lives include a "Some assembly required" involvement. Expect paradoxical phenomena whenever there is a potential discrepancy between the actual unified whole and the various ways to interpret the totality of disconnected parts. Whenever this is true, whenever the "instruction sheet" describing how to connect the parts is dismissed, lost, or ignored, expect the unexpected; anticipate bothersome and unexpected outcomes to arise in a subtle, unexpected manner.

Not only do surprisingly many settings suffer paradoxical behavior, but we can contribute to this wealth of examples with the natural tactic of solving a complicated problem by dividing it into "parts." This separation may be promoted in the name of "efficiency;" it may be rationalized as a means to simplify the analysis. But, this division, this decentralization, this approach we have been taught to embrace, can be a hidden, pernicious "killer assumption" whose existence was forewarned early in the book.

These comments already suggest how this "assassin assumption" of emphasizing the parts forms a natural explanation for differences found so often between the micro and macro examinations of so many disciplines. After all, the explicit purpose of the micro study is to understand the structure of a specified "part" of the field as disconnected from the other structures. The micro approach is a valued, necessary strategy. But, when attempting to understand a macro concern by using information from micro studies, the importance of using "connecting information" among the micro parts must be acknowledged. What "connecting information?" As with Arrow's result, it may be available, even explicitly assumed, but, in subtle ways, not used.

Other illustrations are easy to find. They come, for instance, from the legal world where legislation worrying about "this particular setting over that one" force an emphasis on individual circumstances over the whole. In fact, it is reasonable to wonder whether some of the ever escalating levels of litigation is directed toward resolving these conflicts. Other examples come from economics where standard myopic descriptions of how to determine societal behavior, such as changes in prices, emphasize "local" decisions rather than a global perspective.

Expect examples to arise in engineering. This is because highly complex engineering settings mandates finding approaches to simplify the analysis. A way to address these massive, difficult problems is to deal with the parts, to adopt decentralized organizational structures. But, could this decentralization, which places a strong emphasis on the parts, cause a loss of readily available information? If so, then conflict must be expected; conflict which may be manifested in the form of inefficiencies.

This loss of connecting information most definitely occurs in general decision making whenever the societal outcomes of "parts" has a de facto precedence over the whole. This includes those commonly used procedures, such as agendas and tournaments, which reach a final conclusion in terms of disjoint decisions about "pairs." It includes settings where divided jurisdictions, such as states or local communities, separates information about criminal activities causing inefficiencies in law enforcement. It includes countries which allow the different branches of the military to separately develop resources which, as we now should expect, result in a lack of efficiency and a more costly defense budget.

On a daily basis we probably experience numerous small frustrations — in our dealings with bureaucracy, in committees, in our daily work — which manifest this lack of coordination, this loss of information explaining how the "whole" should be assembled. As such, we should expect the ubiquitous difficulties which cause Arrow's and Sen's assertions to affect us in numerous ways on a regular basis. This reality suggests adopting a cautious, somewhat sceptical attitude about so many aspects of our daily and professional lives — *beware of hidden assumptions.*

## 4.1.2 General approach

The lost information for new examples most surely manifests something different than a violation of the "rational agent assumption" which caused the free rider, Arrow's, and Sen's problems. To discover new examples, consider settings which are similar to where a person tackles a "Some assembly required" project while ignoring the instruction sheet. Namely, examine settings where a discussion about how to assemble the parts is put aside.

The challenge is to anticipate and understand when and where these paradoxes raise their confusing but fascinating heads. Here, we have an advantage; search for part-whole differences in heterogeneous settings. Much like a Tuesday night in a small, rural community, not much happens with homogeneous or replicated settings. Here, it is possible for the parts to capture aspects of the whole. Then, use these heterogeneous settings to identify the nature of the connecting information.

The following examples illustrate this approach while showing how the Arrow type phenomenon extends into other areas. In particular, the emphasis is on informational differences between the parts and the whole. The examples and discussion in sections 4.2, 3, and 6 borrows heavily from my joint research with Katri Sieberg, an academic at the historic College of William and Mary who is interested in economics and political science.

## 4.2   Simpson's Paradox

Let us take a break from this discussion and relax. To do so, let me offer you another opportunity to win good fortune.

> "Do I have a deal! See that nice, new, red Porsche sitting outside? It is yours by winning a simple game of chance. All you do is to choose one of two urns. Both urns contain red and blue marbles. After you select an urn, reach in without looking and extract a marble. If it is "red," you win the car. If it is "blue," well, I keep the car but you will have to pay for it."

A high stakes game. But, what makes your decision problem somewhat easier is that, from an undisclosed source, you learned that the urn marked $I$ has an higher percentage of red marbles than the urn marked $II$. With this information, the optimal choice is clear. Select urn $I$ as it provides a higher likelihood of winning. Once urn $I$ is selected, reach in and hope that you pull out a red marble.

Now suppose that my confederate — let us call him my "business partner" — has a separate set of urns where, as you also discovered from your secret source, the urn marked $I'$ has a higher percentage of red marbles than the one marked $II'$. With this information, your selection problem is obvious; if you encounter either of us, always choose the first urn as it provides a better chance of winning.

This description defines two disconnected "parts;" they are the two separate sets of urns. For each part, sufficient information is provided to make an optimal decision. But on a particular sunny day, suppose that my confederate skipped the scam to spend time at the beach. Since I am stuck with two sets of urns, to simplify the process I

- combine all of the marbles from "good urns" $I$ and $I'$ to create a new urn $I''$, and

- combine all of the marbles from "bad urns" $II$ and $II'$ to create a new urn $II''$.

Which urn now maximizes your opportunity to win? Again, this question appears to qualify as a "no-brainer;" the correct answer for the "whole" —

the combination of the two parts — should be to select urn $I$." After all, this urn combines the two optimal choices of good urns. Most surely the sum of two "good outcomes" is even better; it should not create a bummer.

### 4.2.1  The paradox

What should cause pause is that this urn problem describes "disjoint, disconnected parts" without a discussion about how to assemble them. The disjoint parts are the two separate sets of urns; the "whole" is created by combining the contents to generate urns $I$" and $II$". Maybe we should expect the unexpected from this "parts–whole" setting. If unusual outcomes do result, they most surely manifest "connecting information." As advised, to find examples and the missing information, examine heterogeneous settings.

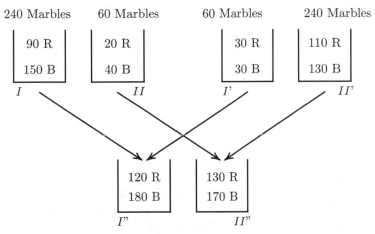

**Figure 4.1.** Marbles in urns

Figure 4.1 depicts such an heterogeneous setting where, indeed, in either collection, the first urn is better than the second. But, when combined, the second urn, $II$", is better than the first combined urn, $I$". In this figure, $R$ and $B$ denote, respectively, the red and blue marbles.

To carry out the computations:

1. For urn $I$, $\frac{90}{240} > \frac{1}{3}$ of the marbles are red; for urn $II$, only $\frac{20}{60} = \frac{1}{3}$ of the marbles are red. As advertised, there is a better chance of winning with urn $I$ from the first set.

2. For urn $I'$, a full $\frac{30}{60} = \frac{1}{2}$ of the marbles are red, while for urn $II'$,

only $\frac{110}{240} < \frac{1}{2}$ of the marbles are red. Again, there is a better chance of winning with urn $I'$ from the second set.

3. When the "good parts" are combined, urn $I''$ has 300 marbles (240 from urn $I$ and 60 from $I'$) of which $90 + 30 = 120$ are red. Hence, the fraction of red in urn $I''$ is $\frac{120}{300}$. Urn $II''$ also has 300 marbles, but the number of red ones is $20 + 110 = 130$. Hence the expected surprise; as these simple computations prove, the higher fraction, $\frac{130}{300}$, of red marbles is in urn $II''$ rather than in $I''$. Urn $II''$, not urn $I''$, provides the better chance of winning. Again, the outcome of the "whole" can conflict with the behavior of the "parts."

This situation where the "overall winner" could have lost all the "battles" brings to mind the efforts of George Washington in the American War for Independence; Washington lost enough battles, but he did win the war. Even more, this sense where the "best" whole comes from combining "poor" parts leaves us with an intriguing question. Could there be settings where the global "optimal" outcome requires putting together "suboptimal" parts?

## 4.2.2   More relevant examples

When described as a game of chance, this example is, at best, amusing. But any oddity involving standard computations — here the computations involve probabilities — most surely occurs in examples that affect daily decisions. The form of the marble example indicates where to find illustrations; search settings where different types — the "successes" or "reds," and the "failures" or 'blues" — are compared and added. A natural example, where E. Simpson first noted this strange behavior, is in medical testing.

To provide a medical interpretation for the Figure 4.1 numbers, suppose a new, experimental medication is tested in Evanston, Illinois, and in Irvine, California. Suppose in Evanston, of the 240 subjects who agree to try the experimental drug, 90 recover. Of the 60 who used the control drug, 20 recover. As with the first set of urns, the values

$$\frac{90}{240} > \frac{20}{60}$$

indicate that the experimental drug is superior. Similarly, in Irvine, of the 60 test subjects, 30 recover and of the 240 control group subjects, 110 recover. As true with the urns, although the Evanston and Irvine results support the experimental drug, the combined data switches the conclusion to support the standard approach.

Examples from other topics and disciplines are equally as easy to find and describe. This phenomenon, for instance, can arise whenever comparing behavior of different groups at different times. To create an example, suppose a university wishes to increase the percentage of women hired to the faculty. To do so, each of two colleges agree to hire a higher percentage of women this year than last year. (So, $R$ denotes the number of women hired.) In the *College of Arts and Sciences*, 90 of the 240 new hires are women; this is an improvement over the 20 women hired out of 60 new CAS hires of last year. Similarly, this year the *Management School* hired 30 women out of 60; again, this is an improvement in the percentages from the 110 women hired out of 240 new Management School hires of a year ago. While the university might rejoice over the success of increasing the percentage of women hired in each unit, an investigation proves that, in fact, the university hired a smaller percentage of women this year than last year.

As the university example suggests, anywhere where comparisons are made from one setting to the next, a Simpson's paradox may occur. Thus, for instance, examples may occur where the crime rate increases in each city even though the national crime rate decreases. Or, in each category, juvenile crimes, adult crimes, violent crime, etc. decrease this year over last, yet the overall crime rate increases. This is not an academic exercise; data exists illustrating this behavior for the above illustrations. In fact, later I give an example about schools in the state of California which suggests that this behavior is fairly robust.

## 4.2.3 Lessons from Arrow's Theorem

The lessons learned about the Arrow and Sen difficulties suggests that an explanation for this *Simpson's Paradox* comes from the way the parts are assembled. Stated in blunter terms, this conflict arises because we ignored the instruction sheet describing the assembly of the parts.

To detect the nature of the elusive missing information, carry out the computation for urn $I''$. Here, the fraction of reds in urn $I$ is $\frac{90}{240}$ while in urn $I'$ it is $\frac{30}{60}$. Imagine your fifth grade arithmetic teacher cringing while groaning that she knew you never would amount to anything if she saw you adding these fraction by summing both the numerators and denominators to obtain

$$\frac{90}{240} + \frac{30}{60} = \frac{(90+30)}{(240+60)} = \frac{120}{300}.$$

This is *not* the proper way to add fractions. *But, it is the correct approach when computing the probabilities for the specified "urns."* After all, the sum of the numerators specifies the number of red marbles while the sum of the denominators specifies the number of marbles.

This addition example identifies a general rule. Should the computations to add probabilities — or to combine items for any process — violate normal fifth grade rules, then the sought after "added information" most surely is embedded within the "unusual computations."

To explain, your fifth grade teacher would be much happier if you would add $\frac{1}{3} + \frac{1}{2}$ as she taught you. First, rewrite the fractions so that they have a common dominator. *Then*, add the numerators to reach the correct *arithmetic* answer of $\frac{1}{3} + \frac{1}{2} = \frac{2}{6} + \frac{3}{6} = \frac{5}{6}$. With this standard addition process, it does not matter whether we add

$$(\frac{100}{300} + \frac{1}{2}) \quad \text{or} \quad (\frac{1}{3} + \frac{100}{200}) \tag{4.1}$$

as both problems are the same; both lead to the same $\frac{5}{6}$ answer.

If, rather than addition, Equation 4.1 represents different combinations of marbles in urns, then the answers for the two settings differ significantly. Rather than a summation, the $\frac{100}{300} + \frac{1}{2}$ expression represents where 100 red marbles are in the first urn but only one is in the second. Common sense dictates that the final answer, where $\frac{101}{302}$ of all marbles in the combined urn are red, must closely reflect the one-third mix of reds in the urn which contributes the most marbles. Similarly, in the $\frac{1}{3} + \frac{100}{200}$ expression from Equation 4.1, the first urn has only one red marble, while the second urn has 100 red ones. The fraction of reds in the combined urn, $\frac{101}{202}$, again closely reflects the even mix of reds and blues in of the urn which chips in the largest number of marbles.

It now is clear. The extra information which connects the parts concerns the relative contributions of the number of marbles each urn makes to the combined whole. Without using this connecting information, the behavior of the whole cannot be understood nor even computed. If this information is not recognized or utilized, then, as described next with a problem that occurred in the state of California, serious difficulties can arise.

### 4.2.4   Simpson problems in sunny California

To create appropriate incentives for struggling schools to improve their performance, in 1999 the state of California instituted an ambitious *Academic Performance Index* (API) program. As stated on their web page, this program "is the cornerstone of California's Public Schools Accountability Act

(PSAA). The purpose of API is to measure the academic performance and growth of schools."

The intent of this program is to impose a "carrot and stick" incentive system where if "a school meets participation and API growth criteria, it may be eligible to receive monetary awards. ... [But if] a school does not meet or exceed its growth targets, it may be identified for participation in [an immediate intervention program]."

How is progress measured? A natural approach is to learn whether students in certain identified groups improve and how the school in general does. The two measures, one emphasizes performance of parts while the other concentrates on the aggregated whole, makes the California program a natural target for a Simpson Paradox. It occurred almost immediately.

A *Los Angles Times* article[1] reported that "[t]eachers and administrators [of a local junior high school] were convinced they would be eligible for rewards, which could include $25,000 checks to teachers. Both Latino and white students, the only two statistically significant groups at the school, exceeded their state-set benchmarks for improvement."

Instead of receiving checks, the school was shocked to discover that they were ineligible for the reward — the "carrot" portion of the program — because of a Simpson Paradox. Even though both groups of students improved, the school's overall score declined. As a consequence, the "stick" portion of the state's program was activated; the school was placed on a list of "underperforming campuses that faced state takeover if scores did not come up within three years." Just imagine the scepticism and sympathy from the public along with a morale drop among the teachers who worked hard to improve student performance. As one administrator commented, "the question our teachers had was 'What more can I do?' "

If only one school had been effected by this API "Simpson" quirk, it could be dismissed as an isolated statistical incident. Instead, it was reported that about 70 schools statewide suffered from this Simpson phenomenon. As true with the above fifth-grade adding explanation, the quirk was caused because comparisons were made with different denominators. For the affected schools, the changed denominators was caused by changing demographics. In the school in question, for instance, the number of white students decreased while the Latino student population went up.

---

[1]On October 18, 200, on page B1 in the Orange County edition.

## 4.2.5    Creating new examples

Because so many California schools were victimized by Simpson's Paradox, we should suspect that this is a fairly robust behavior which should be anticipated. A way to demonstrate that this is the case is to show how easy it is to generate new examples.

Indeed, we can create as many new examples as desired just by mimicking the above way to add fractions. To do so, choose some fraction for the number of reds in the first two set of urns where, to make the first urn better, it has the larger fraction. For purposes of illustration, let them be, respectively, $\frac{1}{4}$ and $\frac{1}{5}$. There is a slight restriction on the choices of the fractions for the second set of urns, but for now, suppose that the first and second urn from the second set are assigned, respectively, the fractions $\frac{1}{2}$ and $\frac{4}{9}$. These four choices are represented in Figure 4.2.

Urns I and I'

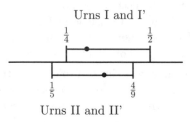

Urns II and II'

**Figure 4.2.** Creating new examples

All that remains is to select the total number of marbles in each set. To keep the number straight, let $F_1$ and $F_2$ be, respectively, the number of marbles in the first and second urns of the First set, while $S_1$ and $S_2$ represent the numbers for the Second set. By combining the urns as described above, a Simpson's paradox occurs if

$$\frac{\frac{1}{4}F_1 + \frac{1}{2}S_1}{F_1 + S_1} < \frac{\frac{1}{5}F_2 + \frac{4}{9}S_2}{F_2 + S_2}.$$

To describe this condition geometrically, the • on the top line between $\frac{1}{4}$ and $\frac{1}{2}$ of Figure 4.2 represents the fraction given by the left side of this inequality. We know how to create such a situation; as the bullet is more to the left, make sure that the urn to the left — the one with fraction $\frac{1}{4}$ — has far more marbles than the one with the fraction $\frac{1}{2}$. To create a paradox, the • on the lower line (representing the mix of reds from the "bad" urns) must be larger, or to the right of the first •. So, an example is generated by making sure that the urn with the $\frac{4}{9}$ fraction makes the largest contribution.

As for the "slight restriction" mentioned above, it is that when the choice of the fractions are graphed as in Figure 4.2, they allow bullets to be placed on the two lines in this relationship.

Actual numbers for this Simpson's Paradox are found by solving some algebra equations. Select a fraction for the upper •, say $\frac{28}{100}$ and a larger one for the lower •, say $\frac{42}{100}$. (I select these number to get a nice answer, but any fractions which can be placed on these lines are fine.) All that remains is to solve the equations

$$\frac{\frac{1}{4}F_1 + \frac{1}{2}S_1}{F_1 + S_1} = \frac{28}{100}, \quad \frac{\frac{1}{5}F_2 + \frac{4}{9}S_2}{F_2 + S_2} = \frac{42}{100}.$$

A simple choice has $F_1 = 88$ and $S_1 = 12$ while $F_2 = 10$ and $S_2 = 90$.

## 4.2.6 Even more general behavior

By understanding the nature of the added information used by the "whole," these examples can be extended in many ways. For instance, the example where a university worries about the low number of women hired to the faculty can be extended from two to any number of divisions. This means that even though each of the 10 or 20 departments in the university hire a higher percentage of women this year than last year, the university, as a whole, could do more poorly. (To create examples, use the approach of Figure 4.2.)

As another extension, why restrict attention to a single level of aggregation? By including more levels — maybe they involve the different administrative levels in an hierarchy where each level involves different information about how to relate the parts — examples as wild as desired can be designed.

To illustrate what can happen, suppose in 16 cities an experimental drug to cure a cold is compared with the standard "warm soup and sleep" approach.

- Each pair of cities reports the data to an assigned county headquarters; there are eight of them.

- Each pair of county headquarters in a state sends the data to the state headquarters; there are four states.

- Each pair of states sends the data to a regional headquarter.

- The two regional headquarters sends the data to a central location.

By using the above, it is a messy exercise in elementary algebra to create "flip-flop" examples where

- in each city, the experimental drug is the better choice,

- in each county, the combined data from the two participating cities shows that the standard approach is better,

- in each state, the combined information from the two participating counties supports the experimental drug,

- in each region, the aggregated data from the two participating states supports the standard approach, and

- at the national level, the data coming from all 16 sites supports the experimental drug.

It is possible to go on and on. For instance, why limit attention to examples with only the two categories of "success" and "failure?" With examples coming from AIDS, TB, and mental illness, the categories might be "cured," "remission," and "failure." Again, within a single site, comparisons are made with fractions; $\frac{1}{3}$ were cured, $\frac{1}{2}$ are in remission, and $\frac{1}{6}$ are failures. Fractions even suffice to compare what happens between sites. But, when combining data within, say, regions, the connecting information concerning the actual numbers of subjects at each site is needed. This extra, connecting information — the information which distinguishes the nature of the parts from the whole — allows paradoxes of almost any kind to occur.

## 4.3   Gambling — and the financial market

The long awaited professional basketball game between the New York Knicks and the LA Lakers takes place next Friday. Bob, from New York, is so confident about his team that he is offering 2:1 odds. This means that if the Knicks win, Bob keeps the money bet with him. But, should the Lakers win, Bob pays $2 for each dollar bet with him. Should we gamble? Quite frankly, even after extensive study of the relative merits of both teams, a bet is, well, it is a gamble.

Sue, who comes from southern California, is so confident about the Lakers that she offers 2:1 odds. So, if the Lakers win, she keeps the money; if the Knicks win, she pays $2 for each dollar bet with her. Again, deciding whether to bet with Sue involves a gamble.

Each disconnected part, each gamble, involves a risk. When determining whether to accept either option, we must decide whether and how much to bet. But, notice; each bet is a "separate, disjoint part." So, our ongoing examination of "parts vs. the whole" should cause wonder whether an advantage can be gained by treating the two bets as a connected whole.

What manifests the significant difference between the invented whole and the separate parts are the newly admissible strategies. For instance, an option not previously available is to bet *against* each team. An individual bet— a bet with each individual "part" —involves risk. But, by betting with the "whole," all risk is eliminated and a profit is guaranteed no matter which team wins.

To illustrate, suppose I bet $100. With the symmetric odds, half is bet on the Knicks with Sue and half on the Lakers with Bob.

- If the Knicks win, I lose $50 to Bob. But, since I bet $50 with Sue, she owes me $100. Thus, my profit is $100 − $50 = $50.

- If the Lakers win, I lose $50 to Sue and receive $100 from Bob. Again, my profit is $50.

No matter what happens in the game, the structure admitted by combining the gambles into a whole, rather than viewing each as a separate entity, guarantees a $50 profit.

The explanation of this outcome is the same. Differences must be expected between the information coming from an assembly of disconnected "parts" and the information about how the separated parts are related to define the "whole." This difference in information content makes a difference in behavior, strategies, etc. In the gambling example, the difference in information radically alters the interpretation and strategies.

This same phenomena arises in finance; it is called "hedging." As an example, suppose we await a judge's opinion on an antitrust decision against, say a well known computer software company. If the judge rules against the company, stock prices will fall; if the judge rules for the company, the prices will rise. Using strategies which mimic the betting example, it is possible to profit whatever happens.[2]

This discussion extends to study of conflict and cooperation — this is called "game theory." By separating a game — an interaction between

---

[2]As the reader might suspect, this is not a hypothetical example. In the fall of 1999, some students in my "Mathematics of Finance" course at Northwestern University profited from this strategy by recognizing that the judge would make a ruling — it didn't matter which way — at a critical juncture during the early stages of the Microsoft trial.

competitors — into disconnected parts, the structure of the game, and the resulting strategies, payoffs, etc., should be expected to differ from those available with the full game. As with Arrow's and Sen's Theorems, the difference involves the coordinating information.

## 4.4  Law

Conflict generated by "part-whole" effects must be expected to occur in areas such as law. After all, legislation often provides only bandaid resolutions of complex difficulties. This means that laws can emphasize particular situations, particular instances, to solve specific problems.

But whenever the legislative concentration is on the "parts" at the expense of the "whole," anticipate all sorts of trouble making opportunities coming from subtle but complex settings hatched by the ignored "connections."

### 4.4.1  Genome mapping

Patent law is an area rich in component "parts" (the individual patents) and "whole" (how various discoveries interact) conflicts. To suggest how this clash can arise, I make an easy prediction of forthcoming events that, most surely, has knowledgeable lawyers salivating over potential legal fees and opportunities while rushing off to brush up on basic microbiology.

The class of problems I have in mind involve the ambitious genome mapping project. The massive undertaking of trying to understand the human genome structure started in 1990; closely related projects include understanding the genome sequencing for grains, such as rice, and even mice. Some of the ways to understand the genome sequencing use high-powered computers, other work involves hands-on research in the lab. All of this effort holds the glittering promise of exciting scientific advances, Nobel Prizes, lots and lots of money for the corporate winners — and considerable amounts of litigation.

A portion of the litigation most surely will manifest the manner in which patents are awarded. Certain high tech companies, for instance, have received patents based on their ability to use computers to determine the sequencing of certain genes. But, full understanding of what they have patented remains unknown. As one actual example, a patent for a human gene turned out, after the fact, to have an effect upon HIV. Who should have the lucrative rights — the group that found the gene, or the group who understood its consequences? Expect conflict between the "wet biology" scientists, who discover the use of the newly discovered genes, and the sequencing community who have discovered the genes with, among other approaches, computer techniques.

But, a "parts-whole" conflict will create even more severe difficulties. This is because, currently, it is not well understood how some genes patented by one group will interact with genes patented by other groups. So, the patents protect the rights of various "parts" (different genes) without knowing how they are coordinated and related. The rest of the story is clear; eventually, connections among these parts — the different patented genes — will be discovered.

It is this coordinating information, it is this information about the whole differs from the sum of the parts, which ensures conflict. If the "connection" leads to an important advance, which "part" deserves the credit — and the lucrative royalties? While the first decade or so of this new millennium probably will recorded in history as an exciting epoch of biological advances, much of the action will take place in the courtroom.

## 4.4.2 Legal cycles

Think of these legal difficulties as manifesting conflicting directions defined by the separate "parts." Let me explain with a simple example which involves mortgages and loans.

If I borrow money from you, it is reasonable for you to demand some form of security to protect your interests. This security notion is captured by the wording of a house mortgage where partial property rights belong to the person, or bank, making a loan. This sense of demanding security for a loan is why the pawn shop demands actual possession of the security — the TV set, or watch, or walking cane — until the borrower can repay them.

To introduce conflict, suppose I want to borrow money to purchase a computer to write the "Great American Novel." Losing physical possession of the computer, in the name of providing security for the loan, is counterproductive; I need the computer to write the book to earn the money to pay off the loan. But, the creditor also faces a problem; if I have the computer, what is to keep me, a starving author, from using the computer as security to borrow money from several others. Who knows; the book might flop, and I might owe far more money to my creditors than the value of my used computer. What should be done? Who should have first priority over the remaining limited assets?

A way to handle the priority question is for the creditor, Judy, to legally register her interest in my computer until I repay the loan. To provide incentives to create a self-enforcing law which encourages Judy to register, the law states that

> if Judy registers, then she has priority over all non-registered people, even if their claims on my assets came earlier.

But Judy has faith in me; she believes that my book will be highly successful. Since Judy is a busy person and since she fully expects me to repay her, she might not get around to registering.

Unfortunately, I quickly need more cash. When I lean on Kay for another loan, Kay learns about Judy's unregistered loan to me. Kay now has an advantage; she can loan me some money and then register. Kay's objective is that if the book flops, by registering, she has priority over Judy on recovering her money from my limited computer assets.

This is not fair; Kay not only knew about Judy's interests, but Kay is trying to exploit the law in a manner to take advantage of Judy. To discourage such tactics, the law now moves in a different direction;

> if Kay *knows* that Judy has unregistered interest in my computer, then Kay cannot gain priority over Judy by rushing off to register her interests.

Both laws are intended to prevent potential injustice. But, as they stretch legal protection off in different directions, they almost invite legal cycles to occur.

To create a cycle, start with the fact that Judy has a legal interest in my computer, but she fails to register it. Kay, who later loaned me money, registers her interest even though Kay is well aware of Judy's actions. This means that Judy has priority over Kay denoted as

$$\text{Judy} \succ \text{Kay.}$$

The book writing is going slowly; expenses are accumulating; I need more money. So, I now borrow money from Lorraine. Lorraine fully understands business, so she immediately registers the loan. But, Kay registered first, so Kay has priority over Lorraine.

$$\text{Kay} \succ \text{Lorraine.}$$

To complete the story, Lorraine has no prior knowledge about Judy's loan. Because Lorraine is registered and because she does not know about Judy, Lorraine has priority over Judy. The relationship

$$\text{Lorraine} \succ \text{Judy}$$

completes the

$$\text{Judy} \succ \text{Kay}, \quad \text{Kay} \succ \text{Lorraine}, \quad \text{Lorraine} \succ \text{Judy}$$

cycle. If my book fails, how should these women divide my meager assets?

The source of the cycle is clear. The laws worry about the individual parts, so coordinating information is missing.

### 4.4.3   If the Catholic bishop would only get married

Other legal cycles are found by searching for examples involving different legal directions where a natural response is, "But, he can't do that!" Consider, for instance, the well intended advice actually advanced to a Catholic bishop that to solve his legal problems. He should marry a nice local girl.

To set the stage, the opening of the Soviet Union and then Russia in the 1990s created tempting opportunities for outsiders with interests ranging from the financial world to missionaries. Many of these ventures were legitimate and positive, while others were, well ...

To protect Russia from "the others," laws needed to be enacted. In 1997, for instance, the Russian parliament passed laws on religion in response to reports that dangerous cults were gaining disturbing numbers of adherents. A simplified version of the resulting conflict is that, for a Catholic bishop to carry out his responsibilities, the laws required him to be the registered head of his organization. The penalties, as with the loan example, are that an unregistered religious leader may be deprived of certain legal rights. This defines one of the legal directions.

To register, the bishop must be a permanent resident. This creates the second legal direction; Russian law makes it difficult to obtain residency status or citizenship. In particular, being a bishop assigned to Russia does not suffice.

As true with most laws, there are loopholes. One way to receive permanent residence status is to marry a local person. In commenting on his legal difficulties, Bishop Jerz Mazur, who is stationed in Irkutsk, a Siberian city near Lake Baikal, stated "They explained to me that if a priest marries a Russian girl, there's no problem."[3]

The promised cycle, then, is

- to be the head of the Catholic Church, the bishop must register,

- to register, the bishop should marry a Russian girl,

---

[3]As quoted in the LA Times, page A2, October 21, 2000.

- if the bishop marries, he cannot remain in the church, so he cannot be the head of the church.

Other examples are found in a similar manner. To indicate how easy they are to find, recall that to ensure a fair election count, the election laws for the state of Florida require a recount, even a manual one if necessary. Another Florida law imposes a strict deadline on when the results must be reported. As the world discovered during the 2000 US Presidential elections when one party demanded a recount and an official from another party demanded strict adherence to the deadline, a cycle could emerge.

- To ensure that all votes are accurately tabulated, a manual recount may be necessary.

- The deadline on when election results must be reported does not permit a full and accurate hand recount.

- Without a full and accurate recount, the state cannot ensure that all votes are accurately tabulated.

## 4.5 Kindness through personal understanding

"I really want to watch the football game tonight, but, instead, let me clear the table and do the dishes." An act of kindness presumably based on an awareness that cleaning up means more to the person's partner than the personal pleasure gained by watching the game. How does this effect, which in academic circles goes under the mouthful title of "intercomparability of utilities" come about? While this issue has been examined and debated at least since the 1870s, my comments are influenced by the persuasive insights of Louis Narens and Duncan Luce, two mathematical psychologists at the University of California at Irvine.

To explore a portion of Narens and Luce's development, consider the needs of David and Sharon. Sharon really would like to watch the game, but she recognizes that after David prepared that splendid dinner, he is tired. Notice, Sharon's act of kindness is based on her ability to contrast her pleasure in watching football against what it means for David to be free from doing dishes. In a real sense, Sharon not only must develop an appreciation and sense of Dave's preferences, but she needs to translate and scale them into her personal expression scheme. After all, by being Nordic, Sharon's spectrum of emotion ranging from unbelievable ecstasy to complete disappointment is captured by slight intonation changes of "That's nice."

David, on the other hand, is an excitable type. Notice, no claim is made that Sharon's perception of David's relative needs is "accurate."

To achieve a reciprocal level of kindness, Dave must understand Sharon's needs and pleasures. In Narens and Luce's framework, they prove that this compatibility between partners requires a very strict mathematical relationship between how each translates the needs and levels of happiness of each other; these conditions are so strict that it is fair to wonder whether complete compatibility ever is possible.[4]

But, compatibility does exist. Couples who have been happily married for a long time can complete the thoughts of a spouse even when nothing is said; each can anticipate the reaction and needs of the other. How is this possible?

Returning to David and Sharon, the impression each has of the other defines the "parts" of our "part-whole" story. When expressed in this manner, the nature of the connecting information becomes clear; something is needed to relate Dave's and Sharon's perceptions of one another. Narens and Luce note that a personal dynamic of being open and carefully explaining needs through, say, a "I'm tired! Is that silly football game more important to you than me also doing the dishes after cooking dinner!" dialogue defines interactions which eventually may lead to such an equilibrium of understanding.

As we should anticipate from our exploration of "connecting information," the form of dynamic interaction can dictate the nature of any equilibrium setting; it will determine how Dave and Sharon will interact on a daily basis. While a reasonably deep result, this Narens and Luce conclusion is embraced by common experience. If, for instance, the dynamics of adjustment always are based on Dave's complaints, then a working relationship favoring David should be expected. If Sharon's quiet but forceful views always dominate, an interaction form favoring Sharon should result. If both express their views, then a third type of relationship will emerge. Again, the final conclusion is based on the form of connecting information.

To continue the story, suppose that after years of comfortably living together, Sharon and David reach a solid working relationship. In precisely

---

[4]Rather than comparing how each person treats different options, Narens and Luce model this understanding in terms of utility levels of each person. Sharon's understanding and translation of Dave's interests is represented by an increasing function $g$; so, Sharon's take on Dave's utility $u_D(X)$ is $g(u_D(X))$. For compatibility, Dave also needs a strictly increasing function; it must be $g^{-1}$. This makes sense; e.g., just by comparing differences in emotions, Sharon's Nordic temperament requires a $g$ which tempers Dave's utility values. Conversely, $g^{-1}$ is the scaling term which escalates the Sharon's subtle differences in emotion into terms David understands.

the same manner, each anticipates the other's reactions when comparing two options. Then, Sharon's mother arrives for an extended visit.

Sharon and her mother managed to survive Sharon's teenage years, so they also have reached a mutual understanding of each other. The question is whether Sharon and Dave's and Sharon and her mother's understandings translate into an appreciation between Dave and Sharon's mother about mutual needs.

Without resorting to bad "in-law" jokes, intuition developed by our "part-whole" study suggests that incompatibility must be expected. Indeed, even in a setting requiring strong understanding among pairs, Naren and Luce prove that this triplet harmony holds only with a very strong condition.[5] For instance, even if both Dave and Sharon agree that

> watching the TV debate of the presidential candidates means more to David than Sharon watching a summary of the week's economic news in Britain.

and Sharon and her mother agree that

> it is more important for Sharon to examine the economic news than for her mother to see the TV show on gardening,

*it does not follow* that David and Sharon's mother agree that

> it is more important for Dave to watch that debate than for Sharon's mother to watch the gardening show.

Aha! A cycle leading to continual squabbles and hurt feelings.

The source of the difficulty is clear. With three pairs, the "parts" are the levels of understanding between each pair. As with pairwise voting cycles, the incompatibility reflects a loss of connecting information — the information which relates the differing levels of understanding among the pairs. Can it be attained? Maybe. But the equilibrium status would be the end result of a "triplet dynamic" of views; it would require comments among David, Sharon, and Sharon's mother to reach a level of mutual understanding. Maybe after Sharon's mother has been visiting long enough, all three will learn to understand one another.

---

[5] As any strictly increasing function defines the pairwise relationship between the members of each pair, compatibility for each of the three pairs is defined by any three increasing functions. Consequently, it is highly unlikely for these three functions to satisfy the appropriate conditions leading to compatibility resembling transitivity. Although the result is not in the literature, just by arranging for the level sets to cross in an appropriate manner, it is easy to prove that "stable" cycles can occur.

## 4.6 Majorities and democracies

To find other examples, select an area — just about any discipline will suffice — and troubling problems of this type can be discovered. A topic which is closely related to our discussions comes from that portion of the political science literature which worries about fundamental concerns facing our democratic system.

In a book nicely summarizing several of these problems, Hannu Nurmi, a political scientist living in the charming port city of Turku, Finland, describes certain kinds of troubling political science behavior. The contribution made here is to explain what happens and why. Be assured; the explanation remains the same; when procedures emphasize the parts, they can dismiss valued information about how the parts are connected — about the whole.

### 4.6.1 Anscombe Paradox

In his book, Nurmi describes the Anscombe paradox. This is a voting paradox which identifies an amusing, yet worrisome phenomenon.

> *It is possible for a majority of the people to be on the losing side on a majority of the issues.*

How can this assertion possibly be true? This claim seems to directly counter all of those warnings about the "tyranny of the majority," about how the minority beliefs can be abused and ignored. Be assured; these concerns remain realistic. But, the Anscombe Paradox can occur.

By now, once told that something unusual happens with *pairwise voting,* we should immediately suspect why the phenomenon occurs, how to construct illustrating examples, and how to explore basic properties. Place all blame on the Condorcet triplet or $n$-tuple. Then, use these profiles to identify all properties.

Wait; something seems wrong. The Anscombe Paradox is not about cycles; this assertion does not even require an alternative to be in more than one pair. In fact, the Anscombe behavior might involve issues as diverse as, say, "yes-no" votes on the school lunch program, a proposal for added lighting on main street, and a bill to provide care for the homeless. Nevertheless, as shown next, it takes only a minor change of names to understand how the Anscombe problem is still another victim of the Condorcet triplet.

**Creating all possible examples**

Start by expressing the Condorcet triplet in terms of pairwise rankings.

| Ranking | $\{A, B\}$ | $\{B, C\}$ | $\{A, C\}$ |
|:---:|:---:|:---:|:---:|
| $A\,B\,C$ | $A\,B$ | $B\,C$ | $A\,C$ |
| $B\,C\,A$ | $B\,A$ | $B\,C$ | $C\,A$ |
| $C\,A\,B$ | $A\,B$ | $C\,B$ | $C\,A$ |

$$(4.2)$$

As we know, this profile defines a cycle. To review, the cycle arises because the pairwise vote drops all information about how voters connect the pairs; in a subtle manner, it loses the information that the voters are rational. Since the Condorcet triplet defines an "heterogeneous" setting for voter preferences, it is reasonable to expect modifications of this profile to create scenarios where the pairwise vote loses information about the voters.

To convert this cycle into a "Yes-No" setting, or into any other pairwise decision problem, replace a pairwise ranking with "Yes" if it agrees with the winning outcome for the specified pair, and "No" otherwise. Next, change the pairs into "issues" to generate the table

| Voter | Issue 1 | Issue 2 | Issue 3 |
|:---:|:---:|:---:|:---:|
| Voter 1 | Yes | Yes | No |
| Voter 2 | No | Yes | Yes |
| Voter 3 | Yes | No | Yes |
| **Outcome** | Yes | Yes | Yes |

$$(4.3)$$

The example I design to illustrate the Anscombe Paradox will involve five individuals where the above three define the "majority." To choose the remaining two individuals, notice that Condorcet influence forces each issue in Table 4.3 to win with a 2:1 tally. To exploit this tally, select the preferences of the remaining two individuals, who form the minority to be

| Voter | Issue 1 | Issue 2 | Issue 3 |
|:---:|:---:|:---:|:---:|
| Voter 4 | No | No | No |
| Voter 5 | No | No | No |

$$(4.4)$$

It is clear from the two Tables 4.3, 4.4 that the minority group consisting of voters 4 and 5 *always* enjoy a "No" victory over all issues. But each of the first three voters — this defines a majority — are on the losing side on a majority of the issues (two out of three).

Incidentally, because the Condorcet portion of a profile affects a sizeable percentage of normal voting settings, it is reasonable to expect that this Anscombe behavior, where a majority is frustrated in a majority of instances, is not merely an hypothetical concern. Indeed, Katri Sieberg and I developed a theoretical approach which demonstrates the surprisingly strong likelihood of this and wide range of related kinds of perversities. The message of our research is to expect this unexpected behavior.

If this disturbing behavior is theoretically likely, then we should expect to observe it in our elections. It does arise; among others, Steven Brams, a political scientist from New York University, and his collaborators showed how this behavior occurs with those proposals which clutter the ballot in the state of California.

That the above example relies heavily upon Condorcet's triplet is not a coincidence; with slight modifications, it follows from arguments I developed to study pairwise voting that *all examples illustrating the Anscombe Paradox* — or the Ostrogorski Paradox which is introduced and described in the next section — *must involve portions of the Condorcet profiles as modified in the above manner.* This observation suggests that by adding voters and issues, even more dramatic examples can be designed. Again, all of possible examples — whether they are based on theoretical discussion or on empirical data — are consequences of Condorcet tuples.

To further illustrate this behavior with a four-issue example, start with the Condorcet four-tuple. In the same manner as used above, an example is created where the "Yes" votes win by 3:1 over each of the four issues. By adding three more voters who vote "No" on each issue, an Anscombe Paradox example results. Here each member of the majority (these are voters 1-4) are on the losing side on three-fourths of the issues.

| Voter | Issue 1 | Issue 2 | Issue 3 | Issue 4 | |
|---|---|---|---|---|---|
| Voter 1 | Yes | Yes | Yes | No | |
| Voter 2 | No | Yes | Yes | Yes | |
| Voter 3 | Yes | No | Yes | Yes | (4.5) |
| Voter 4 | Yes | Yes | No | Yes | |
| Voters 5-7 | No | No | No | No | |
| **Outcome** | No | No | No | No | |

By creatively modifying the Condorcet cycles (as done in the last chapter when designing agendas and tournaments), even more is possible. Examples can be generated to demonstrate the sizeable "super majority" vote which is needed to overcome this phenomenon, or to describe settings where nobody accepts the final outcome, or .... Since these examples involve modified forms of the Condorcet triplet or n-tuple, the explanation for the Anscombe

Paradox remains the same. A majority of the people can be frustrated because pairwise voting loses all connecting information.

**Who cares?**

Perhaps this "connecting" information is of value only when the issues are actually related. To explain, why worry about the Anscombe behavior with disconnected issues such as whether the price of coffee should go up, whether Monday night football should continue, and whether the comedy clubs in Chicago are better than those in LA. Who cares if each of a specific majority of identified individuals suffers defeat on most votes?

To explain these comments, start with the fact that the Anscombe phenomenon is caused by a loss of connecting information. As with pairwise voting, "issue by issue" voting strips away all information about who voted for what collection of issues. In other words, the Anscombe Paradox occurs whenever this loss of connecting information allows for a "shifting majority;" the identity of who belongs to the winning voting majority can change with the issue. But, if the concerns already are disconnected, if the issues are not related, who cares? Here, any "connecting" information that Bob likes Chicago comedy clubs and hates Monday night football is artificial. Here, it does not matter if the pairwise vote strips the spurious connecting information to allow for shifting majorities.

However, when three, or four, or several issues are intimately related and even serve as parts of an overall program, such as an air pollution program involving gas additives to reduce automobile pollutants, exhaust fumes from factories, and the burning of the rain forests, then this paradox is disturbing. Here, the election oddity acquires a "divide to conquer" status where a division into parts becomes a strategy to frustrate majority opinion. With connected issues, then, as with our other discussions, procedures such as the Borda Count which are capable of capturing these connecting elements must be used. On the other hand, while "bundled voting" where all alternatives are assembled in one bill can provide connections, it also can be abused; here the associated "parts-whole" problems are even more worrisome (This theme is further developed in research with Sieberg.)

## 4.6.2   Ostrogorski concerns

In his book, Nurmi also describes the Ostrogorski election oddity. This is where the identity of the dominant party can differ if we emphasize the party where most voters like its stands over most issues, or if we emphasize the party which wins a majority of the issues by majority votes.

Aha! As this is another election oddity which involves the "majority pairwise vote," the behavior must be manifested by Condorcet triplets or n-tuples. Even more, the Condorcet structure is central for all profiles supporting this oddity; this remains true whether they are constructed examples or based on empirical observations.

| Voter | Issue 1 | Issue 2 | Issue 3 | Supported Party | |
|---|---|---|---|---|---|
| Voter 1 | Yes | Yes | No | OP | |
| Voter 2 | No | Yes | Yes | OP | |
| Voter 3 | Yes | No | Yes | OP | (4.6) |
| Voter 4 | No | No | No | PS | |
| Voter 5 | No | No | No | PS | |
| **Outcome** | No | No | No | | |

The Table 4.6 example uses Tables 4.3, 4.4. To create parties, suppose the *Optimist Party* (OP) cheerfully supports all issues. As expected, the grumpy *Pessimist Party* (PS) is against everything. With these five voters, which party is the dominant one? As Table 4.6 illustrates, we can announce with good cheer that the *Optimist Party* is dominant. After all, a full 60% of the voters (voters 1, 2, 3) support a majority of the Optimist's views.

While it is arguable that the Optimist Party is the dominant party, the Pessimist Party wins on *all issues*. Maybe they are the dominant party. Which party is dominant?

In his book, Nurmi points out that, previously, it was thought that the Anscombe and Ostrogorski Paradoxes are essentially the same. They are the same in terms of the source of the problems — both manifest subtle consequences of the Condorcet tuples and the loss of connecting information — but not in terms of the definitions. To dismiss this fallacy, Nurmi constructed an example, similar to the one which follows, which supports the Ostrogorski phenomenon but not the Anscombe Paradox.

To be an Ostrogorski example, the OP party must lose a majority of the issues; they must come up short on at least two of the three issues. To avoid creating an Anscombe illustration, only a *specified* minority of the voters can be on the losing side of most issues. With five voters, then, no more than two voters can be frustrated on more than one issue. To create an example, just change the views of one PS voter, say voter 4, on one issue. As Table 4.7 shows, only voter 2 is frustrated on a majority of the issues (actually, all of them) even though the OP party loses a majority of the votes.

| Voter | Issue 1 | Issue 2 | Issue 3 | Supported Party |
|---|---|---|---|---|
| Voter 1 | Yes | Yes | No | OP |
| Voter 2 | No | Yes | Yes | OP |
| Voter 3 | Yes | No | Yes | OP |
| Voter 4 | Yes | No | No | PS |
| Voter 5 | No | No | No | PS |
| Outcome | Yes | No | No | |

$$(4.7)$$

Finding actual examples of the Ostrogorski Paradox is not difficult. Just check the US Congress where the minority party always tries to encourage renegade members of the majority to vote against the majority party. By selecting three or four issues where the minority succeeded, the paradox is illustrated. In other words, while our legislators might not appreciate the theoretical reasons for these various surprises, they fully understand and exploit the pragmatics of them.

By using the Condorcet structure as amended here, we can construct many other examples. Finding properties of all of these examples just involves examining and understanding the role of the Condorcet portion of general profiles. While the approach is known, the information resides in my technical papers which, as I confessed earlier (page vi), can "challenge the patience of even the experts."

## 4.7   Learning how to cause trouble

Let me describe how to become a world-class, intellectual troublemaker. A way to achieve this distinction is to learn how to uncover problems and peculiarities which are almost guaranteed to occur even with established procedures. For real infamy, select procedures which deliver important conclusions. One example is developed here; others are easy to find.

The approach exploits our attitudes toward "fairness," or "envy" which start with the all too familiar, "Mommy; Johnny got more than me!" Embedded in our cultural expectations since childhood is the sense that "fairness" involves comparing the gains of any two individuals. You have done this; at some time you discovered someone whose grade in a course, or salary, or promotion relative to yours was "unfair." Extending the notion to almost everything, "fairness" tends to be equated with pairwise comparisons between individuals, corporations, states, and even countries. But, as parents, employers, and teachers quickly learn, universal fairness does not exist.

In restricted settings, "envy-free" procedures can be designed so that everyone prefers what they got over what anyone else got. Consider, for instance, two siblings sharing a small cake. This setting flashes images where cries of "She got more than me!" sabotage the best laid plans for a joyful treat. How can the cake be cut? A solution is for one person, say the sister, to cut the cake and the other person, the brother, to make the first choice. If the sister is envious of her brother's choice, it is her fault; she did the cutting. With his first choice, the brother should have no envy.

Whenever fairness and envy-free are of prime importance, these procedures are fine.[6] But, beyond preserving familial harmony, a weakness with envy-free procedures is that pandering to egos can create inefficiency and a loss of effectiveness. I resist illustrating this point with a gruesome biblical type story where two brothers vie for a pet dog, so one gets the head and .... But business pages and news accounts describe attempts at "envy-free" divisions where a thriving firm or farm suffers the same fate as that pet dog when partners, or divorcing spouses, or siblings in an inheritance case insist on their "fair share." Indeed, the principle of primogeniture, where the eldest (usually the eldest son) inherits the entire estate of one or both parents, reflects the need to prevent "fairness" from damaging economic feasibility.

Remember when you patiently waited on a traffic-free day for a light to change to make a left turn, and, just as the red light flickers, a long stream of on-coming traffic unfairly prolonged your stay. "Fairness" competes with efficiency and even safety on a daily basis. Insisting on fairness by worrying about pairwise comparisons, or comparisons of this group versus that one, emphasizes the "parts." You know the rest of the message. With a sufficiently heterogeneous setting and using a procedure where the outcomes involve interactions and connecting information, the societal outcome can conflict with impressions developed by comparing individual parts.

This sense of "measuring fairness by comparing parts" is central to Arrow's concept of binary independence. In the Chapter 2 ice skating example used to motivate this axiom, I purposely emphasized the "unfairness" of Surya Bonaly beating Nicole Bobek because of Michelle Kwan's superb performance. (As a personal note, I watched this competition and wanted Bobek to win, so I *did* find the outcome to be unfair.) The earlier California example (on page 110) where the students did better but the school did worse is another illustration. But the heavy cost associated with requiring group outcomes to honor pairwise comparisons includes the risk of

---

[6]By imposing realistic assumptions on the outcome, a reasonably direct application of Arrow's result shows that these envy-free settings are restricted.

introducing societal confusion through cycles, inappropriate outcomes, or a dictatorship. To eliminate these evils, useful group outcomes must incorporate the information which unites the parts.

In turn, with a sufficiently heterogeneous setting, anticipate conflict between societal outcomes and what is "justified" through pairwise comparisons. This gap, this conflict, provides magnificent opportunities for troublemakers. By using "Johnny got more than me" comparisons, it is possible to be outraged about unfair societal distributions. By invoking fairness and equity, and who can be against that, a first class fuss can be made. This is not speculation; although a couple of my acquaintances are unaware of any theoretical explanations, they have developed reasonable careers as political and social nags in this manner. On the other hand, while trouble can be created with most procedures, it can be particularly easy when the procedure and associated societal outcomes are just plain lousy; they are in desperate need of repair.

## 4.7.1   Apportionment of US Congress

A world class troublemaker selects procedures where the outcomes matter; e.g., political power. A major American "power broker" is the procedure used to apportion congressional seats.

As the number of seats assigned to a state equates to political power, and as the outcomes of the current procedure are prone to claims of "unfairness," it is reasonable to predict that within the next decade or so, problems will occur. Moreover, these problems will generate so much political and legal fuss that the issue will need to be decided by the US Supreme Court. The basis of this bickering will involve a misguided understanding of "fairness" and the relationship between the "whole and the parts." Alternatively, as I firmly believe, the complaints might legitimately reflect an awareness that the current US apportionment method has problems — serious problems.

To set the stage, every decade the US House of Representatives is apportioned according to the results of the decennial census. The actual assignment uses a "fairness" scheme which resembles the *proportional voting* election approaches used so widely around the world. This scheme is one of five proposed by the Harvard mathematician E. V. Huntington during the 1920s, a decade full of controversy about appropriate ways to apportion Congressional seats. The actual approach was based on a recommendation made by a select committee of the National Academy of Sciences.

The object of an apportionment method is to assign each state a number of representatives which is proportional to the state's population. This means that a state with 1/3 of the total US population should receive 1/3 of the representatives. With a house size of 15, then, the state should receive five seats. But, with house size 16, well, a problem is created because now that state is entitled to $5\frac{1}{3}$ seats. As it is doubtful whether a third of a representative can be effective, the apportionment problem requires "rounding off." Does this state deserve five or six seats?

This is not the place to describe "rounding off procedures" and their problems; the concluding chapter with technical notes has references so that the interested reader can further investigate this issue. For now, be assured, with more than two states, and the US has 50, subtle difficulties plague any procedure. For instance, while it seems natural to round $5\frac{1}{3}$ down to 5, the fractional parts from the other states could be even smaller. If so, then rounding up, rather than down, is more appropriate. But other examples prove that rounding up can be the wrong approach.

| State | Population | Exact | Integer | Fraction | Final |
|:-----:|:----------:|:-----:|:-------:|:--------:|:-----------:|
| A | 1320 | 1.320 | 1 | 0.320 | $1 + 1 = 2$ |
| B | 2310 | 2.315 | 2 | 0.315 | 2 |
| C | 3135 | 3.135 | 3 | 0.135 | 3 |
| D | 3220 | 3.230 | 3 | 0.230 | 3 |
| **Total** | 10,000 | 10 | 9 | 1 | 10 |

$$(4.8)$$

To illustrate, suppose the total population of 10,000 is divided among four states as specified in the second column of Table 4.8. The third column identifies each state's exact apportionment for house size 10 as determined by the population figures. The exact apportionments involve fractions, so the fourth column assigns each state the integer value. Adding these four integer values proves that nine, not ten, seats have been allocated. This means that one seat remains to be assigned to some state.

With this example, the usual rounding off learned back in elementary school does not apply because no state has a fractional portion even as large as one-third. To escape from this quandary, notice that since state A has the largest fractional part, it probably is the most deserving. So, a natural approach, as indicated in the last column, is to assign A the remaining seat. The US used this allocation procedure, advocated by the American politician and statesman, Alexander Hamilton, for decades.

Returning to our goal of becoming trouble makers, we need to identify the "connecting information." It is easy to find; as this example proves, the apportionments for a specified house size requires using information about the fractional values of *all* states. (While Hamilton's method is but one approach, for our purposes it suffices to declare that all apportionment methods involve *connecting information* about all of the states.) *This is the trouble making opportunity*; by emphasizing individual comparisons — the parts — conflict most surely can be found. As we also have learned to expect, the more heterogeneous the population distribution, as true for the US, the more likely it is to discover some sort of conflict.

## 4.7.2   Causing problems

OK, where are the trouble making opportunities? Since "rounding off" compares fractional values, the same fractional comparison holds when comparing two states. No conflict can occur here, so where are the promised opportunities?

Potential troubling settings occur where the above computations are of little value. For instance, by adding another seat to the ten-seat example, *new calculations are needed* to distribute the eleven seats. Suppose a new state is added, or some state, say Michigan, is divided to make the Upper Peninsula the state of Superior, or several states combine because of regional interests. Suppose there is a population shift. In each of these settings, *new computations are needed*. The need for the new calculations suggests that the conclusions for these different parts may be partially divorced.

*We* may anticipate a connection, a relationship, among the parts. We may expect, for instance, the apportionment of house size ten to be related to that of house size eleven. But, just as with Arrow's and Sen's results, such relationships may be more in our expectations than a natural consequence of our computational tools. To illustrate this assertion, among the several factors that can be varied to create an "injustice," three choices involve the house size, the definition of states, and shifting populations.

### House size

The US abandoned Hamilton's method because apportionment difficulties arose with changes in the house size. To explain in terms of the "parts-whole" analysis, the computations for different house sizes have little to do with one another. Thus, each of the two apportionments define "disjoint parts." The "whole" involves comparing the two allocations.

To illustrate with the Table 4.8 figures, Table 4.9 shows what happens by adding one more seat to the mix to have a house size of 11. This *increase* in the house size moves state A from having the largest to the smallest fractional value. Consequently, by increasing the house size, state A *loses* a seat. How unfair! Honoring the state of Alabama, an early American victim of this phenomenon, this behavior is called the *Alabama Paradox*.

| State | Population | Exact | Integer | Fraction | Final |
|-------|-----------|-------|---------|----------|-------|
| A | 1320 | 1.452 | 1 | 0.452 | 1 |
| B | 2310 | 2.541 | 2 | 0.541 | $2 + 1 = 3$ |
| C | 3140 | 3.454 | 3 | 0.454 | 3 |
| D | 3230 | 3.553 | 3 | 0.553 | $3 + 1 = 4$ |
| **Total** | 10,000 | 11 | 9 | 2 | 11 |

$$(4.9)$$

This behavior resembles Simpson's Paradox in that adding to the total reduces a component. To understand what happens, notice that a quick way to find a state's *exact* apportionment after the house adds a seat is to add the state's fractional portion to its previous exact apportionment. To illustrate, with house size ten state A has the exact apportionment of 1.320. As state A has $1320/10,000 = 0.1329$ of the total population, A's exact apportionment for house size eleven is its apportionment for ten seats, 1.320 *plus* the addition 0.1320 seats it is awarded from the increase of one in house size; it is $1.320 + 0.1320 = 1.452$.

This computation explains what happens; larger states have a larger fraction of the total population, so this addition allows a larger state's exact apportionment to leapfrog over that of smaller states. As one might expect from this description, this is not a rare, isolated incident. Instead, as I proved elsewhere, for most population figures, this phenomena eventually occurs with some house size. In fact, a more unusual quirk occurs; the more accurate the census figures, the more likely it is that something unexpected will occur, and even with a smaller house size.

Not only can this behavior occur, but it has — several times. Indeed, as an attempt to avoid this troubling phenomenon with the 1910 census figures, the US adjusted the size of Congress to the current figure of 435 representatives.

### Region versus states

Economic, cultural, and other interests can place a stronger emphasis on regions over individual states. Two states, for instance, might represent rural interests while two others might share urban problems. Do our apportionment methods respect these de facto divisions? Not necessarily.

By now we should anticipate this assertion. The establishment of coalitions creates a connecting whole, but the economic and regional interests inspiring the creation of a coalition have nothing to do with the computations of allocations for the "parts;" the individual states. As such, expect a "part-whole" conflict where regional interests can be short changed.

To illustrate this assertion with the Table 4.8 populations and the house size ten, suppose that states A and C represent western interests, while states B and D reflect eastern interests. Table 4.10 demonstrates that the Table 4.8 figures need not respect regional needs. To explain, the next to the last column shows that the combined B & D region has the largest fractional part. From a regional perspective, they should receive the one extra seat. However, since the apportionment emphasizes the "parts" of each coalition (the states), the actual apportionment in the last column (the sum of seats assigned by Table 4.8) favors the region with a smaller population.

| State | Population | Exact | Integer | Fraction | Actual |
|-------|-----------|-------|---------|----------|--------|
| A&C   | 4460      | 4.460 | 4       | 0.460    | 5      |
| B&D   | 5540      | 5.540 | 5       | 0.540    | 5      |
| Total | 10,000    | 10    | 9       | 1        | 10     |

$$(4.10)$$

### 4.7.3   Shifting populations

Suppose, as part of a population change, a bloc of people move from one state to another; there are no other changes in their populations. At apportionment time, we might assume that the state welcoming this bloc will be favored in the apportionment of seats. Not necessarily.

To use an example from an earlier book *Basic Geometry of Voting*, consider a scenario where the census figures given below lead to the following distribution of a 200 seat house.

| State | Population | Exact  | Integer | Fraction | Actual |
|-------|-----------|--------|---------|----------|--------|
| A     | 1570      | 1.57   | 1       | 0.57     | 1      |
| B     | 26630     | 26.630 | 26      | 0.630    | 27     |
| C     | 171800    | 171.80 | 171     | 0.8      | 172    |

$$(4.11)$$

But state B recognizes that a block of 20 who moved from A to B is not reflected by the census. As a result, corrections are made to the census figures leading to the correct values, and final apportionment, of

| State | Population | Exact   | Integer | Fraction | Actual |
|-------|-----------|---------|---------|----------|--------|
| A     | 1550      | 1.52    | 1       | 0.52     | 2      |
| B     | 26650     | 26.11   | 26      | 0.11     | 26     |
| C     | 175900    | 1721.37 | 172     | 0.37     | 172    |

$$(4.12)$$

In other words, state B ends up losing a seat while state A gains one. By focussing just on states A and B, this appears to be an injustice; by examining the total picture, it becomes clear that state C's increased population is what caused the problem.

### 4.7.4 Other apportionment methods

Thanks to the frustrations of the Alabama Paradox, the US no longer uses Hamilton's method. Instead, the apportionment starts with each state receiving a seat. Then, the $51^{st}$ seat is awarded to the most deserving state based on a "fairness" principle. The $52^{nd}$ state is awarded to the new, most deserving state. The process continues until all 435 seats are allocated.

To understand the trouble making opportunities of the current apportionment procedure, notice how this method purposely avoids the information needed for Hamilton's method. This ensures that situations exist where a state with a smaller fractional part of an exact apportionment receives a seat instead of a state with a larger fractional part. Illustrating examples are readily available from the apportionment based on almost any census.

A more perverse behavior, discovered by the Huntington during his analysis of apportionment methods, is where a state's apportionment can be rounded up or down by *several seats.* To explain, a state with the exact apportionment of $23\frac{1}{5}$ should receive either 23 or 24 seats. However, depending on the method and the populations of the other states, this state might receive, say, 19 or 26 seats. This *is* unfair. Actually, the number and kinds of perversities goes on and on. Quite frankly, with a fixed house size, Hamilton's method seems to be superior to the other methods.

## 4.8 Strategic Voting

When I gave a lecture at a college in Michigan right after the March 2000 Presidential primary, I met an Alan Keyes supporter. This voter recognized that his candidate had, in his words, "about as much of a chance as a snow ball in hell" to win the Republican Party primary. Since his true first choice most surely would lose, he attempted to obtain a personally better election outcome by voting for George Bush in his futile strategic effort to prevent the eventual Michigan winner, John McCain, from winning.

An unfortunate consequence of this commonly used strategic "Don't waste your vote" behavior is that it might prevent a third party candidate who could win, from winning. Early on election day in 1998, Jesse Ventura boasted how his third party candidacy for governor of the state of Minnesota succeeded because his strong showing scared the establishment. Hours later he discovered he did much more; he was elected. But, Ventura might not have been victorious if more of his supporters heeded the standard advice that, rather than "throwing away their vote," they should strategically vote for their second choice.

Jesse Jackson's two runs to become the Presidential candidate on the Democratic ticket occurred during the years of the Reagan administration. With the country comfortably settled into the conservative side of the political spectrum, Jackson wanted to move the Democratic party back to certain of its traditional liberal policies. This secondary role of elections, where the ballot also serves as partial referendums on policies, created turmoil with certain voters; should they vote sincerely for Jackson and "send a message to Washington," or should they vote for a more viable candidate? Jackson would not have won the candidacy of his party, but his protest movement would have received more support and influence had all of his supporters resisted the temptation to vote strategically to avoid "wasting their vote."

Stories upon stories of this type add importance to the need of developing an election procedure which is "strategy-proof;" a procedure where it never is in your best interests to vote strategically. Independently, Allan Gibbard and Mark Satterthwaite tackled this design project in the early 1970s. Instead of developing such a method, independently they showed that this is impossible to do; once there are at least three candidates, then, with the exception of a dictatorship, no strategy-proof procedure exists.

Both finished their results about the same time unaware of the activities of the other. Gibbard had his research published. But Satterthwaite's work was his Ph.D thesis from the University of Wisconsin, so his submission for publication was delayed by the usual academic bureaucracy. Adding to the frustration, because both works were so similar, the delay meant that Satterthwaite's research could not be accepted for publication as it stood. In response, Satterthwaite provided a new slant; he developed and wrote a new paper showing how this result about strategic behavior is intimately related to Arrow's Theorem.

An inkling that the Gibbard-Satterthwaite and Arrow results *might* be related is suggested by how both results involve dictatorships and both need three or more candidates. As a reading of Satterthwaite's paper proves, the actual connections are more subtle and concrete; they involve the binary independence condition.

To understand the connections between binary independence and strategic action, imagine an election between your favorite, Maria, and her opponent, Nancy. As your only two choices are to vote for Maria or for Nancy;

you vote, of course, for Maria. If Nancy is winning in this two person race, there is no alternative way for you to strategically cast your ballot to provide added help for Maria. Stated more generally, in a two candidate, or in a "binary independence," world, the only voting option is to vote sincerely.

The set of available options, however, significantly increases with more candidates. If Olga is a third candidate, a Maria supporter now has three ways to vote to prevent Nancy's victory.

$$M \succ O \succ N, \quad M \succ N \succ O, \quad O \succ M \succ N.$$

Presumably, one of these rankings is sincere. So, in addition to the sincere ranking, there are two other ways to mark the ballot where Maria is ranked above Nancy. These two extra options form strategic possibilities for the voter to try to achieve a personally better outcome. A personally preferred election outcome, of course, might be to elect Maria, or it might be to prevent Nancy from winning.

The role of binary independence in strategic voting, then, is how it limits a voter to the single choice of voting sincerely; binary independence deprives the voter of strategic opportunities. In non-dictatorial settings with several candidates and with transitive outcomes, however, situations always must exist where a voter can be tempted with added choices; the extra options form the strategic alternatives.

This argument suggests that examples of strategic behavior should be roughly related to those examples illustrating where a procedure fails binary independence. Indeed, my earlier example (page 44) showing that the Borda Count fails binary independence also shows how certain voters could strategically use these "extra voting options" for their personal advantage. As for plurality elections, the cries of "Don't waste your vote!" which often accompany three candidate plurality elections indicate one of the associated strategic actions. For instance, in the US 2000 Presidential elections, a voter with

Nader $\succ$ Gore $\succ$ Bush

sincere preferences might fear that a vote for the consumer advocate Ralph Nader is a de facto vote for Bush. As a result, this voter might strategically vote as though his preferences were

Gore $\succ$ Nader $\succ$ Bush.

As both rankings have the same "Gore-Bush" relationship, this strategy resembles the examples used to illustrate that the plurality vote fails binary independence. Incidentally, this is not a hypothetical example. Weeks before (and forever after) the November 2000 election, the polls indicated a statistical tie, so even allies of Nader pleaded with him to encourage his supporters to back Gore. In fact the vote trading, the strategic behavior, became so explicit that Nader voters in some states publically promised to vote for Gore if they could find a Gore supporter in a state where Gore was predicted to win easily who would promise to vote for Nader.

This binary independence connection suggests how to find strategic behavior in multistage elections such as runoffs, tournaments, and agendas. If the last stage of this procedure involves a pair, such as in a runoff or an agenda, then, the sole possible vote at this stage provides no strategic opportunities. Thus, a successful strategic action has to occur earlier; it must influence which candidates are advanced to the final stage. To illustrate, I describe what can happen with an agenda.

Start by using the ranking wheel of Chapter 3 to derive a Condorcet profile. That is, suppose the preferences for three voters are

$$A \succ B \succ C, \quad B \succ C \succ A, \quad C \succ A \succ B.$$

The resulting cyclic $A \succ B, B \succ C, C \succ A$ societal rankings ensure that whomever is voted on last in an agenda will win. In particular, if confronted with a

"the winner of $A, B$ is advanced to be compared with $C$"

agenda, and if your preferences are $A \succ B \succ C$, then the candidate you fear, $C$, will win. This is because $A$ beats $B$ at the first stage to advance to be compared with $C$. In the last election, $C$ wins.

Is there a way to prevent $C$ from winning? In the final $\{A, C\}$ binary election, you are powerless. You can only vote for $A$ or $C$, so a sincere vote for $A$ is the only option. With advanced thought and planning, however, $C$ can be prevented from winning by using a $B \succ A \succ C$ strategy. In the first election, rather than voting for your favorite $A$, vote for $B$. Once $B$ is advanced to the final stage, she will beat $C$.

Actually, these kinds of strategies are widely used. In primary elections, for instance, it is not unusual for voters to vote in the "other party's primary" to help elect a "weaker" opponent for the general election.

# Chapter 5

# More Perversities

It is this dismissal of valuable but available information, this loss of connections, which makes the area of economics so rich in problematic examples. What makes these peculiarities from economics particularly frustrating is that, as with the Arrow and Sen assertions, it could be that the needed information is explicitly assumed or provided. But, it may be that relevant data is not being used to determine final outcomes and conclusions. Instead, economic procedures may ignore crucial aspects of the information.

As a slight digression, let me mention a positive development. Although the "parts-whole" conflict is not mentioned, the field of economics is addressing some of these difficulties. In the late 1960s, an economist from the University of Minnesota, Leonid Hurwicz, raised questions about the various economic solution concepts. To roughly paraphrase his more precise technical comments, "OK, these are nice notions, but are they any good? If these concepts truly model economic environments, then how do people find the solutions? Presumably, individuals find the price equilibrium, or other economic concepts, by interacting. But, how? Who says what to whom?"

This search for the "Who does what? Who says what to whom?" connecting information gives birth to a wide range of notions. It is the origin of the "mechanism design" literature where the goal is to specify the interactions needed to achieve a specified purpose. The design, for instance, might involve appropriate incentives to make the system self-policing; people do what they are supposed to do primarily because it is in their best interest. The design might be an organizational chart which outlines the responsibilities and chain of command of different individuals and groups.

From the perspective of this book, this literature searches for the subtle connections that are needed to realize a specified goal. But, although mech-

anism design is an intriguing topic, I continue with my description of the
difficulties caused by the loss of connecting information.

After describing certain difficulties of economics, potential explanations
of efficiency problems in engineering are explored. Some of the better engineering firms fully understand, at least intuitively, that a part-whole conflict
occurs. In some manner, their use of "facilitators" — individuals whose assignment is to ensure that different groups are working toward, rather than
inadvertently conflicting with, corporate goals — can be treated as an empirical attempt toward "mechanism design." The extent and way in which
it is addressed, however, underscores the seriousness of the conflict.

Finally, to address some remaining concerns from the introductory chapter, the final section returns to the simpler setting of voting. By showing
how problems arise even with large "parts," I identify another source of
voting difficulties.

## 5.1   Economics: Supply and Demand

Much of our understanding of the market place comes from the wisdom of
the moral philosopher Adam Smith. According to Smith,

> "It is not from the benevolence of the butcher, the brewer, or
> the baker, that we expect our dinner, but from their regard to their
> own interest."

In one philosophical stroke, Smith cut the complexity and diversity of economic interactions to the simple force of conflicting self-interest; conflicts
which presumably interact with one another in a manner to reach the state
of efficiency where supply equals demand.

> "Every individual endeavors to employ his capital so that its
> produce may be of greatest value. He generally neither intends to
> promote the public interest, nor knows how much he is promoting
> it. He intends only his own security, only his own gain. And he is
> led by an invisible hand to promote an end which was no part of his
> intention. By pursuing his own interest he frequently promotes that
> of society more effectively than when he really intends to promote
> it ... "

This invisible hand explanation has influenced economic decisions and
governmental policy, it is the story which lies behind the analysis found in
the morning papers, on the evening news, and embraced by our politicians.

But, is it true? Surprisingly, even though Smith's narrative has been around for more than a couple of centuries, nobody really knows.

A result casting huge stones at this story was an example constructed by Herb Scarf, an economist at Yale University. Scarf's example uses three economic agents where each enjoys all of the nice characteristics usually assumed in that first economics course. To ensure that only Smith's story of marketplace pressures is being considered, all other complications are assumed away. To do so, Scarf required each of the three individuals to have a separate commodity — think of them as the butcher, the brewer, and the baker — which they trade among each other in a self-interested manner. In this highly idealized setting, nobody has wealth; all money earned to purchase other commodities comes from selling a portion of what the person has at the going price.

By dismissing complications, the resulting commodity prices are based on marketplace dynamics; they are based on who wants what at different prices. The punch line of Scarf's example is that even with this idyllic setting, the prices — governed solely by the market place pressures — *always move away* from the price equilibrium to cycle forever. Ouch! This example compromises the validity of Smith's Invisible Hand story.

## 5.1.1 Sonnenschein, Mantel, Debreu

Other theoretical results go beyond Scarf's model with its cyclic behavior to indicate that Smith's Invisible Hand story suffers serious difficulties. For instance, Hugo Sonnenschein, an economist who also was the president of the University of Chicago, proved that even a particularly simple version of Smith's approach — a story so elementary that it can be described in an introductory course of economics — can generate behavior so wild and complex that the economic system never reaches the desired state where supply equals demand. Again, to avoid complications, the story is restricted to pure market place pressures of the type we might expect to see in a flea or fish market where the face-to-face encounters determine prices.

Sonnenschein's result was sharpened by the Argentinian economist Rolf Mantel and improved to its current state by Gerard Debreu, the winner of the 1983 Nobel Prize in economics. This result strongly suggests that we should dismiss Smith's Invisible Hand as just another wishful story.

While fascinating, this Sonnenschein, Mantel, Debreu assertion, denoted as SMD for simplicity, appears to conflict with observations. After all, it suggests that the economic world can be a far more chaotic environment than what we observe and experience.

Is it? In that first economic course, in news reports about how national economic decisions are made, we have been taught about the wisdom of "trusting the marketplace." The story is so wide spread that it is natural and easy to accept Smith's claim that the economics of our society — if left alone — generates a smooth movement of prices converging to the promised land of a price equilibrium.

The SMD result asserts that this soothing scenario need not be true. Instead, it follows from SMD that anything — even the wildest imaginable behavior — can describe the economic dynamics. As a consequence, their claim even invites you to visit your local mathematics department to find the latest, most outrageous form of chaotic motion. Then, according to SMD, preferences can be designed for the economic agents so that the resulting price dynamics mimics that highly chaotic behavior just borrowed from your friendly mathematician! This is bothersome.

Grasping for straws to preserve the story, one might conjecture that the accompanying preferences so pathological that any economist would immediately dismiss them as unrealistic. No; the preferences are of the type found in many standard articles.

## 5.1.2   A misleading theory?

Is this assertion of wild behavior a flaw in the described theory, or in our observations? The fault probably resides in both camps. The actual marketplace dynamics, for instance, probably are more complicated and chaotic than we recognize. On the other hand, a conflict causing misleading theoretical assertions is that certain basic, standard economic assumptions have the effect of losing "available, crucial information." (Sound familiar?) Actual people don't lose this information; the theory does. Whenever this happens, the economic analysis must be expected to offer misleading predictions.

As one example which borrows from Smith's observation that the butcher and baker act in a self interested manner, the economist assumes that at a given situation and price, the rational economic person seeks to buy and sell what is personally best; the person finds his or her optimal deal. This is a reasonable assumption.

The problem arises in the way this "self-interest" assumption is implemented. The problem is that, inadvertently, optimization techniques can convert a wise person into a highly myopic agent who dismisses a considerable amount of useful information. The information is readily available, but the particular modelling of "rationality" dismisses valued data.

To explain, optimizing techniques tend to be "situation specific" — they find the "best" solution in each situation. By emphasizing each specific situation, they can create an economic agent who is ignorant about what he might do with even a minuscule change in prices or personal wealth. It admits, for instance, agents who make radical changes in purchases with trivial price changes, even a penny, or minor changes in wealth, say by finding a nickel on the floor. Actual day-to-day decisions incorporate what might be done with minor changes; the added information moderates how we behave. But, our theoretical "rational person" is forced to ignore this valuable, more general information. It is this myopic ignorance which unleashes the wild and chaotic economic theoretical behavior allowed by SMD.

Clearly, this loss of available information should cause misleading assertions. It does; the lost information, for instance, generates highly chaotic price behavior. But by using assumptions which reintroduce the information about what a rational agent would do with slight changes in circumstances, it follows, as I showed, that aspects of the wild price behavior are tempered. In particular, the troubling SMD result no longer holds in its full generality.

## 5.1.3 Subeconomies

To describe even wilder conclusions, consider an economy where a certain good no longer can be traded. Each person has to consume what she or he has. Examples include where the commodity is a certain cigarette with a funny smell, or some discontinued computer software. For the converse of this story, suppose a new product suddenly appears on the market.

The goal is to understand the relationship between the two economies. If, for instance, the economy with a larger number of commodities is well behaved because the prices move smoothly in a highly predictable "Invisible Hand" manner to reach the price equilibrium, could the smaller economy be erratic enough to to create chaos-envy among mathematicians or physicists?

Surprisingly, this wild scenario, a behavior which would cast further doubt on Adam Smith's story and other economic procedures, can happen. Even more disturbing, I proved that the behavior of each possible subeconomy — created by dropping different choices and/or number of commodities — can have any desired behavior. This means you can specify in advance the kind of price dynamic you want for each subeconomy; in doing so, be as iconoclastic as you wish. Then, fixed preferences for the economic agents can be constructed so that each economy behaves as stated.

This assertion means that a three commodity economy of steak, fish, and lobster, can be created where the price dynamics of the full economy behaves in an orderly fashion. Yet when the same people encounter the "fish and steak economy," the prices become highly erratic and chaotic. When they are in an economy of fish and lobster the price dynamic is cyclic where prices never approach the sole equilibrium. This economic result, in other words, mimics the Table 2.1 example (page 27) where the plurality election over four candidates differs from any three candidate election outcome. While this economic assertion is technically more difficult to prove, the conceptual difficulty involves the same loss of connecting information.

Words are required to prevent the reader from dismissing this behavior as another theoretical anomaly removed from reality. The "lost information" turns out to be how economic agents make substitutes. For instance, at each price each person has a certain demand for steak, fish, and lobster. Perhaps steak is emphasized only because of money earned by selling lobsters. If lobsters are removed from the market, well, fish might be all that can be afforded. So, demand can and does change character depending on what is available to buy and sell. Notice how this explanation closely resembles, as it must, the "lost information" story for Arrow's result and voting paradoxes.

This economic behavior is easier to understand by considering changes in demand when introducing new commodities. As an illustration, recall how individual demand radically changed from the distant days of carbon paper to photocopying, or from typewriters to PC computers. Changing the alternatives can profoundly effect the economy's demand structure.

## 5.2   Individual demand and consumer benefits

When vacationing in a small town in Northern Michigan, an enjoyable way to spend a Sunday morning while supporting the local fire department is to attend the annual pancake breakfast at the fire hall; the hall is located at the corner of Central and California.[1] Let me see; to get there, we could walk west on Main, then north on Central. Or, we could walk north on Michigan and then west on California. The order of travel does not matter; either route will end with a delightful breakfast of pancakes and sausages.

The different segments of this journey constitute "parts." In walking to the fire hall, the sum of the parts *is* the whole; geography does not complicate the journey by imposing subtle, unexpected connecting information. There are no cliffs, swamps, or abandoned mines along the way. But, as we discovered earlier with the agenda manipulation scenarios, the landscape changes radically when moving from the comfort of geography to the complexity of the social sciences. In the social sciences, a strong indicator that

---

[1]The rural fire hall we support has one street; the state highway.

valued connecting information exists and is not being used occurs when the order of the parts influences the final outcome. To illustrate this theme, the story described next is based on the insightful research of the economists John Chipman from Minnesota and Jim Moore from Purdue.

The story begins with some prices dropping, others increasing, and a new tax structure. Are you better or worse off? Economists have wrestled with this problem using terms such as "consumer surplus" and "compensating variation," as part of their cost-benefit analysis. One approach is to use an individual's wealth as a way to measure this change.

The idea is simple and natural. It mimics arguments used to try to win a salary increase; "Gee, boss; with the price changes I need more money just to stay even." The approach is to determine how much your wealth would have to change to make you equally as pleased as you were. Notice, your wealth does not change; this is just a hypothetical measure introduced to determine whether you are better off or poorer. If, for instance, it would require a decrease in your wealth to bring you to the previous level, then you now are better off. Similarly, if an infusion of money is required to regain a previous status, you currently are worse off.

How is this change in status be measured? Part of the answer comes an economist's blackboard covered with all those upward and downward sloping lines with different areas shaded in. These graphs describe clever ways to use an individual's demands for a certain good to determine the accrued benefits, or losses, from price changes.

Suppose, for instance, that the price of milk changed from $1.30 to $1.50, the price of bread changed from $1.40 to $1.10, and the price of fish changed from $3.40 to $3.50. One approach is to measure the effect of the price change of milk, holding the other two fixed. Then, once the effect of changing the price of milk to $1.50 is measured, measure the effect of the bread change, and finally the effect of the fish change. This resembles a "go west on Main, then north on Central" approach to reach the final destination. The question is whether the same answer results by taking other route — a "go north on Michigan and then west on California" change; say, first study the effects of a change in fish, then bread, and finally milk.

If the answer can change depending on the route, can we trust any conclusion? To appreciate the potential impact, return to that argument for a salary increase. Imagine, for instance, that one order of computation proves that you are in serious need of a salary increase just to remain the same, while another order of computation proves that you are much better off. Which approach do you think your boss will support? As true with the earlier comments about strategic behavior, extra options offer manipulative opportunities.

If different routes can generate different answers (and this is precisely what happens), then valued (maybe unexpected) information about how these parts are connected is being dismissed. In turn, this suggests that a version of Arrow's Impossibility result is lurking out there. To avoid being sidetracked by technicalities, I outline the ideas showing how to establish a result which mimics Arrow's assertion. To do so, I show what plays the role of each of Arrow's conditions.

In Arrow's world, *binary independence* requires the societal outcomes to be computed in terms of the parts. The parallel concept for the cost-benefit world, call it "Computation of parts," is where the outcome is computed by changing one price at a time. As with binary independence, changes in the other prices are assumed to have no effect on this analysis.

From a technical perspective, the principal role played by the *Pareto* condition in Arrow's result is to ensure that each pair — the parts — does not have a rigid, fixed outcome. So, for economics, replace Pareto with the requirement that a change in an individual's demand structure forces a change in the measure of the benefit. This makes sense; if I like fish, and if the price of fish drops significantly, I am personally better off.

Arrow's condition about transitive societal ranking requires the societal pairwise outcomes to be assembled in a specified structured manner. The parallel condition for the cost-benefit world is to require the final outcome to be the same independent of the order in which the results from the different prices are assembled.

The conclusion of Arrow's dictator is that for all possible inputs (all possible profiles), the only way to ensure this orderly outcome is to strongly restrict the inputs to those of a single person; a dictator. In the cost-benefit world, the parallel for Arrow's dictator is if, for all possible price and wealth changes, the only way to realize this story of determining the final outcome by taking any route is by highly restricting the individual's preferences.

With some technical considerations purposely omitted, this comparison with Arrow's Theorem captures the results of Chipman and Moore. They prove that there are settings where it is impossible to carry out this story; the outcome always can change with the path. They then prove that there are other settings where the only way the scenario — this cost-benefit story where the path of analysis does not matter — can hold is if the person's preferences are tightly restricted. Their conclusion, then, is an analogue of Arrow's dictator. In other words, a subtle "parts-whole" conflict damns the procedure; it does not work as anticipated.

Problems should be expected. In the last section, we explored what can happen in a lobster, fish, steak economy should a commodity be missing. Rather than dropping a commodity, price changes can alter what a person can afford; demands for different commodities at different prices most surely are connected. Procedures which artificially divorce these parts — even if the division is not intended — must be expected to provide misleading conclusions. Many other results of this type from economics are available. They arise whenever differences occur due to the route taken or the alternatives considered.

## 5.3 Can excellence breed inefficiency?

When confronted with a complex problem, we know what to do.

> Divide a difficult problem into smaller parts. Then, solve each of the component parts.

This standard wisdom makes sense. It is unrealistic to expect a highly complex problem to be solved without dividing it into manageable components. An extreme illustration is the successful construction and design of the Boeing 777 airliner. No one person could understand all of the issues and problems. Success could be achieved only by breaking the construction and design issues into smaller components.

This "solution by division" strategy is so valued that, in different forms, it is widely used throughout modern society. This includes the forms of decentralization manifested by the different units of our government, court systems, legal firms, financial firms, and on and on. Remember the "genius" title assigned to Henry Ford? Ford's clever insight was to "decentralize" manufacturing with the assembly line.

These examples reflect an appreciation that handling massive concerns requires localized expertise. A "jack of all trades but master of none" might have spelled success in a simpler time, but it is not likely to do so today. Instead, mastering complexity requires a "divide to conquer" decentralization. Nothing can go wrong here; or can it?

Problems can and do arise. "Conflict" almost arrives with gusto by complicating predictions made by the micro and macro study of so many topics. Indeed, this inherent conflict between the "parts and the whole" has become a research concern which transcends individual disciplines. To focus the discussion, recall the earlier comments about the inefficiencies which can plague engineering; it is worth wondering whether some of these difficulties might reflect various decentralized approaches.

### 5.3.1   A simple decentralization model

To understand these concerns, treat Arrow's Theorem as a model of decentralization. Namely, view it as questioning whether it is possible to compute the transitive societal rankings in the decentralized manner of separately determining each societal binary outcome. This twist converts Arrow's Theorem into an insightful, delightfully simple example of a decentralization that goes astray. The problem has nothing to do with how each part is separately computed; this computation may manifest excellence by determining the optimal ranking of the pair according to the available information.

This model is particularly useful because we understand what goes wrong and how to fix it. The problem, of course, is the decentralization; it unleashes an "information assassin" which kills information needed for the desired final product. The "fix" is to find ways to reintroduce the relevant information.

It is reasonable to suspect that other forms of decentralization suffer problems and enjoy resolutions similar to the Arrow model. The difficulty, as already discussed, is to detect the appropriate information needed to relate the individual parts. In particular, when searching for the "connecting information," ignore "good intentions;" in Arrow's world, the "good intention" of inviting only rational voters was subverted by the decentralization. Also, do not be impressed by "redundancies" introduced to ensure that all information is used. In Arrow's setting, the inclusion of *all* binary parts ensured a considerable overlap of information about the "parts," yet a negative conclusion resulted. In fact, it is reasonable to wonder whether this combination of "good intentions" and "information overlap" were the blinders which delayed a deeper understanding of why Arrow's result holds.

### 5.3.2   Inefficiency in engineering?

Do similar "informational blinders" introduce "inefficiencies" in manufacturing and engineering design? The examples of Chapter 1 make it is clear that one "inefficiency" culprit is the choice of a decision procedure. Selecting a correct decision procedure for engineering and design purposes can be complicated; the answer must incorporate the needs, characteristics, and peculiarities of a specific engineering project. However, as indicated later in this chapter, when assigning "points" to alternatives in a multi-criteria process, a wise choice is the Borda Count; it is the unique method where the outcome avoids most of the unpleasant paradoxes. Indeed, when ways to circumvent the difficulties of Arrow's Theorem are examined in the next chapter, only the BC survives all of the different requirements.

Beyond multi-criteria decisions, a more subtle issue involves the monstrous scale of many engineering design projects. Decentralization is a must; it is a way to use the excellence and expertise to attack assigned "parts." Just considering the immense effort of logistics and careful coordination brings forth a new appreciation for their work. Yet, could this decomposition which is intended to harness excellence cause troubles? Could subtle aspects of this search for excellence contribute to inefficiency?

The surprising answer is that, yes, a decentralized search for excellence can breed inefficiency. Suppose the goal is to design a new airplane, or a new digital TV, or even a new kind of washing machine. Different projects are farmed out to different units; each unit strives to achieve excellence. Notice, this is the same story as with Arrow's model; the computed ranking for each pair could be the optimal choice. Excellence within the individual units is not the issue; as with the Arrow model, inefficiency may reflect the loss of an overview, the loss of connecting information.

In designing a plane, for instance, the optimal choice of a navigation system might be too large for the optimal cockpit design; the optimal choice of a wing design might conflict with the design of the body; the optimal body design might be too heavy for the wings. Oh, after one group returns another group's proposal as impractical, a more appropriate design will be advanced — it is not optimal in isolation, but it may be relative to the total project. (This iterative process contributes to inefficiency.) Stated in words similar to the question raised about the meaning of Simpson's paradox (page 108), the optimal choice for the total project might require suboptimal decisions for the parts.

This is not idle, theoretical speculation; this is an engineering reality. Without knowing the decision theoretic reasons, the engineers are well aware of the problems. And, they are searching for answers. Again, help about what to do comes from Arrow's Theorem. While my discussion about how to avoid Arrow's difficulties starts in the next chapter, we know what to do; find ways to make the decision procedures use the information about the rationality of the voters. Similarly, in engineering, a way to reduce inefficiencies is to find methods which promote an appropriate information transfer among the different decentralized units of a project. The engineering model is more difficult, however, because we really do not fully understand what available information is lost through decentralization.

Let me support these comments with examples. The first one involves a high placed manager from a well known automobile company who told me how his company improved morale by having the managers from different units get together for weekly coffee, some social interaction, and a general discussion. An unexpected result of this gathering was an improvement in efficiency. Morale might be part of the answer, but the real answer probably is that some of the previously "lost" information was being recovered and transferred during these discussions.

A more explicit example comes from comments made by someone very knowledgeable about a highly regarded, large firm. He acknowledged that this company suffered the coordination problems which are predicted by Arrow's result. The problem is so severe, he claimed, that some of their employees needed to serve as "facilitators;" part of their responsibilities is to ensure a coordinated interaction among various units. Rather than a surprise, the message from Arrow's Theorem is that this is a necessity. What is a surprise is the large percentage of employees charged with at least some of this responsibility — over half![2]

I could go on and on. For instance, because of the different talents needed for different tasks, a new product often is divided into the

- the design stage where the new product is designed,

- the implementation stage where the design is fleshed out into all requirements needed for the actual production, and

- the actual manufacturing stage.

With three separate units, problems manifesting a loss of connecting information must be expected. They occur; in part, it is due to the lack of complete information about what is currently possible at different stages. The common result has the plans from one stage returned to another to be redone to match what is currently possible. Each iterate cause inefficiency (by losing time and money), and it is precisely what can be predicted by using Arrow's result as a model of decentralized activity.

## 5.4   Elections with triplets, or ...

Our quick trip through statistics, apportionments, law, economics, engineering and other topics showed that changing the set of available alternatives — maybe by dropping or adding an alternative — can radically alter the societal conclusion. To better understand this puzzling behavior, return to simple decision problems where, instead of computing the societal rankings

---

[2]I do not identify the company only because my source seemed embarrassed by the use of so many facilitators. But, this large percentage may contribute to the high regard the company enjoys.

with pairs, use something else. After all, if decisions based on binary comparisons cause troubles, then maybe we should compute the societal outcome in terms of how society ranks the triplets. Why not construct the societal ranking with their rankings of four-tuples, or five-tuples? How about using the societal rankings of $k$-tuples for a specified value of $k$ between 2 and $n$?

While this project sounds reasonable, we already know from the plurality election of Ann, Barb, Candy, and Deanna with the Table 2.1 preferences (page 27) that serious conflict can arise. To recall, this profile demonstrates that the four-candidate plurality conclusion can directly oppose the plurality ranking of each triplet. I introduced this example to create a sense of mystery, but by now we can anticipate the source. Namely, expect that by independently computing each triplet's outcome — so information about a voter's rankings of one triplet is not used in the computation of another triplet — we can lose valued, available but subtle portions of information.

What information? Let me offer the reader a challenge; before continuing, try to identify it. (It differs from the "loss of individual rationality" explanation of binary independence.)

## 5.4.1   An Arrow-like Theorem

To make these comments precise, extend "binary independence" into a natural definition for "triplet independence." The idea is to require the societal outcome for each triplet to depend strictly upon each voter's relative ranking of that triplet. In terms of the ice skating example, this means that the societal ranking of {Bobek, Bonaly, Kwan} will not be influenced in any manner by how the judges rank, say, Kwiatkowski. Consequently, and this is where the loss of information comes in, the ranking of any triplet is determined in a disconnected manner from the ranking of any other triplet.

**Definition 8** *A social welfare procedure (that is, a decision procedure which ranks the different alternatives) satisfies* Ternary Independence *if and only if the following conditions hold. Let $A$, $B$, and $C$ be any three social states or alternatives. Suppose $\mathbf{p}_1$ and $\mathbf{p}_2$ are any two profiles where each voter's $\{A, B, C\}$ ranking in $\mathbf{p}_1$ agrees with the voter's $\{A, B, C\}$ ranking in $\mathbf{p}_2$. The group's $\{A, B, C\}$ relative societal ranking for both profiles are the same.*

To analyze what can go wrong, observe that the inputs and the outputs are divided into "disconnected parts" of triplets. Based on our experience, this suggests that should the society be sufficiently heterogeneous, then the myopic processing nature of the procedure, where it emphasizes triplets, probably will confuse the actual society of rational voters with a different, *nonexistent* society of partially rational voters. To illustrate that this is the case, use the ranking disc of Figure 5.1 to generate the Condorcet four-tuple. As we know, this ranking disk profile places each candidate in each position exactly once. Therefore, as already discussed, the election outcome for *any* positional method is the complete tie

$$A = B = C = D.$$

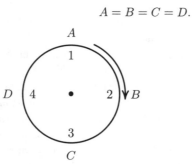

**Figure 5.1.** Four candidate ranking disk

To facilitate comparisons of this tied outcome with the outcomes of the triplets, the following table separates the triplet portions of each ranking.

| **Ranking** | $\{A, B, C\}$ | $\{B, C, D\}$ | $\{A, C, D\}$ | $\{A, B, D\}$ |
|---|---|---|---|---|
| $A B C D$ | $A B C$ | $B C D$ | $A C D$ | $A B D$ |
| $B C D A$ | $B C A$ | $B C D$ | $C D A$ | $B D A$ |
| $C D A B$ | $C A B$ | $C D B$ | $C D A$ | $D A B$ |
| $D A B C$ | $A B C$ | $D B C$ | $D A C$ | $D A B$ |

This messy table has an interesting feature; for each triplet, three of the four rankings form a Condorcet triplet. For instance, the first column of $\{A, B, C\}$ rankings has a Condorcet triplet plus an extra $A \succ B \succ C$ ranking. Consequently, whatever positional method is used with these triplets, the contribution of the three rankings in the Condorcet triplet define a complete tie. This tie is broken by the remaining ranking; the preferences of the fourth, remaining voter.

This suggests the start of conflict! Disharmony occurs because all positional methods define a complete tie for the four-candidate Condorcet tuple. But, since each triplet's ranking from this tuple is determined by the ranking of the one remaining voter, the outcomes of the triplets must disagree with the four-candidate outcome. Indeed, most positional methods rank the triplets in the conflicting (and cyclic) manner

$$A \succ B \succ C, \quad B \succ C \succ D, \quad C \succ D \succ A, \quad D \succ A \succ B.$$

(These rankings correspond to the orderings of triplets in the Figure 5.1 ranking disk in the indicated direction.) The only procedures with different outcomes are where voters vote for one (plurality method) or for two candidates; the plurality outcomes are

$$A \succ B = C, \quad B \succ C = D, \quad C \succ D = A, \quad D \succ A = B.$$

while the outcomes for the method where we vote for two alternatives are

$$A = B \succ C, \quad B = C \succ D, \quad C = D \succ A, \quad D = A \succ B.$$

The explanation for this conflict follows the lead of Table 3.6 (page 85). Namely, the anonymity respected by voting procedures allows the parts to be reassembled in any desired manner. So, rather than our actual rational society, the various ways the parts can be reassembled identify the large number of different kinds of societies the procedure believes it is serving.

In particular, the above table allows the transitive rankings to be confused with a profile where two voters share the same cyclic ranking

$$A\,B\,C, \quad B\,C\,D, \quad C\,D\,A, \quad D\,A\,B$$

while the other two "partially rational" voters have preferences

$$B\,C\,A, \quad C\,D\,B, \quad D\,A\,C, \quad A\,B\,D$$
$$C\,A\,B, \quad D\,B\,C, \quad A\,C\,D, \quad B\,D\,A$$

which also fail transitivity. Notice; although each voter in this hypothetical world can rank any triplet in a transitive manner, *the voter is incapable of transferring information about his ranking of one triplet to his ranking of another one.* In particular, these partially rational creatures fail to preserve how a pair is ranked from one triplet to another. For instance, notice that the last two voters reverse their relative ranking of the only common pair in each successive pair of triplets; what air-heads! But, this kind of society is unexpectedly admitted by our tacit assumption.

The point is, there is only one way to assign triplets from a specified Condorcet profile to define a transitive, four candidate profile. The many other ways to assign them to voters generate unintended "rationally challenged" societies. So, as the ternary independent procedures cannot distinguish these wild constructions from the intended society, outcomes based on triplets need not reflect our "rational voter" world. Instead, thanks to the decentralization of ternary independence, the outcomes may reflect what happens in a fictional world of short term memory where voters can rank triplets, but they forget how they did it when they rank another triplet.

What is the "lost information" caused by ternary independence? It is that when a *rational voter* ranks a triplet, the voter must use the *same binary rankings for each triplet*. The voter cannot change the ranking of a pair from one triplet to another. Because this subtle form of available, crucial information about the actual voters is lost, we must expect an Arrow type conclusion. This is the case.

**Theorem 7** *Let F be a social welfare function with transitive outcomes for four or more candidates. Assume that the strictly transitive preferences of the voters satisfy the Universal domain condition. If F satisfies ternary independence and Pareto, then F is equivalent to a dictator.*

There is nothing special about binary, or ternary comparisons. The same difficulty occurs whenever the emphasis is placed on finding the societal rankings for a subset. Thus, "ternary" in Definition 8 can be replaced with "*k*-ariness," where sets of *k* candidates are ranked separately, and the same word change leads to another version of Theorem 7.

## 5.4.2   Consequences for our elections

What does all of this mean about our daily affairs where decisions are made by a show of hands? In the market place, at work, during elections, and so forth, we are not worried about abstractions as captured by these theorems; we face the far more pragmatic concern of determining *who is the correct winner*. To be specific, we know that the "Let's have a show of hands" plurality vote can be bad. But, how bad can it get?

The answer is that the plurality outcomes can be as bad and perverse as you wish. By this I mean that you can create as pathological of an example as you desire, and it creates an example that can occur.

To be specific, the 2000 US election campaign started in August, 1999, with ten declared candidates for the Republican presidential candidate. In mid-August, nine of these candidates participated in the Iowa Republican Party straw ballot — an election with non-binding results. For fun, consider the actual ranking where George W. Bush came in first, Steve Forbes second, Elizabeth Dole third, and so forth. This ranking does not include the one missing candidate, Senator John McCain from Arizona, who did not participate, but who made an impressive showing in later primaries. What would have happened had he taken part? What if Pat Buchanan, or former

Vice President Dan Quayle had not participated? Would the ranking remained much the same? Maybe Lamar Alexander, who did so poorly that he then withdrew from contention, could have been the front runner with one of these scenarios.

Unfortunately, information about each voter's ranking of the ten candidates is not available, so I cannot determine what actually would have occurred with these different scenarios. Theoretically, however, the answer is "anything could have occurred." The basic result, which I discovered by using notions from "chaos" at the end of the 1980s, states that you can rank these ten candidates in any desired manner. Next, consider the ten possible situations where one candidate drops out; rank the remaining nine candidates in any desired way — be perverse. So far, we have rankings of 11 sets, where the rankings can be as far apart as desired.

Next, consider all situations where two candidates decide not to compete, or three candidates, or four, or ... Choose a ranking for each set of two or more candidates; they can be weird; they need not have anything to do with one another. (By doing this, rankings are selected for 1013 different sets of candidates.) The result asserts that an example of rational voter preferences can be constructed so that the voters' sincere ranking of each subset of candidates is the one you selected.[3]

To illustrate, move away from the Republican party to consider the election from among { *Jennifer, Katri, Lillian, Monica, Nancy, Olga, Pat* }. An example can be constructed where

- Katri beats all candidates in pairwise elections (she is the Condorcet winner),

- Lillian wins all three candidate elections,

- Monica wins all four candidate elections,

- Nancy wins all five candidate elections,

- Olga wins all six candidate elections,

- Pat wins the seven candidate election,

- Jennifer is bottom ranked in all elections except the seven candidate election where she is second ranked.

---

[3]These elections behaviors are more fully described in my book *Chaotic Elections! A Mathematician Looks at Voting.*

The point is, whatever listing of rankings is specified for each set of candidates, an example can be created where that ranking is the sincere outcome. This result is troubling for democracy. But, the problem does not stop at voting; Deanna Haunsperger, a mathematician at Carleton College in Minnesota, proved that similar problems can trouble statistical procedures.

By now, the reason for this outcome should be intuitive. If the voter preferences are sufficiently heterogeneous, then these preferences can be subdivided into different sized parts and rearranged in all sorts of ways. The different arrangements indicate the different, imaginary societies that the voting procedures are trying to service. The differences in elections indicates the serious loss of available information about the voters.

### 5.4.3   Resolution?

Surprisingly, a resolution for these problems can be found. While the technical explanation is not offered here, the best way to reflect voter preferences is to use the Borda Count. Recall, for nine candidates, this is where ballots are tallied by assigning 8, 7, $\ldots$, 1, 0 points respectively to a voter's top-, second-, $\ldots$, eighth-, and ninth-ranked candidate. Can other number choices work? Surprisingly not; only this particular selection and obvious modifications have the desired properties. In the next chapter, when discussing resolutions of Arrow's Theorem, the Borda Count again plays a central role.

## 5.5   Still more examples

It is possible to go on and on and on providing more examples from law, psychology, and economics. It is possible to construct a more general, formal theorem about what goes wrong. However, the point has been made; emphasizing parts carries the cost of losing available but valued information. This mantra holds not only for choice results such as those by Arrow and Sen, but also for any area and any topic. At this stage, I invite the reader to discover and/or construct his or her own examples.

# Chapter 6

# A Search For Resolutions

## 6.1 Introduction

We now understand these problems from Arrow's and Sen's theorems, Simpson's Paradox, gambling, economics, inefficiencies of complex, decentralized systems, and on and on. The paradoxical behavior reflects the inadvertent loss of crucial but available information about how the disjoint parts are related. Worse than being "lost," this information can be purposely dismissed whenever we use or design procedures — whether decision, economic, or statistical — which emphasize the "disjoint parts" over the "whole."

As illustrated, by understanding why problems occur, a wide selection of unexpected examples from a variety of areas can be discovered. Quite frankly, by now, we should view with suspect any conclusion from any subject area which involves the surgical separation of "parts" from one another. Definitely worry when this separation is advertised in terms of noble intents such as "efficiency" or preserving the "integrity of the outcome."

A more ambitious goal is to find resolutions. At least in principle, we know how to do this; reintroduce the lost information. But, how? To provide guidance in doing so, I tackle the obvious challenge of showing how not to, and then how to, circumvent the fundamental difficulties imposed by Arrow's and Sen's theorems.

To start, recall that Arrow's theorem requires a sufficiently heterogeneous society; this causes the Arrovian procedures to lose information about the rationality of the voters. So, to find a useful resolution, maybe we should design ways which avoid highly heterogeneous settings, or which require — in a "to-be-determined" manner — the decision process to use the previously dismissed information.

## 6.1.1   Homogeneity

When buying a car or another consumer good, if we discover that insisting on certain features leads to disaster, then it is time to re-evaluate the basics. For instance, if demanding a sexy body style for a car leads only to vehicles with limited performance, then, difficult as it may be, "sexy body styles" may have to be sacrificed. Similarly, when confronted with the consequences of Arrow's dictatorial conclusion, maybe we should seek more forgiving "axioms" (i.e., basic properties) than those proposed by Arrow.

Alas, as indicated next, for the most part this popular approach almost always leads to frustration. As a preview, *any approach* which fails to remedy the "lost information" phenomenon is doomed for mediocrity if not abject failure. As continually shown, expect to suffer "lost information problems" if a procedure emphasizes "disconnected parts."

If reasonable modifications of the axioms, the defining properties, fail to provide realistic satisfaction, then an alternative method is to

*do nothing and hope for the best.*

After all, if Arrow's negative result requires a "sufficiently heterogeneous society," and if we belong to a fairly "homogeneous" club, social group, or society, then why worry? Perhaps the commonality of agreement found among our friends and neighbors, the members of our social or political group, ensures that an appropriate level of consensus will be reached. Perhaps our community sense of essential agreement will make *our* decision procedure immune from the wrath of Arrow's dictatorial assertion. Stated as a wishful myth, maybe *our* particular society is free from these difficulties.

This reasonable sentiment has motivated considerable research. Unfortunately, the conclusions prove that "hoping for the best" is, well, another futile exercise in wishful thinking. While a certain level of homogeneity among the voters' preferences does mitigate some of Arrow's difficulties, serious problems remain. Surprisingly, even if a society is free from the confusion caused by the mixed, motley opinions which characterize both the best and the worse features of a fully heterogeneous setting, the resulting societal conclusions need not mean what we think they do — at least as measured by Arrow's properties.

A way to prove this discouraging assertion is to characterize *all possible* non-dictatorial procedures which satisfy Arrow's conditions for the different homogeneous societies. Are they clumsy! Not only do they suffer a complete lack of social graces, but they are devoid of even a token appearance of "democratic behavior." No realistic rational society would have anything to do with them.

Phrased in another manner, since no reasonable society would want these awkward methods, then, even with reasonably homogeneous beliefs, our widely used, standard procedures still violate Arrow's properties. The argument is simple; if our standard procedures satisfied all of Arrow's conditions, they would be in the list of admitted procedures. As they are not, these standard procedures remain suspect even when used only in homogeneous societies. These methods still must suffer in the quality of their decisions — as measured by Arrow's properties.

The reason Arrow's difficulties keep haunting us is a continuation of the earlier "donkey and cart" explanation. If constrained to develop decision procedures with Arrow's assumptions — assumptions which, inadvertently, emphasize the needs of the unsophisticated, irrational who cannot sequence preferences into a transitive structure — the resulting procedures still strip and dismiss valued information about the rationality of voters' preferences. No matter how homogeneous the society, Arrovian procedures always treat the transitivity of societal outcomes as an accident rather than an intended (by us, not the procedure) expression of the voters' rationality.

## 6.1.2 Free rider

An alternative approach toward handling these difficulties can be illustrated and motivated with the earlier free rider "beer party" example (page 83). This beer party conflict does not pose an insurmountable difficulty; with even limited experience, we can solve it. One way to ensure that each person pays enough to cover the costs for the beer party is through moral persuasion. "Come on, Bill; we know you will drink far more than for what you are paying. Cough up more money!"

When dealing with a small group of people who interact with each other on a daily basis, shame is a particularly effective strategy. Our challenge is to incorporate the "shaming of Bill" into a workable decision procedure. Going beyond small friendly groups, our method needs to be effective even with the cold, indifferent interactions which can characterize large groups, After all, "shaming" works only if we know Bill's bad habits and if Bill cares. More generally, something needs to be built into the procedure to accurately coordinate the parts.

But if the "free rider problem" is caused by divorcing the crucial components — the collection of money to buy the community good is separated from the levels of individual consumption of the community good — then reunite them. How about using a "cash bar" where you pay for each drink. It does not matter how deviously Bill tries to "free-ride;" everyone — including Bill — pays for what he or she consumes. The difference between the cash bar and the original story introducing this free rider effect is that by coordinating the parts in the intended manner — how much you pay and how much you enjoy — eliminates free riding.

A crude but useful way to evaluate the effectiveness of this "cash bar" solution is to check whether it excludes that hypothetical, irrational person who (with the original procedure) sincerely believes in low cash contributions and high beer consumption. By needing to pay cash for each drink, this person cannot participate. So, a consequence of excluding the dead-beat irrationals is to frustrate the free rider whose strategic actions mimic our innocent irrational person.

A similar approach holds for choice procedures. If binary independence severs the assumption of individual rationality from computations, then impose new conditions which do what we thought was being done. To do so, we need to modify "binary independence" so that a new version requires admissible procedures to process and use the rationality connections. As with the beer party solution, a way to check proposed modifications is to determine whether they admit irrational voters.

### 6.1.3   Sen

Even after satisfying Arrow's problem, there still is Sen's concern for liberalism. Here, the remedies differ from those which are useful for Arrow's problem. For instance, the Borda Count turns out to be a natural way to handle Arrow's difficulties. But, the Borda Count is useless for Sen's problem if only because the BC requires each voter to express an opinion over all alternatives. It is this inclusiveness, this use of all voters' preferences over *all alternatives*, which forces the BC to violate Sen's goal of reserving certain choices to appropriate decisive voters.

While we might not know (at this stage) *how* to do it, we know *what* needs to be done. Modify Sen's setting to require the use of information about the rationality of voters. In carrying out this dictate, it is delightful to discover how some of the resulting procedures capture the old "Do unto others ... " philosophy. As an advance notice, the "individual vs. societal rights" resolution described here supports those laws banning the loud playing of music late at night or while driving down a metropolitan street. In flavor, these remedies agree with aspects of the Borda Count while, maybe, disagreeing with Minnesota Governor Jesse "The Body" Ventura. [1]   Similar

---

[1]See the reference to the Duluth, Minnesota noise law in Chapter 1.

answers, described in the next chapter, hold for certain settings modelled by the Prisoner Dilemma (page 64).

## 6.2 Altering assumptions

An active research theme has been to try to sidestep the Sen and Arrow conflicts by modifying their original assumptions. The cynical part of me argues that a hidden goal of this research is to quickly publish a paper that describes still another cheap impossibility theorem before annual salaries are determined; the dominant idealistic part of me accepts that the object is to explore and examine those properties which may lead to positive conclusions. Whatever the motivation, most of these attempts have failed.

By now, you know the reason; as long as the newly imposed conditions allow decisions to be made with the parts — pairwise information — the associated procedures still will vitiate the crucial assumption of individual rationality. As such, those published negative results dramatically underscore the reality that useful assertions are unlikely as long as the procedures lose fundamental information about the voters. But, as shown in Section 6.5, by using this informational perspective as a guide to select replacement properties for Arrow and Sen, fruitful positive conclusions emerge.

### 6.2.1 From a new pope to an oligarchy

When the Catholic Church is forced to replace a pope, the media patiently waits outside of the Vatican for the appropriate colored smoke to slowly make its way up the chimney. While we never are supposed to learn about the deliberations, we do know what procedure the cardinals use.

For an overly simplified description, the winning candidate must receive a two-thirds vote. So, to be rejected in a pairwise competition, a candidate must receive less than a third of the vote. This difference between acceptance and rejection creates a huge region of indifference. It means that if a candidate manages to receive between one-third to two-thirds of the vote in a pairwise competition, then, as far as the election outcome is concerned, both candidates are "essentially tied." No wonder the conclave can continue for such a long time.

Procedures, such as the pope selection process, replace "transitivity" with a more general notion. To explain, we have no trouble with non-transitive comments such as

Misha is essentially as tall as Robert, Robert is essentially as tall
as Ezra, but Misha is taller than Ezra,

or

the coffee can is about as heavy as this milk bottle, and the
milk bottle is about as heavy as this package of chicken, but the
package of chicken is heavier than the coffee can.

To describe this relationship, recall that the concept of transitivity borrows heavily from concepts about the relative positions of points on the line.
(This discussion started on page 34.) The weaker form of transitivity described next — *quasitransitivity* — finds its definition by capturing aspects
of this "almost the same" measurement.

**Definition 9** *A set of binary rankings over alternatives is* quasitransitive *if
for any three of them, the rankings $A \succ B, B \succ C$ imply that $A \succ C$.*

Be careful with this definition. Just as any parent listening to a teenager
trying to describe the previous night's activities knows only too well, the
crux of the definition is not so much in what is stated, but in what is
*not* stated. In particular, this definition imposes no condition about what
happens should two alternatives be ranked "essentially the same." Since the
alternatives are not exactly equal, but "almost," put a little twist in the "="
sign to have $A \approx B$. By being silent about what can occur, the definition
allows somewhat perverse settings where

$$A \approx B,\ B \approx C,\ \text{but } A \succ C$$

as captured by our size examples.

To understand Arrow's Theorem, it is silly to offer the voters the added
flexibility and opportunities of this "relaxed transitivity." After all, their
stricter transitive preferences already suffice to jeopardize the individual rationality assumption. Using my earlier comparison, providing more options
to the voters is akin to dumping another load of hay on that stack hiding
the proverbial needle. Therefore, apply this relaxed form of transitivity, quasitransitivity, only to the societal outcomes such as in the pope selection.
Unfortunately, even adding this flexibility leads to failure; the only minor
gain is to replace Arrow's dictator with an oligarchy.

**Definition 10** *An* oligarchy *is a specified set of voters with the power to
decide on the society ranking of a pair when all members of the oligarchy*

*are in agreement. Namely, for any pair of social states $A, B$, if all members of the oligarchy have the ranking $A \succ B$, then that is the societal ranking. However, if even one member of the oligarchy disagrees with the assessment of the other members on the ranking of the pair, then the societal ranking is $A \approx B$; the choices are essentially tied.*

The following version of Arrow's result, first discovered by Gibbard and then modified and extended by others, becomes the following.

**Theorem 8** *Suppose we have a social welfare function with quasitransitive outcomes for at least three candidates and at least two voters. Assume that the strictly transitive preferences of the voters satisfy the Universal domain condition. If our social welfare function satisfies binary independence and Pareto, then it is equivalent to an oligarchy.*

In other words, relaxing Arrow's requirement that the societal outcomes must be transitive — now they need only be quasitransitive — slightly relaxes Arrow's dictator into a chummy group who belong to an oligarchy.

Why does this negative conclusion arise? The answer shadows my earlier explanation for Arrow's and Sen's assertions; as long as the procedure satisfies the reasonable sounding but disabling binary independence assumption, crucial and available information about the system is lost. Again, the nature of the lost information (from the ranking disk construction of Condorcet profiles) allows binary independence to confuse the actual preferences with those from an imaginary irrational society of cyclic voters. The only procedures allowing even quasitransitive outcomes has privileged voters joined by a commonality of preferences — an oligarchy.

To see an oligarchy in action, suppose the preferences over the alternatives Buy, Sell, or Trade of the four members of a stock buying club, Peter, Paul, John, and Judas, are

| Name | Ranking | Name | Ranking |
|------|---------|------|---------|
| Peter | $S \succ T \succ B$ | Paul | $S \succ B \succ T$ |
| John | $B \succ S \succ T$ | Judas | $T \succ B \succ S$ |

Because of Judas, and only because of Judas's contrary views, this oligarchy can never reach decisive conclusions; Judas's contrary views forces the outcome to be the complete tie $S \approx T \approx B$. Just the disagreement between Judas and Paul about each pair proves that unanimity over the ranking of any pair is impossible.

By expelling Judas from the select group, the oligarchy now consists of Peter, Paul, and John. All three agree on the $ST$ ranking, but on nothing else, so the societal outcome is the quasi-transitive ranking

$$S \succ T, \quad T \approx B, \quad S \approx B.$$

To explain this result in a different manner, Arrow's result mandated a dictator because, after binary independence severed all coordinating information about transitivity, the only way to ensure a transitive societal outcome is to concentrate on a single voter's preferences; when this voter is rational, the societal outcome is transitive. An advantage gained by using the more forgiving quasitransitive societal rankings is that an indifferent societal ranking for a pair causes no damage; it does not severely limit the societal choices for the rankings of the other pairs.

But if "societal indifference" avoids causing problems with quasitransitivity, then all damaging effects must be due to the strict societal rankings of pairs. For this damage control reason, an oligarchy responds only to settings where all members are in complete agreement. Namely, to avoid sliding into a societal cycle, to avoid problems caused by shifting coalitions, the procedure assigns the safe "essentially tied" outcome for a pair of alternatives hampered by even minimal conflict.

Is an oligarchy an improvement? The answer probably depends on whether we have privileged membership in the ruling group; if not, there is no reason to embrace this elitist approach.

## 6.2.2  Tinkering with other assumptions

While all sorts of other modifications can be proposed, they are so technical that, even though I discovered some of them, they appear to belong to the "get a life" category. (Nevertheless, I invite the technically inclined reader to read (Saari [51]) for proofs and extensions of what follows.)

To offer a flavor of these comments,

- maybe positive results can be found by dropping the Pareto condition.

Nice try, but it is unsuccessful. Quite frankly, the only technical value of the Pareto condition is to ensure that there are two or more societal rankings for each pair. Consequently, the Pareto condition can be replaced by requiring that a pair never is stuck with a fixed outcome; for each pair of alternatives, require that at least two of the three societal rankings occur. So, for the $\{A, B\}$ pair, at least two of the

$$AB, \quad A = B, \quad BA$$

societal rankings must arise. Even more; there is no need to even assume
that a pair's societal rankings agrees with what the voters want. But, even
this replacement for Pareto allows an Arrow-type negative assertion.

This new result has an interesting flavor. By replacing Pareto with the
above more permissive assumption, the societal rankings need not agree with
what any voter wants. Instead, this more general setting allows perverse
situations such as a *negative dictator* where the outcome always reverses
the wishes of the designated individual. Some readers may have witnessed
such a procedure; think about how a group might react toward a particularly
annoying member — whatever he wants, we mandate the opposite. Another,
new, strange procedure is where, even with strict preferences, the dictator
can be stuck with a completely tied outcome.

To be more imaginative, instead of worrying about the obvious, staid
(and realistic) approach where the voters preferences about a pair determines the ranking of *that pair*, how about designing procedures where what
a voter thinks about one pair influences the outcome of a different pair.
Why not create a procedure where, say, the {Alice, Beth} societal outcome
is determined by how certain voters view {Alice, Beth}, how other voters
view {Beth, Crystal}, and how still other voters view {Alice, Crystal}.

Nice try; again, failure. Quite frankly, whenever the pairwise outcomes
are divided into pairs, where the societal outcome for each pair is determined
by pairwise inputs of "something" — even if the names of the pairs are
scrambled — the same Arrow type conclusion holds. The only difference is
that, now, a "twisted dictator" can emerge whose views, say, over {Beth,
Crystal} strictly determines the societal {Alice, Beth} outcome.

The basic, disturbing point remains; whenever a procedure allows something resembling binary independence where information is segregated and
disconnected, the data can be scrambled in a way which causes crucial assumptions (here, about transitive preferences) to be lost. If so, expect to be
stuck with a distorted procedure which fails any test of responsible democracy. Good answers cannot be obtained in an environment allowing "lost
but available and needed information."

## 6.3   Profile restrictions

My sermon for this section is that Arrow's axioms resemble false gods; by
blinding us to other explanations, they have led us in wrong directions. After all, although it was suspected almost immediately upon the publication
of Arrow's result that binary independence caused his assertion, the po-

litical correctness of pairwise comparisons has blinded our thinking about the fundamental traits of choice procedures. Even today procedures are criticized if they fail the binary independence test. This condition has so colored our thinking that, rather than questioning and modifying "binary independence," it is more popular to explore what happens by tinkering with Arrow's other assumptions. This approach resembles the old story of the drunk losing his car keys in the bushes but searching for them under a street light where it is easier to see. One assumption — an academic street light — which has been particularly investigated is "Unrestricted Domain."

The goal of this line of inquiry is to determine whether reasonable procedures emerge should we be willing to pay the price of prohibiting some voters from having certain preferences. While this comment accurately describes this research direction, it sounds like a particularly horrible form of dictatorial thought control. So, let me offer a spin which suggests a more benign interpretation.

This "restrictions on profiles" research is based on the recognition that many groups are surprisingly homogeneous. The hope is that a sufficiently homogeneous group might be able to find and use non-dictatorial decision methods which satisfy Arrow's conditions. Rather than an overt intent to abridge basic principles of democracy by restricting who can believe what — by specifying who can have what preferences — the objective is to determine the degree of homogeneity which is needed by a society for it to have reasonable decision procedures.

This area has a "bad news, good news" flavor where the "bad news" results have dominated the literature. The new twist provided here is to show that, with what we now know, these negative assertions must be expected. The new "good news" conclusions of Section 6.4 have been toyed with since the days of Condorcet. For instance, Sen made interesting contributions using these ideas for three-candidate societies. The basic conclusions given here, however, are new with some recent papers and this book.

## 6.3.1   Bad news

Nobody worries about the election procedure used by a highly dictatorial — or even a professional — society. The reason is clear; if all voters have essentially the same sanctioned ranking of the candidates, then who cares about the procedure; the societal ranking remains essentially the same. This suggests that by imposing sufficiently severe restrictions on the preferences the voters can assume, all sorts of reasonable decision procedures might be suddenly released from the tight hold of Arrow's conditions.

To show that this assumption is correct, start with an extreme constraint on voter preferences over four candidates. The most extreme setting is unanimity; as everyone must have the same ranking in this dictatorial society, all sorts of Arrovian procedures are allowed.

But, unanimity is boring; nothing happens. So, very slightly relax this extreme restriction by allowing each voter to select a preference only from the two rankings

$$ABCD, \quad BACD \tag{6.1}$$

Even with four candidates, the restrictions are so tight that several non-dictatorial methods with transitive societal rankings can serve this particular society; these procedures satisfy both binary independence and Pareto. The pairwise vote, for instance, works quite well — here. To prove this assertion, recall from Section 3.3.3 (page 84) that the pairwise vote fails Arrow's properties only because it allows non-transitive societal outcomes.

This non-transitivity flaw never mars the restricted Equation 6.1 world. After all, with the exception of $\{A, B\}$, all voters unanimously agree on the other five pairwise votes leading to the unanimous societal rankings

$$AC, AD, \quad BC, BD, \quad CD.$$

So far, these results define the ranking

$$[A, B] \succ C \succ D; \tag{6.2}$$

the only suspense concerns the ranking of the top two candidates $A$ and $B$. But whatever the $\{A, B\}$ societal ranking, it just adjusts the ranking of the two top candidates in the top bracket, so these binary rankings always define a transitive societal ranking.

### A four, or a two candidate society?

The success of the pairwise vote for the Equation 6.1 society also identifies why it is a useless profile restriction. Any claim that this society truly involves four candidates is, at best, a weak illusion. In reality, this highly restrictive society offers only a two candidate $\{A, B\}$ election where the only mystery left on election night is whether $A$ or $B$ is top ranked. The Pareto condition dictates the societal rankings of all other pairs, and their inferior status relative to $A$ and $B$ ensures a transitive societal ranking.

So, this strong restriction on the freedom of expression permits the Borda Count and the pairwise vote, among many different procedures, to easily satisfy binary independence and the rest of Arrow's assumptions. This is not a surprise; it is to be expected.[2]

### Borda Count

It is worth indicating why the BC satisfies binary independence in the artificial world of Equation 6.1. With the $\{A, C\}$ pair, verification of binary independence requires studying the BC rankings for any two allowed profiles $\mathbf{p}_1$ and $\mathbf{p}_2$; in each profile each voter keeps the same $\{A, C\}$ ranking. But the Equation 6.1 world requires *all voters* to prefer $A \succ C$. Thus, $A$'s BC score always is higher than $C$'s; the $A \succ C$ ranking remains invariant — for this particular society.

The only interesting Equation 6.1 setting is the $\{A, B\}$ ranking. But if two profiles $\mathbf{p}_1$ and $\mathbf{p}_2$ have the same voters preferring $A$ to $B$ and $B$ to $A$ *while satisfying the Equation 6.1 constraint*, then the two profiles are identical. Binary independence is satisfied because identical profiles have identical outcomes.

To appreciate why the severity of this restriction allows the BC to be a "binary independence method," slightly relax the constraints. To explain, the three candidate setting where voters can choose only between

$$A B C, \quad B A C$$

mimics the Equation 6.1 society where the BC and a host of other methods are binary independent. After all, the universal negative attitude toward $C$ causes a

$$[A, B] \succ C$$

ranking where the only effort is to rank the alternatives stuck in the bracket. As the bracket is separate from any other alternative, $A$ and $B$ can be ranked in any manner without hurting transitivity.

However, slightly augmenting this list to include $A C B$, so the voters' admissible preferences come from

$$A B C, \quad B A C, \quad A C B, \tag{6.3}$$

disqualifies the Borda Count as a binary independent procedure. Even if each voter has the same $\{A, B\}$ ranking in the two profiles, $\mathbf{p}_1$ and $\mathbf{p}_2$, voters

---

[2] A minor surprise is that even in this restrictive setting the plurality vote does not satisfy Arrow's assertion. It does satisfy binary independence with the Equation 6.1 restriction, but it violates the Pareto condition with $C$ and $D$; even though all voters prefer $C D$, the plurality outcome has them tied.

who prefer $ABC$ in $\mathbf{p}_1$ may prefer $ACB$ in $\mathbf{p}_2$. As demonstrated earlier with these preferences (page 43), this slight variation suffices to ensure that the BC fails binary independence.

**Extremes**

A spectrum of tradeoffs — where more severe restrictions imposed on voter preferences qualify more procedures — is emerging. At one extreme, complete freedom of expression as ensured by the "Unrestricted Domain" allows only dictators to be acceptable procedures. At the other extreme, by severely abridging what the voters can believe, as in Equation 6.1, the pairwise vote, BC, and many other decision methods work quite well.

This balancing between the level of the freedom of expression and the restrictive nature allowed by the admitted procedures suggests that somewhere between the two extremes is a profile restraint which allows the voters limited freedom of choice with reasonable decision procedures. But, what are the restrictions and the accompanying procedures?

## 6.3.2 Non-dictatorial procedures

As I show next, it takes only a surprisingly slight constraint on voters' preferences to avoid Arrow's dictator conclusion. But, the resulting asymmetry of the decision methods, where some voters have significantly more power than others, make these procedures useless for a democratic society.

**Erik the partial dictator**

The weakest possible alteration of the Universal Domain assumption for three-alternatives is where only one voter is prohibited from selecting just one specified ranking. To illustrate with the Presidential candidates of Anneli, Brigid, and Carola, suppose, for unexplained reasons, Erik never can have the $ACB$ preference; any of the five remaining rankings are fine. With the exception of Erik, all remaining voters can rank these candidates in any desired transitive manner.

As this restriction on Erik's choices violates Arrow's Universal Domain assumption, we might hope to design non-dictatorial procedures which receive a passing grade with Arrow's other properties. The good news is that a non-dictatorial procedure can be designed; the bad news is that the resulting procedure so closely resembles a dictator that it is difficult to claim that any progress has been made.

In particular, don't waste any tears on Erik because of the restriction imposed on his preferences. To the contrary; these constraints endow Erik with considerable power. This is because the only non-dictatorial method for this society designates Erik as a "partial dictator." To explain, this non-dictatorial method uses Erik's preferences, and only his preferences, to determine the societal rankings for $\{A, C\}$ and $\{B, C\}$; the opinions of the other voters are totally ignored. Erik's powers continue; whenever he prefer Brigid to Anneli, well, that also must be the societal ranking independent of what the other voters want.

The only time Erik's dictatorial role over the $\{A, B\}$ ranking is relinquished is when he prefers Anneli to Brigid. In this one setting, and only in this setting, can the rest of society have a voice; it can determine the $\{A, B\}$ ranking by using, say, a majority vote.

To illustrate with numbers, suppose Erik's preferences are $C\,A\,B$. The other voters split where 100 of them prefer $A\,B\,C$, and 102 prefer $B\,A\,C$. The information table becomes

| Voter | $\{A, B\}$ | $\{A, C\}$ | $\{B, C\}$ | |
|---|---|---|---|---|
| Erik | $A\,B$ | $C\,A$ | $C\,B$ | |
| 100 | $A\,B$ | — | — | (6.4) |
| 102 | $B\,A$ | — | — | |
| **Outcome** | $B\,A$ | $C\,A$ | $C\,B$ | |

The four slots in the table indicate where the information from 202 voters is irrelevant because Erik makes the societal decision for these pairs. Information is not dismissed for the 202 voters' $\{A, B\}$ rankings *only because Erik prefers $A\,B$.* Remember, this is the *only* situation which offers a limited franchise for the other voters. While the democratic solution (use the plurality, Borda Count, or pairwise vote) would have Brigid top-ranked but nearly tied with Anneli with Carola as a distant third, the societal ranking of this distorted procedure is $C\,B\,A$ where, not surprisingly, Erik's good friend Carola wins even though all other voters have her bottom-ranked. The satisfying power of being a partial dictator!

Do such procedures exist? Of course they do. Any academic frustrated with the veto power of an administrator probably has experienced versions of this "Erik the Partial Dictator" approach.

**Stilted methods**

Other restrictions can be imposed, and many (not all) admit non-dictatorial decision procedures. But, as with Erik the partial dictator, all of these restrictions are unsuccessful; they require highly stilted, dictatorial-like procedures; procedures that none of us would rush to the UN to advance as models for newly emerging democratic societies.

As we now know, difficulties must be anticipated whenever a decision tool for a sophisticated society is constructed with the limited, crude parts that reflect the needs of an irrational group. Namely, binary independence unintentionally handicaps all efforts to construct sophisticated procedures by requiring the methods to be usable by the actual rational voters *as well as* by the hypothetical irrational voters with cyclic preferences. It is this unintended conflict of simultaneously trying to serve the needs of the irrational while also trying to provide transitive rankings for rational voters which causes Arrow's dictator, or the oligarchy, or the partial dictator. Once a rational society is sufficiently heterogeneous — and this requires only two voters with differing opinions — the information dismissed by binary independence can force the societal pairwise rankings to be so scrambled that a transitive ranking is impossible. Only by concentrating on the views of a single person — Arrow's dictator — can the disjointed societal pairwise rankings always be assembled in a transitive manner.

**Crumbs from a dictator**

This same argument explains why only stilted methods are allowed by societies with different levels of homogeneity. As binary independence restricts what information can be used, designing procedures becomes a frustrating pursuit for gaps where the profile restrictions erode the dictator's powers. Quite frankly, designing non-dictatorial procedures is a search for crumbs left behind by the idiosyncratic nature of the dictator's preferences; treat it as combing the data for slight windows of opportunity where other voters can participate. This is no way to create tools for a democracy.

To illustrate what happens without being overly technical, let me describe the emergence of Erik the partial dictator. Start by assuming that "'Erik the Finn" is a full Nordic dictator; what Erik wants for each pair of alternatives, Erik gets as the society ranking. But Erik's allowable preferences permit only five possible societal outcomes. It is this missing outcome which offers the small crumb allowing other voters to become minimally involved.

Erik never has the $A \succ C \succ B$ preference, so when he prefers $A \succ B$, his preferences — and the societal outcome — are one of the remaining two rankings with $[A \succ B]$; it is either

$$[A \succ B] \succ C \quad \text{or} \quad C \succ [A \succ B].$$

Either case allows the ranking in the brackets to be changed to $A = B$ or $B \succ A$ without harming transitivity. Thus, when Erik likes $A \succ B$, the restriction on his preferences create a small opportunity for other voters to decide the societal $\{A, B\}$ ranking while preserving transitive societal outcomes. What is not obvious, but true, is that no other procedure allows even this limited freedom. (Compare this argument with the one associated with Equation 6.2.)

To further illustrate this argument, suppose Erik prefers $B \succ A$. With full dictatorial powers, a possible societal ranking is $B \succ C \succ A$ where $C$ *separates* $A$ and $B$. The problem is that by allowing other voters to tinker with the $\{A, B\}$ ranking, they might change it to $A \succ B$ which would define the forbidden societal cycle $A \succ B$, $B \succ C$, $C \succ A$. In other words, when $A$ and $B$ are not ranked adjacently, allowing any other voter to have a voice can introduce a change which destroys transitivity. Erik remains a dictator if only to preserve transitivity.

This argument allows us to anticipate the kinds of procedures associated with different profile restrictions. For instance, restrict Erik's preferences so that $C$ *never* is middle ranked; e.g., Erik's possible preferences are

$$[A \succ B] \succ C, \qquad [B \succ A] \succ C,$$
$$C \succ [A \succ B], \qquad C \succ [B \succ A].$$

Here, Erik's preferences — and the societal ranking he would determine as a dictator — always have $A$ and $B$ adjacently ranked. Consequently, this new profile restriction permits Erik the partial dictator to determine the societal $\{A, C\}$ and $\{B, C\}$ rankings, but authorizes the other voters to select the societal $\{A, B\}$ ranking.

### Choice of restrictions

Useful profile restrictions for Arrow's world, then, are those which create settings where some pair is adjacently ranked in all associated societal rankings. To demonstrate with an negative example, extend Erik's original restriction so that he now is prohibited from having any preference where $A \succ B$. This severe restriction suggests that it is possible that maybe more freedom can be offered to other voters. But, no; this demanding restriction returns us to an Arrovian dictator. This is because Erik's three allowed rankings,

$$C \succ B \succ A, \quad B \succ C \succ A, \quad B \succ A \succ C,$$

never create societal outcomes where the same pair of alternatives remains adjacently ranked. Consequently, as this example demonstrates, it is not the size of the profile restriction that matters, but how you use it.

The traits of an useful profile restriction are emerging. Binary independence strips and dismisses the information that the pairs of alternatives are to be transitively sequenced, so all sequencing must be imposed by the profile restrictions. In other words, the voters' preferences need to be so severely restricted that the societal outcome is essentially inherited, rather than computed. This description almost suggests ordering the alternatives along a line and then requiring the voters' preferences to respect that imposed ordering. While this approach sounds totally undemocratic, it is widely used in economics and political science.

### 6.3.3  Black's Conditions

One of the more successful constraints imposed on voter preferences was developed by an influential pioneer of this area; the Welsh political scientist Duncan Black who was from the University College of North Wales. Since Black's condition is so widely accepted as a way to understand and analyze certain (restrictive) properties of voting and economic procedures, it is worth spending a couple of pages to motivate and explain what Black's condition is, and what it can and cannot do.

Start with the "garbage in, garbage out" fear that the structure of the inputs — the voters' preferences — governs the structure of the societal outcomes and the admissible procedures. An extreme version of the "garbage in" fears are the severe Equation 6.1 restrictions. By allowing only two types of preferences, this restriction is so strict that it is akin to placing two points on the line and letting each voter select "either this one or that one." A natural extension, then, is to allow the voters to select preferences which reflect, in some manner, the orderly properties of points situated on the *same* straight line. This description essentially describes Black's condition.

**Single issue concerns**

To define a "line of preferences," consider settings where society's attention is directed toward a single issue, say the amount of money to be spent to develop a new community park, or to improve a local school, or the portion of a state budget designated toward ecology. The dollar amounts attached to the three alternatives $\{A, B, C\}$ allow them to be plotted as points on the Figure 6.1a line. Each voter's *ideal point* — the voter's idealized and preferred value for the specified project — is indicated in Figure 6.1a with an arrow labelled by the voter's name (number).

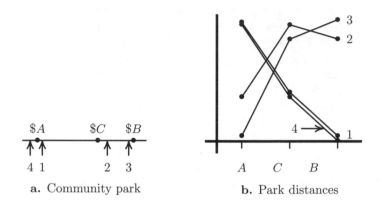

$A \qquad \$C \quad \$B$

4 1       2   3          $A \quad C \quad B$

**a.** Community park          **b.** Park distances

**Figure 6.1.** Special preferences

A natural premise about the voters is that the closer an alternative is to the voter's ideal point, the more the voter likes it. After all, if I believe that precisely \$300 should be spent on a project, then I prefer the proposal of spending \$305 over the \$370 proposal. By using "distance" to characterize rankings, the Figure 6.1a geometry determines each voter's preference ranking. For instance, voter one's ideal point in Figure 6.1a is very close to point $A$, next closest to $C$, and farthest from $B$, so his preference ranking is $A\,C\,B$.

The expectation, maybe it is a hope, is that preferences created in this fashion must, in some manner, reflect inherited traits from the straight line. They do; they avoid the cyclic complications caused by Condorcet tuples. For instance, because alternative $C$ sits between $A$ and $B$, no voter can have $C$ bottom ranked. In fact, the preferences are

- Voters 1 and 4 prefer $A\,C\,B$,

- Voter 2 prefers $C\,B\,A$, and

- Voter 3 prefers $B\,C\,A$.

To connect this profile restriction with the earlier discussion, I show below why $C$'s preferred status, where she can never be bottom ranked, prevents cyclic majority vote outcomes.

**Toward Black's condition**

Unfortunately, the Figure 6.1a characterization is limited to decision problems where the individual rankings are described in terms of a distance. This restriction eliminates even simple examples such as the choice of a common beverage for a party, the location of a family picnic, or the election of officers for an organization. Fortunately, however, this "distance" limitation can be removed while preserving essential geometric properties.

Toward this end, plot the Figure 6.1a preferences in graph form as displayed in Figure 6.1b. This figure purposely reflects our "more is better" prejudice where "larger" numbers represent better situations. For instance, we know what a graph of the stock market on the evening news means when it has an upward sloping line. To create a similar "higher is better" representation, instead of plotting the distances from each voter's ideal point to the different alternatives, *subtract* this distance from an idealized starting value. Treat, if you wish, the starting value as an ultimate level of happiness which can be attained only should your ideal point be selected. Subtracting the distance, then, reflects the wear and tear you suffer when a proposal fails to meet your high expectations. The actual starting value does not matter; it is an artificial device introduced to ensure that the higher the position of a point, the more preferred the alternative.

To illustrate this construction, consider voter three's preferences as given by the Figure 6.1b graph labelled with a "3" in the top-right corner. The height of the graph over $B$ is the largest. It should be because, according to Figure 6.1a, $B$ and voter three's ideal choice are very close. So, the height of this point on the graph is determined by subtracting the small distance from a specified starting value. Similarly, the value for $C$ on this graph is somewhat lower to reflect $C$'s greater distance from voter three's ideal choice. In the same manner, the graphs for all four voters are determined.

We still need to divorce "distances" from the discussion. The approach to do so is to identify a feature which reflects the notion that these graphs represent a highly homogeneous society. The characteristic noted by Black is that each curve has a single peak. The graph for voter 2, for instance, has its peak over alternative $C$, while the monotone graphs for the remaining three voters have their peaks at one end or the other.

This "single-peaked" geometric trait allows us to dispense with the notion of "distances." Instead of needing to compute and subtract distances, treat each point as capturing a voter's "utility level" or "happiness level" for an alternative. Namely, the height of a point on a graph measures the person's "utility," or "level of delight," which is associated with the alternative where "more is better."

This interpretation makes Figure 6.1b more general than Figure 6.1a because, by relying on utility functions from an unspecified source rather than measured distances on a line, the graph captures a wider variety of ways to characterize preferences. The measure of "homogeneity" remains;

each graph must have a single peak.

### Black's Condition

This "single peaked" characterization of voters' preferences is widely used with voting and decision procedures. Its strength comes, in part, from a sense of freedom; it does not matter whether the graph is defined by distances between ideal points and alternatives, by utility considerations, or whatever. The following gives a precise definition.

**Definition 11** *Preferences over a finite set of alternatives satisfy Black's single-peaked condition if the alternatives can be ordered on a line in a fashion so that a utility function representing each voter's preference ranking has a single peak.*

A four-alternative illustration of this definition is demonstrated with the preferences in Figure 6.2a. Ed's graph, for instance, displays his low opinion of alternative $C$, his slightly better view of $A$, his high regard for $D$, and his slightly lower ranking of $B$ leading to his $D\,B\,A\,C$ preference. Similarly, Fred and George have the respective rankings of $A\,C\,D\,B$ and $C\,A\,D\,B$

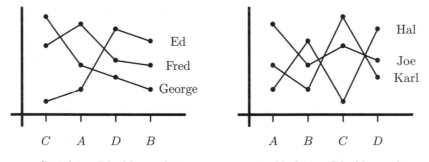

**a.** Satisfying Black's condition          **b.** Violating Black's condtion

**Figure 6.2.** Black's single peaked condition

The important point about the Figure 6.2a graphs is that all of them have a single peak; those for Ed and Fred have their single peak in the interior; the graph for George has its peak at the left most point over alternative $C$. Thus, these preferences satisfy Black's geometric condition.

For comparison, each graph in Figure 6.2b has two peaks, not one. For instance, Hal's graph has peaks over the second and fourth listed alternatives creating a gully between them. If just one graph has a gully, here Hal's gullies causes difficulties, then Black's condition is not satisfied.

**Advantages of Black's condition**

An advantage offered by Black's condition is that the pairwise vote no longer allows irrational societal outcomes.

**Theorem 9** *(Black) For any finite number of alternatives, if the admitted preferences satisfy Black's single-peaked condition, then the pairwise outcomes cannot be cyclic.*

Black's condition prevents cycles only because his condition imposes strong constraints on the voters' wishes. To explain, binary independence requires the computations for the $\{A, B\}$ societal outcome to have nothing to do with the $\{B, C\}$ determination; how society ranks Allison and Barbi has nothing to do with how it ranks Barbi and Connie. It is this severing of connections which causes Arrow's troubling conclusion. The power of Black's condition is that it *does* impose connections among the various societal rankings; what society thinks of Allison and Barbi can determine their Barbi and Connie ranking. Whenever such societal links and connections exist, we must anticipate some kind of positive conclusion.

The idea behind Black's condition is as simple as asserting that

> if most people are standing to the left of John, and if John is standing to the left of Jake, then most people are standing to the left of Jake.

To see how this statement captures the essence of the proof, in Figure 6.3 the "first" and "second" division points designate the midpoints, respectively, between $A$ and $B$ and between $B$ and $C$. Call these points, respectively, "John" and "Jake."

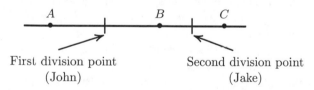

First division point          Second division point
      (John)                          (Jake)

**Figure 6.3.** Analyzing Black's condition

Suppose, for instance, that the voters' preferences allow $A$ to beat $B$ in a majority vote. The only way $A$'s victory can occur is if most voters' ideal points are to the left of "John," the first division point. But, if most points are "standing" to the left of John, then they also are to the left of Jake, the second division point. Namely, the $A\,B$ outcome also requires $A$ to beat $C$ and $B$ to beat $C$ leading to the societal $A\,B\,C$ ranking.

Similarly, if $C$ beats $B$, then most of the voters' ideal points are to the right of Jake, the second division point; this ensures that the societal ranking is the transitive $C\,B\,A$. The remaining case is where most of the voters' ideal points are caught between the two dividing points. The argument is equally as simple; $B$ in the middle beats both $A$ and $C$ leading to a societal $B \succ [A, C]$ outcome. Just as with the "Erik the partial dictator" scenario, whatever ranking the bracketed $\{A, C\}$ assumes keeps the societal ranking transitive.

**Weaknesses of Black's condition**

To have a transitive societal outcome, the societal pairwise rankings must satisfy a particular sequencing condition. But binary independence, by stripping the profile of the needed sequencing information, prevents a procedure from lining up these rankings in a correct manner. Consequently, this orderly structure can only be inherited from the data by imposing a tight restriction on the voters' preferences. This description captures the spirit of the above where if $A$ beats $B$, then both $A$ and $B$ must beat $C$.

Even though Black's restriction avoids cyclic outcomes, it spawns a new breed of problems. As a way to explain, it is clear that a child still years away from understanding numbers cannot be expected to pick up number blocks in a methodical "1" first, "2" second, "3" third. On the other hand, it is possible to entertain tolerant neighbors with this feat by lining the blocks in the correct fashion along the child's crawling path. But the orderly outcome reflects the systematic positioning of the blocks, not the child's reasoning. The same story explains the success of Black's condition. As long as a procedure, such as the pairwise vote, satisfies binary independence, an orderly outcome is *not* a consequence of the procedure processing information about the rationality of each voter's preferences. As with the child's blocks lined up in a row, the success of Black's condition reflects the strongly restricted orderliness of the preferences.

To find the difficulties which can accompany Black's condition, search, as always, for informational differences. For instance, since Black provides a transitive ordering of pairwise outcomes from the restricted nature of the profile, rather than the rationality of the voters, conflict should arise with procedures which *do* use the rationality information. This prediction just uses the obvious notion that if procedures use different information, then they can have different conclusions.

To demonstrate, with examples developed in my work with the French economist Fabrice Valognes, suppose

- 9 voters prefer apple pie $\succ$ cherry pie $\succ$ blueberry pie,

- 4 voters prefer cherry pie $\succ$ blueberry pie $\succ$ apple pie, and

- 8 voters prefer blueberry pie $\succ$ cherry pie $\succ$ apple pie.

As no voter has cherry pie bottom ranked, these preferences satisfy Black's condition. Indeed, as ensured by Black's Theorem, the pairwise rankings form the transitive societal ranking of

$$\text{cherry} \succ \text{blueberry} \succ \text{apple.}$$

While Black's structure imposes order on the pairwise vote, these outcomes can conflict with procedures which do incorporate the rationality information. In particular:

- The *plurality ranking* of apple $\succ$ blueberry $\succ$ cherry has apple pie, the pairwise vote's bottom choice, as the winner.

- Compounding the electoral confusion, blueberry pie is the top choice when ballots are tallied by assigning 7, 2, 0 points, respectively, to each voter's top, second, and bottom ranked alternative.

- Cherry pie wins when voters vote for two alternatives.

Confusion continues even after imposing Black's constraints.

As an aside which addresses concerns from the introductory chapter, it is worth worrying why different voting methods deliver conflicting outcomes. The explanation, which is essentially the same as for Arrow's and Sen's results, involves another misuse of information. To illustrate, the plurality vote dismisses all information about a voter's second and third ranked alternative. As such, we should expect the above plurality result because information concerning the favored status of cherry pie is ignored. Similarly, voting for two candidates only identifies which pie we dislike; the procedure dismisses information about our top ranking. Finding the "correct" level of information needed for a reasonable outcome is a delicate problem that only recently has been resolved; surprisingly, the answer is the Borda Count.

**Verifying Black's condition**

Even in the world of pairwise voting, another weakness of Black's condition comes from the requirement that the preferences are single-peaked *with an appropriate permutation of the alternatives.* What is an *"appropriate permutation of the alternatives?"* How does one find it?

To illustrate, Figure 6.4 depicts a situation which is so bad that *each* of three graphs fails Black's single peaked geometry. But, rather than implying that these preferences fail Black's condition, these gullies just mean that this particular $A - B - C - D$ ordering of alternatives does not work.

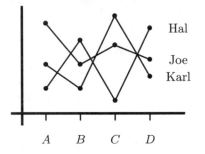

**Figure 6.4.** Violating Black's condition?

The complexity is captured by the fact that each example demonstrating a negative conclusion means essentially nothing; it just means that this particular choice is not successful. Black's condition requires examining the geometry of *all possible* graphs for all other orderings.

The task again resembles the search for that proverbial needle in a haystack; each failure where a straw is grasped does not mean the needle is not there, it just means more work is required. Similarly, with Figure 6.4, our negative conclusion just means that we need to check the graphs with the ordering $A - B - D - C$, or $A - D - B - C$, or .... As there are 24 different sets of graphs that can be constructed, the failure of any ordering (because at least one graph has gullies) only means that more work, maybe much more, is needed. To illustrate, let me invite the reader to determine whether the Figure 6.4 preferences satisfy Black's condition.

Actually, finding the appropriate permutation of the alternatives to satisfy Black's condition is easier, and faster, than one might expect. But the approach is technical so it is relegated to elsewhere. By the way, the answer for my challenge is that the Figure 6.4 preferences do satisfy Black's condition. Figure 6.4 is just Figure 6.2a where Ed = Hal, Fred = Joe, and

George = Karl, and the ordering of the alternatives is scrambled.

**Higher dimensions**

While a useful theoretical aide, Black's approach, which models an overly idealistic, homogeneous society, is of dubious practical value. With the community park example, for instance, individual decisions are clouded by side issues involving, say, how the outcome will affect the funding available for the improvement of roads, the local school, and so forth. Other examples involve, say, the choice of the chair for a social group or department. Here a candidate's administrative effectiveness competes with personal concerns about how the choice will affect us. In other words, it is difficult to imagine settings with alternatives so clearly and cleanly defined that they can be reduced to a single issue. Realistic circumstances are more appropriately modeled with multiple issues. But multiple issues unleash the curse of dimensionality to cause cycles.

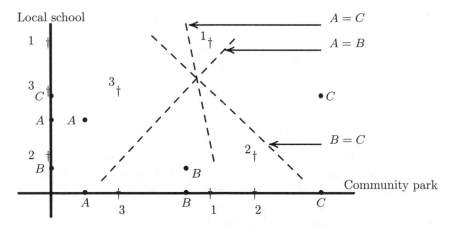

**Figure 6.5.** Alternatives with connecting issues

Represent a second accompanying issue, say, support for the local school, by values along the vertical axis. To illustrate, point $B$ in Figure 6.5 indicates a proposal supporting a moderate level of development for the community park accompanied by low support for school improvement. Again, each voter's preferences reflect the distance to the various proposals.

To assist these comparisons, the dashed lines in Figure 6.5 define points of equal distance from two proposals. If a voter's ideal point, denoted by a †, is on such a line, then the voter is indifferent between them. But when the first three points from Figure 6.1a, which allowed a rational outcome, are plotted to reflect accompanying joint concerns, the resulting profile defines a Condorcet profile. (Voter 3, for instance, prefers $A \succ B \succ C$ while voter 2 prefers $B \succ C \succ A$.) Viewed separately, the preferences over each issue become points on a line, so they satisfy Black's condition. But by combining the two concerns to reflect trade-offs in how the money should be spent, we return to a setting with a pairwise cycle rather than a transitive conclusion.

I leave it to the reader to modify Figure 6.5 to discover another "parts which disagree with the whole" conflict. It is possible, for instance, to select ideal points to create a conflict between how these voters would rank any one issue and the combined package of issues.

## 6.4    Good news

Maybe the failure of finding appropriate and reasonable profile restrictions is a "burning bush" signal that considering the wrong kind of restrictions. Maybe "success" requires selecting restrictions which more accurately reflect the technical reasons for Arrow's assertion.

Not only is this the case, but clues about how to carry out this program come from the source of Arrow's and Sen's problems. Namely, parts of the profile are confused with the wishes of an irrational society. So, by prohibiting these profile portions, positive assertions should follow.

### 6.4.1    Trouble causing profiles

We know the trouble-making profile combinations; they are the Condorcet $n$-tuples and portions of them. As continually demonstrated, paradoxes and troubling outcomes persistently arise with these profile portions. Problems result from the inability of the pairwise vote to distinguish this profile from imaginary ones which involve irrational voters with cyclic preferences.

Surprisingly, the Condorcet profile completely characterizes this heterogeneity *for binary independence.* So, by forbidding a profile from having any part of a Condorcet $n$-tuple, we should obtain resolutions for Arrow's puzzle; by removing this Condorcet portion of the profile, we must expect success.

**Theorem 10** *(Saari) For a decision problem with $n$ voters (or $n$ criteria), suppose all parts of the profile with any portion of a Condorcet component have been removed. With the remaining profile, there are many non-dictatorial methods which satisfy all of Arrow's other properties. In par-*

*ticular, this restriction allows the pairwise vote, the Borda Count, agendas, etc. to satisfy both binary independence and the Pareto condition. Moreover, all of these procedures elect the same candidate; all of those which provide rankings offer the same societal ranking.*

*Of particular importance, the BC ranking with the original profile always agrees with the BC ranking coming from the profile with the removed Condorcet part.*

Contrary to Black's condition, this profile restrictions avoids Arrow's difficulty in a manner which allows all admissible methods to agree; they all yield the exact same outcome. Rather than the earlier worries where the outcome can depend on which procedure we happen to inherit, this theorem states that by eliminating the Condorcet portions of a profile, the remaining information always provides the same outcome for a large class of procedures. Not all procedures, but a large and useful class of them.

## 6.4.2   New problems?

While providing comfort, this theorem raises questions.

1. What information is lost by excluding the Condorcet portions from a profile? Arrow's problem arises by dismissing, in a subtle manner, information about the voters. Similarly, by throwing out data about the voters, are we tossing the baby out with the bath water?

2. What does it mean to exclude "all parts ... with Condorcet components?" Is this highly technical? Even worse; this sounds like the crafty machinations of a cigar chumping political boss. Are we sabotaging democratic principles by "tossing out ballots?"

3. It can be difficult to check whether Black's condition is satisfied; does the same problem arise here? After all, even an appealing approach can be dismissed if it is difficult to implement. Are there reasonable ways to find this common ranking?

### Lost information?

Addressing these concerns in the order posed, the answer for first item uses the ranking disk construction of Condorcet $n$-tuples. This disk ensures that each candidate is treated in an identical manner; each is in first, second, ..., last position precisely once. In fact, the symmetry of treatment of the alternatives is so complete that it is difficult to identify any societal ranking, other than a complete tie, that should be associated with this profile.

So, by excluding the Condorcet terms, no ranking information is lost; the Condorcet terms should indicate a tie. The real danger is to allow this information to be used by procedures incapable of recognizing the subtleties of rational preferences. By doing so, we risk contaminating the societal outcomes by falsely interpreting the Condorcet portion as representing the cyclic preferences of irrational voters. There should be no debate; the real cost comes from using, rather than dropping, these Condorcet portions.

**Trouble in removing troubles**

The answer for the second part of item 2 is easy. No ballots are actually lost or ignored. Instead, treat the "dropping" of these terms as a convenient counting scheme. First, gather all ballots that do not favor any candidate, such as the Condorcet collection. Then, break the tie by counting the remaining ballots. This is similar to counting ballots in a two candidate race between Margaret and Zelda. First, match up pairs of ballots where one vote is for Margaret and one vote is for Zelda. This gathering of all such pairs defines a tie; this tie is broken and the winning candidate is determined by the ballots remaining after the cancellation.[3]

The answer for the first part of item 2, where the concern is to remove all troubling traces of Condorcet tuples, is subtle. In fact, removing all parts of a Condorcet tuple usually results in a profile with "fractional" number of voters for different preferences.

To explain with an analogy, suppose an unidentified plane is traveling 600 MPH in a north-east direction. If this plane crosses the national boundary of *Serendipity*, the Serendipean air force will scramble to investigate. As the proud country of Serendipity lies directly east of the current location of the potential intruder, rather than the plane's speed, our radar attendant must determine how fast the plane is moving to the east. He needs to know the eastern component of the velocity to determine when to push the alert button. Thanks to his high school trigonometry course, he computes this value as $600/\sqrt{2}$ MPH — an "irrational" number.

The point is, even though the plane's velocity has an integer representation, *a particular component* might be a fraction, or even an irrational value. Similarly with voting, by extracting those components of a profile that are

---

[3]When my results describing the source of voting paradoxes were described in a February 2000 *Economist* article, some readers in an internet exchange incorrectly argued that this cancellation approach is subversive. Oh, my.

free from the Condorcet taint, the answer can involve fractional terms. This is no difficulty; as with the radar attendant trying to protect *Serendipity*, the fractional values are artifacts of the computations needed to achieve a particular purpose.

Instead of trying to eliminate the Condorcet portions, why not impose the restriction that admissible profiles cannot have any Condorcet components. A nice try, but it is not very useful; indeed, even a unanimity profile fails this condition.

Wow! *Even an unanimity profile does not satisfy the non-Condorcet property!* To verify this unexpected assertion, suppose when a voter considers brands of soda, his preferences are $A\,B\,C$. The Borda Count outcome agrees with this voter's preference; it is $A\,B\,C$ as supported by the tally 2:1:0. While the pairwise vote offers the same ranking, the pairwise tallies fail to reflect the $A$'s superiority over the other choices. Yes, $A$ does beat both $B$ and $C$, but the same 1:0 pairwise tally fails to capture the voter's stronger preference of soda $A$ over $C$. Compare this weak conclusion with the Borda Count tally which gives $A$ a stronger 2:0 margin over $C$. The source of this seemingly arcane behavior is that a slight Condorcet component is embedded within the unanimity profile. This component "twists" the societal pairwise tally to weaken $A$'s victory margin over $C$. By removing this distorting term, even the pairwise vote gives $A$ her just top-standing.

**An easy answer**

All this "coordinate component" and "fractional voter" tech talk makes Theorem 10 seem impractical and restricted only to those weird "number-crunchers" whose sense of a "hot Saturday night" is checking new web features while designing a C++ program.

Fortunately, this is not the case. What saves us from this nerdy fate is the assertion that all outcomes (and tally differences) are reflected by the Borda Count tally. Consequently, an efficient and quick way to achieve the goals of the theorem is to *compute the BC outcome for the original profile — no elimination of Condorcet terms is needed!*

Some words are required to suggest why the BC accomplishes this particularly comfortable conclusion without having to worry about the extent of the Condorcet contamination. As each alternative in a Condorcet triplet

$$A\,B\,C,\quad B\,C\,A,\quad C\,A\,B,$$

is listed the same number of times in each position, and as the Borda Count assigns points to alternatives according to how they are ranked, the BC cancels the effects of any Condorcet portion. If, for instance, Heili and Torik are in a Condorcet swirl, the total number of points Heili receives comes from when she was top, and second, and third, and ... ranked. As Torik has the same rankings, he receives the same score.

**Why not the plurality vote?**

This argument showing why the Borda Count is not affected by the Condorcet terms holds equally well for any other method, such as the plurality vote, which assigns points to candidates according to how they are ranked. So, why not use the plurality vote, or the method where voters vote for their top two candidates, or voting by assigning 7 and 3 points, respectively, to a voter's first and second ranked candidate, or ....

Even after the removal of the Condorcet terms, each of these methods still violates Arrow's binary independence property. This observation suggests that these procedures continue to lose information. Recall, binary independence causes problems because it forbids the procedure from distinguishing whether certain preferences come from the actual rational society, or from an irrational society with cyclic preferences.

Somewhat related problems plague these other methods. For example, by considering only who a voter has top-ranked, the plurality vote cannot distinguish between the data from the actual rational voter and an hypothetical, non-existent voter who has partially cyclic preferences. This suggests, as with the Condorcet problem, that we can unwittingly make bad decisions with these procedures.

To illustrate, consider two irrational voters trying to rank school board candidates where one prefers A to all other alternatives while the other prefers D to all other alternatives. As for the other candidates, the first voter has the cyclic ranking

$$B C, \quad C D, \quad D B$$

while our second voter ranks them in the cyclic fashion

$$A B, \quad B C, \quad C A.$$

A reasonable outcome for these two voters is $[A = D] \succ [B = C]$ because only candidates $A$ and $D$ receive any favorable treatment; all others are treated equally. This ranking is their plurality outcome.

For the same election, suppose a husband and wife strongly disagree about the candidates as they have completely opposite views of $A B C D$ and

$D C B A$. While they cannot agree on politics, they do agree that a splendid way to spend the afternoon is to go to the beach rather than voting. After all, why vote when their directly opposing views will only cancel?

This natural cancellation is respected by the Borda Count, but not with the plurality vote or many other voting procedures. In fact, the plurality outcome of $[A = D] \succ [B = C]$ reflects the procedure's inability to distinguish between our loving, but contentious husband and wife, and the two irrational voters; for either group, this voting procedure just registers that one voter likes $A$ while the other likes $D$. By using the earlier argument of computing all profiles that the plurality vote views as being identical, we discover why the plurality vote is such a bad procedure — it, too, loses crucial information about the rationality of the voter's preferences.

Elsewhere, when I technically characterized this "lost information," I showed that the only procedure which does not lose information by confusing actual rational voters with non-existent hypothetical voters is the Borda Count. This research makes it arguable that only the Borda Count offers an accurate accounting of the voters' preferences.

## 6.5 Resolutions through new axioms

If dictatorial conclusions arise because "binary independence" separates information about voter preferences into disjoint parts, then any resolution must reintroduce these connections. Stated in another manner, if binary independence forces us, unintentionally, to attend to the needs of the irrational, then revise the property to force the procedure to recognize and admit only rational voters.

To carry out this program, we first must identify features about binary rankings which distinguish between transitive and cyclic preferences. Whatever is this new property, it must be able to distinguish between the pairwise rankings $A \succ B$, $B \succ C$, $A \succ C$, which define the transitive $A \succ B \succ C$, and the binary $A \succ B$, $B \succ C$, $C \succ A$ cyclic ranking. To add to the challenge, the added information about one pair must not use the rankings of other pairs.

Intuition about how to solve this problem comes from the closely related problem of finding ways to distinguish the Figure 6.6 ordering properties of the points $a$, $b$, $c$ on the line from those on the circle. To be more concrete, pretend that these points describe the seating arrangement for three people; the line has them seated on a bench while the circle has them around a table. To rank the points on the circle, notice that $b > c$ on the line segment means that $c$ is seated to the left of $b$. So, for the circle, say that $b \succ c$ if $c$ is seated on $b$'s left side. This convention defines $a \succ b, b \succ c, c \succ a$ table ordering; a cycle. As with our ranking problem, something in addition to the inequalities $a > b$, $b > c$, $a > c$ is needed to determine whether the points are on a line or the circle.

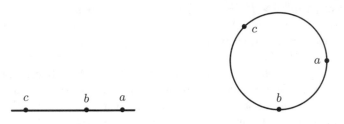

**Figure 6.6.** Points on a line — or on a circle?

This comparison of points with people offers clues for our puzzle. Recall, the points on a circle represent people seated at a round table, and the points on a line correspond to people seated on a bench. There is a distinction; for those on the bench, someone is in the middle. But, for the table, who is in the middle? In other words, points on a line allows us to determine whether others are "between" them; $b$ is sitting between $a$ and $c$ with the Figure 6.6 line segment. But is $b$ between $a$ and $c$ on the circle?

To describe the separation feature for points on a line, start with the inequality defined by the two points. Next, specify the number of other points that lie between them. With the Figure 6.6 line segment, we have

- $(a > b, 0)$, where the zero means that the $a > b$ inequality is "weak" because no point from the set separates the pair,

- $(b > c, 0)$ which, again, is a "weak" ranking because these two points are not separated by another admissible point, and

- $(a > c, 1)$, where the "1" implies that the $a > c$ inequality is stronger (than $a > b$ or $b > c$) in the sense that the points $a$ and $c$ are separated by one of the other admissible points ($b$).

Since the properties of a line are used to define transitivity, it is reasonable to transfer this "betweenness" or "intensity" property to the rankings of alternatives. By directly mimicking the $a > b > c$ ordering of points on the line, the pairwise rankings for the $A \succ B \succ C$ transitive ranking become

- $(A \succ B, 0)$ and $(B \succ C, 0)$ to represent 'weak" preferences in the sense that for each pair, the ranking of this pair is not separated by any of the other alternatives, and

- $(A \succ C, 1)$ to reflect the "stronger" preference — the stronger intensity of this ranking — as manifested by the fact that one of the admissible alternatives is used to create a separation in this ranking.

This leads to the following definition.

**Definition 12** *The intensity of a pairwise ranking, say $A \succ C$, is the number of admissible alternatives used to separate these two alternatives. If the number is $k$, the intensity ranking is denoted as $(A \succ C, k)$.*

To see how this intensity information distinguishes between transitive and cyclic preferences, notice that the $A \succ B \succ C$ transitive ranking has the intensity information

$$(A \succ B, 0), \quad (B \succ C, 0), \quad (A \succ C, 1)$$

where one pair has a "1" intensity level. But if the same rankings come from an irrational voter with no concept of "betweenness" or a transitive ranking, then he fails to comprehend that $B$ is between $A$ and $C$. Thus, his rankings are

$$(A \succ B, 0), \quad (B \succ C, 0), \quad (A \succ C, 0).$$

This same "zero-intensity," weak binary rankings can characterize the cyclic ranking setting — or a seating arrangement around a table — where the information becomes

$$(A \succ B, 0), \quad (B \succ C, 0), \quad (C \succ A, 0).$$

The informational difference separating the two settings is that with a transitive preference, one pair must have a strong intensity level. While this is only a minor difference, it suffices to solve Arrow's mystery. The following definition is used to create a "revised," positive version of Arrow's result.

**Definition 13** *A social welfare function — a decision procedure which ranks the alternatives — satisfies Intensity of binary independence (IBI) if society's relative ranking of any two alternatives is determined only by*

- *each voter's relative ranking of the pair,*

- and the intensity of this ranking.

*That is, for any pair of alternatives* $\{A, B\}$, *if each voter's relative ranking and intensity of this ranking is the same for two profiles* $\mathbf{p}_1$ *and* $\mathbf{p}_2$, *then society's relative ranking of this pair is the same for both profiles.*

## 6.5.1   Intensity of binary independence

As the intensity version of binary independence, IBI, requires a procedure to use only slightly more information about the voters than binary independence, it is a minor extension. All binary independence procedures are IBI procedures; they just ignore the added intensity information.

IBI makes a difference. The Borda Count, for instance, satisfies the intensity property, but it fails Arrow's binary condition. For instance, when I illustrated (page 43) the failure of the BC to satisfy binary independence, I used two profiles where every voter had the same relative ranking of $\{A, B\}$ *but with different intensity levels.* While Arrow's condition ignores this important difference in individual preferences, the new IBI property includes it in the decision process. Stated in another manner, "binary independence" is interested only about who is seated to the left of whom; "Intensity of binary independence" also worries about whether they are seated on a bench or around a table.

As shown next, this minor IBI change finally offers a way to escape the perplexity and worry of Arrow's Theorem.

**Theorem 11** *(Saari)    The Borda Count is a nondictatorial procedure that always has transitive outcomes and that satisfies Unrestricted Domain, IBI, and Pareto.*

Recall, the Borda Count assigns $n-1, n-2, \ldots, 0$ points, respectively, to a voter's first, second, $\ldots$, bottom ranked candidates. So, for four candidates, the assigned points for this reasonable and natural method are 3, 2, 1, 0, while for three candidates they are 2, 1, 0. So, this theorem means that a slight change in binary independence converts Arrow's sense of frustration complete with dictators and paradoxes, into a hopeful setting which admits reasonable procedures to rank the candidates.

To show why the BC works, first, clearly the BC is nondictatorial; it even satisfies anonymity (i.e., the "names" of the voters do not matter). The outcomes are transitive; the BC assigns number scores to each candidate, so its ranking reflects the ordering properties of points on the line.

Clearly there are no restrictions on how the voters rank the candidates *as long as this is done in a transitive manner.* In other words, the BC satisfies "Unrestricted Domain" while monitoring whether the voters are, or are not rational; the pairwise vote cannot do this. To appreciate this monitoring capability, try to use the BC to tally the ballots for a voter with the cyclic ranking $A \succ B, B \succ C, C \succ A$. As with the dice example (page 31), the cyclic effect of this voter's preferences frustrates any attempt to identify the maximal element — it is impossible to determine who should receive two points and who should get one point.

So, the BC excludes irrational voters; it is designed and intended only for rational voters. Compare this comment and the Theorem 11 conclusion with the Chapter 2 claim that *if we want rational outcomes, we need to use procedures which recognize (and demand) the rationality of voters.*

To show that the BC respects Pareto and IBI, start with the simple addition problems

$$14 = \quad 2 + 1 + 6 + 5$$
$$10 = \quad 4 + 2 + 3 + 1. \tag{6.5}$$

A way to find the difference between the two sums, $14 - 10 = 4$ is to add the differences between the terms being added; namely,

$$14 - 10 = (2 - 4) + (1 - 2) + (6 - 3) + (5 - 1). \tag{6.6}$$

This last expression is how the relative BC ranking of two candidates, Lillian and Connie, will be compared. Namely, the difference between their BC tallies is computed by adding the differential of points assigned by each voter to these two candidates.

Suppose there are four voters and seven candidates. Information about the BC scores of candidates Connie and Lillian for the voters is

| Voter | C's Ranking | C's BC pts | L's Ranking | L's BC pts | Ranking |
|-------|-------------|------------|-------------|------------|---------|
| Dana | 3 | $7 - 3 = 4$ | 5 | $7 - 5 = 2$ | $(C \succ L, 1)$ |
| Hal | 5 | $7 - 5 = 2$ | 6 | $7 - 6 = 1$ | $(C \succ L, 0)$ |
| Don | 4 | $7 - 4 = 3$ | 1 | $7 - 1 = 6$ | $(L \succ C, 2)$ |
| Jeff | 6 | $7 - 6 = 1$ | 2 | $7 - 2 = 5$ | $(L \succ C, 3)$ |
| **Total** | | 10 | | 14 | $L \succ C$ |

To compute the $14 - 10 = 4$ difference between Lillian's and Connie's BC scores, first compute the difference between the number of BC points assigned to Lillian and to Connie by each voter. Then, add these differences; this is the Equation 6.6 computation.

Another way to find this same value of 4 is to add unity to each of the intensity points associated with the $L \succ C$ rankings, and compute the sum of $(3 + 1) + (2 + 1) = 7$. Next, do the same with the $C \succ L$ rankings to obtain $(1 + 1) + (0 + 1) = 3$. Finally, subtract Lillian's sum from Connie's to obtain $7 - 3 = 4$.

The equality of these two computations is no accident. This is because the "intensity number" always is one less than the difference between BC scores. In other words, the BC relative ranking of two candidates can be computed just by how each voter ranks this pair and the intensity of this ranking. Consequently, the BC satisfies the IBI conditions.

Pareto follows because this intensity level, and the differential of points, always favors the candidate unanimously preferred. This completes the proof. (Experts will note that the relative ranking of all positional methods — methods which assign points to candidates according to how each voter ranks them — can be expressed as the sum of differentials. Only the BC differential, however, uses the intensity information. Consequently, *the BC is the only positional method to satisfy Theorem 11.*)

## 6.5.2    Other acceptable procedures

By knowing that the BC satisfies this minor modification of Arrow's conditions, it becomes a simple game to design all sorts of other methods. To see how to do this, recall my earlier example (page 42) where I became a de facto dictator by hogging the BC ballots. This example suggests that other procedures acceptable to this theorem include a BC election where some voter has more ballots than other voters, but not enough to be a dictator. This is called a *weighted voting method;* some voters ballots are counted as though they were cast by a specified number of voters rather than one.

Common examples of weighted voting procedures come from law firms or stock meetings where a vote depends upon factors such as ownership shares of a company. Historically, the Catholic Church used weighted voting in electing a pope where the votes of the "holier" Cardinals carried more weight. As long as the voting weight does not make a voter equivalent to a dictator, these weighted BC methods are admitted by the theorem. But, changing this weight defines a continuous scaling of weighted voting which slides into a dictatorship.

To exclude weighted voting, require each voter's vote to have the same impact. A natural way to do this is to require *anonymity*. This means that interchanging the voter's names while keeping the preferences fixed, has no effect on the outcome. While this condition expels weighted methods, it keeps, in addition to the BC, a procedure invented by Duncan Black which is a hybrid of BC and pairwise voting.

In *Black's procedure*, first rank the candidates by pairwise voting. If some candidate wins all pairwise elections (the *Condorcet winner*), then she is selected. If not, then the BC winner is selected. A modified Black's method is where if the pairwise rankings define a transitive ranking, then that ranking is used. If not, then the BC ranking is adopted. To see that the modified Black's method satisfies the theorem, we only need to show that it satisfies IBI. (We already know that both the pairwise vote and BC satisfy all other conditions.) But, the pairwise vote is an binary independence procedure, and, as noted, a binary independence procedure satisfies IBI.

This modified Black method resembles trying to repair the "donkey and cart" transportation system by saying that when things become too bad, call a BC cab. After all, Black's method inherits failings from the pairwise vote. An easy way to exclude Black's method is to prohibit one of its weaknesses; e.g., impose the requirement that if a candidate is winning, then she still wins when more voters supporting her decide to vote.[4]

## 6.6 What next?

After exploring various ways to get around the massive, negative barricade imposed by Arrow's Theorem, we find that a surprisingly simple solution is to amend Arrow's binary independence condition so that it now includes information about the rationality of voters. This intensity of binary information is just one approach; there are others. It is interesting that the various ways to include this rationality information usually identify the Borda Count as a means to side step Arrow's conclusion.

But, what about Sen's puzzle? Clearly, the Borda Count plays no role here. Nevertheless, as described in the next chapter, the answer also uses the intensity information.

---

[4]These conditions come close to creating an axiomatic representation of the Borda Count in terms of Arrow type axioms.

# Chapter 7

# From Sen To Prisoners and Prostitution

The state of Michigan consists of two peninsulas; the much prettier upper one separates Lake Superior from Lake Michigan while the lower one separates Lake Michigan from Lake Huron. The Upper Peninsula, where the residents proudly call themselves "Yuppers," is a remote, heavily forested, beautiful area known for its excellence in fishing and hunting. Manufacturing never made it this far north and the days of active, productive mining are decades past. Today the main industries center around activities such as tourism, logging, and several prisons positioned in the midst of deep woods — locations carefully selected to discourage the "big city guests" from thoughts of prematurely leaving the facilities. The northern most region of this remote north territory is Keweenaw County. It is easy to find this region on a map — the Upper Peninsula resembles a left hand with its thumb jutting into Lake Superior; Keweenaw County is the thumb nail.

During the "Copper Rush" of 1848, an event which never could compete with the glamour of a 1849 rush in California for a different metal, Keweenaw County was an active mining region. Its furthest north city of Copper Harbor even had a fort built to provide protection against the never threatening Indians. With the days of copper mining decades behind us, "exploration" of the area now involves hiking, biking, kayaking, and cross country skiing. Rather than searching for the red metal, the richness resides in the beauty of the county's extensive wilderness and shorelines.

If one wants to experience peace, quiet and solitude, this area, where the population of deer and bear exceeds that of permanent human residents, is the place to go. But, even this calm, scenic area, where one could hike through the forest for days without ever seeing another person, has its Sen-type conflicts. Even in the midst of the wilderness, voters must determine how the county government can best mesh individual and societal rights.

In July 1999, the county proposed an ordinance which reads, in part, "The County of Keweenaw ordains:

> It shall be unlawful for a person to disturb the public peace and quiet by shouting, whistling, (exhibiting) loud boisterous, or vulgar conduct, ... playing ... musical instruments, phonographs, radios, televisions, tape players ... at any time or place so as to unreasonably annoy or disturb the quiet, comfort and repose of persons in the vicinity."[1]

As Keweenaw County Sheriff Ron Lahti explained to a local newspaper, the importance of this statute is "to control people who ... want to be loud or obnoxious. ... By no means are we looking ... to stop people from having parties or going about their daily lives, but we need an ordinance to fix serious problems before they get out of hand."

In this chapter I show how and why Sheriff Lahti's attitude, an attitude which is noteworthy primarily because it took until the end of the millennium before Keweenaw County needed it, captures the spirit of a natural way to resolve Sen's problem. It does more than this; it also indicates what needs to be done to resolve Prisoner Dilemma settings. The sense of the approach is that individual rights are allowed, but only if they do not "unreasonably annoy," disturb, or interfere with the rights of others.

## 7.1   Annoying others

To discuss Sen's behavior, a version of Table 2.5 (page 57) is reproduced.

| Voter | $\{A, B\}$ | $\{B, C\}$ | $\{A, C\}$ | |
|---|---|---|---|---|
| Bob | $A \succ B$ | $B \succ C$ | — | |
| Jim | — | $B \succ C$ | $C \succ A$ | (7.1) |
| Others | — | $B \succ C$ | — | |
| **Outcome** | $A \succ B$ | $B \succ C$ | $C \succ A$ | |

To identify this example with the difficulties of Keweenaw County, suppose

---

[1]This ordinance and the quotes from Sheriff Lahti come from a front page article of 7/24/99 of "The Daily Mining Gazette," Houghton, Michigan. The Sheriff's Finnish surname is pronounced "LAW-ti."

- $A$ is where Bob plays his radio as loudly as he wishes,

- $B$ is where Bob plays his radio at a reasonable volume, and

- $C$ is where Sheriff Lahti sends Bob straight to jail.

Bob's preferences are $A \succ B \succ C$; he wants to play his music and he most surely wants to avoid jail time. The preferences of all other voters, including Jim, are $B \succ C \succ A$; they want to preserve the serenity of Keweenaw County even at the expense of sending Bob to jail. Until arrested, Bob will do what he wants. With his established preferences, expect to hear loud noises masquerading as music.

## 7.1.1 Source of the problem

To provide insight into the source of the Sen dilemma, characterize these preferences with the "intensity of binary ranking" terminology already introduced (page 189). Recall, this definition specifies the number of alternatives which separate two identified alternatives in a ranking.

In our example, Bob's preference over his decisive pair $\{A, B\}$ is the weak $(A \succ B, 0)$ as no alternative separates them. By being decisive over this pair, Bob imposes on society the loud $A \succ B$ outcome. This boisterous behavior offends the "strong" contrary $(B \succ A, 1)$ feelings of all others. Supporting Sheriff Lahti's concern about overly loud, obnoxious people, the other people find that Bob's choice of $A$ strongly annoys and disturbs them. This "strong" feeling is represented by the "1" in their IBI ranking which means that "one" alternative separates these two choices.

On the other hand, Bob finds Jim to be a strong annoyance. After all, if Bob has to spend a night in jail, which he *strongly* opposes with his $(A \succ C, 1)$ belief, it is because Jim calls Sheriff Lahti. Jim's actions reflect his *weak* $(C \succ A, 0)$ preference. While we leave Bob and Jim to their continual Sen conflict, what we should take from their battles is that

> Sen's cycle arises because the societal outcome determined by each decisive agent's *weak* preference creates a strong negative externality; namely, it offends someone's *strong* contrary feelings.

Rather than an anomaly, the Bob and Jim story, a story which captures the role of strong negative externalities, characterizes *all possible examples* illustrating Sen's problem. The universal nature of this explanation follows from the earlier description (page 79) showing how to construct all examples which demonstrate Sen's result.

## 7.1.2   Negative vibes

To review, all Sen type examples can be constructed by starting with an unanimity profile of cyclic rankings. Select these rankings to agree with the intended societal cyclic outcomes. Next, select the pairs assigned to the decisive voters so that each voter's ranking over at least one pair in each cycle is irrelevant for the decision process. By being irrelevant, the information about how a voter ranks this pair is dropped from the information table.

The dropped information creates a sense of ambiguity; it no longer is clear whether a voter's preferences are the original cyclic ones or a transitive choice. Of course, the difference between the two settings is how the missing pair is ranked. In the original setting, the voter's pairwise ranking created a cycle. But, by reversing at least one of these pairwise rankings for each cycle, the cycle is transformed into a transitive ranking.

My "negative externality" argument uses the observation that some of the newly reversed pairwise rankings are "strong;" namely, the new transitive ranking has alternatives separating the pair. To illustrate, start with a three-voter example with societal cycles $A \succ B$, $B \succ C$, $C \succ A$ and $B \succ C$, $C \succ D$, $D \succ B$. The information table for the hypothetical profile of irrational voters where everyone has these cyclic preferences is

| Voter | $\{A,B\}$ | $\{B,C\}$ | $\{A,C\}$ | $\{B,D\}$ | $\{C,D\}$ |
|---|---|---|---|---|---|
| Adrian | $A \succ B$ | $B \succ C$ | $C \succ A$ | $D \succ B$ | $C \succ D$ |
| Bruce | $A \succ B$ | $B \succ C$ | $C \succ A$ | $D \succ B$ | $C \succ D$ |
| Carl | $A \succ B$ | $B \succ C$ | $C \succ A$ | $D \succ B$ | $C \succ D$ |
| **Outcome** | $A \succ B$ | $B \succ C$ | $C \succ A$ | $D \succ B$ | $C \succ D$ |

Next, assign pairs to decisive voters so that, for each voter, one binary ranking from each cycle is irrelevant for the decision. Making Adrian decisive over $\{B,C\}$ dismisses information about that pair (which handles both cycles) for Bruce and Carl. To allow Adrian to have transitive preferences, let Bruce be decisive over $\{A,B\}$ (which handles the first cycle) and Carl be decisive over $\{B,D\}$ (the second cycle). This defines the information table

| Voter | $\{A,B\}$ | $\{B,C\}$ | $\{A,C\}$ | $\{B,D\}$ | $\{C,D\}$ |
|---|---|---|---|---|---|
| Adrian | — | $B \succ C$ | $C \succ A$ | — | $C \succ D$ |
| Bruce | $A \succ B$ | — | $C \succ A$ | — | $C \succ D$ |
| Carl | — | — | $C \succ A$ | $D \succ B$ | $C \succ D$ |
| **Outcome** | $A \succ B$ | $B \succ C$ | $C \succ A$ | $D \succ B$ | $C \succ D$ |

To convert Adrian's original cyclic rankings into a transitive ranking, reverse the pairwise rankings in his two slots. (Keeping the same ranking for either pair keeps a cycle in his preferences.) This means that Adrian's preference ranking MUST be either $B \succ C \succ A \succ D$ or $B \succ C \succ D \succ A$. For either choice, Adrian strongly opposes (his ranking separates the alternatives) the decisions made by Bruce and by Carl.

Adrian's strong negative opinion of Bruce's $A \succ B$ decision occurs because Adrian reversed his original $A \succ B$ ranking to have a transitive $B \succ C \succ A$ preference over this triplet. So, the new pairwise $B \succ A$ ranking is strong; $C$ separates them.

To step away from arguing with a special case, let me use a "purple moon analysis" to show why this always must happen. *If* this reversal allowed Adrian to have the weak $(B \succ A, 0)$ preference, then $A$ and $B$ would be ranked next to each other. By being adjacently ranked, his preference for the triplet is either $[B \succ A] \succ C$ or $C \succ [B \succ A]$. As the bracket involve adjacent alternatives, this ranking can be reversed to the original state without affecting transitivity. This means that Adrian started with transitive preferences; he did not. This false conclusion tells us that the original $(B \succ A, 0)$ assumption is false. The same phenomenon occurs when converting the original cyclic preferences assigned to Bruce and Carl into transitive preferences.

More generally, in this conversion of cycles to transitive preferences, if the ranking always is "weak" with a $(E \succ F, 0)$ representation, then the alternatives must be adjacent to each other in the final transitive ranking. But, as with the "Eric the Dictator" discussion (page 172), when two alternatives are adjacent in a transitive ranking, they can be interchanged without jeopardizing transitivity. This cannot be the case; reversing the ranking of this pair returns us to the original cyclic ranking. Thus, some new pairwise ranking for each voter must be "strong."

## 7.2   Thou shall not annoy others

As shown, when cyclic outcomes occur with Sen's properties, the decisive voter's choice negatively affects some other voter in a strong manner. This "negative externality" not only measures the annoyance effect, but it also captures the sought after indicator of rationality. This is because, if a voter has a "strong" ranking, then by definition the voter cannot have cyclic preferences; his preferences enjoy at least some level of transitivity.

These arguments suggest how to resolve Sen's difficulty. We know we must reintroduce the rationality of the voters into the decision process, and we also know that a Sen problem occurs when the decisive outcome *strongly* annoys (an indicator of some level of rational preferences) someone. Following the lead of Keweenaw County, perhaps an individual's decisive rights should be abridged only when they *strongly* infringe on the rights of others. This suggests replacing Sen's Liberalism with the following.

**Definition 14** *The* Unintrusive Liberalism *condition is where an agent is decisive over an assigned pair of alternatives as long as the agent's choice does not create a strong negative binary ranking for some other agent.*

Back to Bob playing his radio in Keweenaw County of the Upper Peninsula of Michigan. Suppose when Bob decides to play his radio overly loud, he is surrounded by friends who also enjoy jeopardizing their ear drums. By their choice, Bob's actions do not create a strong negative externality, so Sheriff Lahti need not be involved. Let's carry this a step further. Suppose John, who does not particularly like Bob's choice of music, shows up. While John is annoyed by Bob's actions, John is only "minimally annoyed" as his reversed preferences are "weak" — they are not separated by the remaining alternative of calling Sheriff Lahti. Because John has a weak negative ranking, Bob remains free to do as he pleases.

**Theorem 12** *(Brunel and Saari) For three or more alternatives, suppose the decisive pairs of alternatives assigned to different agents have the property that no two pairs have a common alternative. There exist procedures which satisfy the Unintrusive Liberalism and the Pareto condition while always generating transitive societal outcomes.*

Again, an answer for this quarter century problem involves reintroducing the lost, crucial information. In this setting, which is the joint effort with Anne Brunel, an economist at the Université de Caen, the lost information involved the rationality of the voters. It is interesting how the connecting information introduced in this result resembles the familiar "Do unto others . . . " charge. Resolutions for all of these complexities, whether for Arrow's or Sen's problems, must follow a similar pattern.

## 7.3   Return to the Prisoner's Dilemma

At the end of the second chapter (starting on page 63), the difficulty of the Prisoner's Dilemma was introduced and then connected to Sen's result. But now that we have a positive resolution for Sen's Theorem, we must whether it is possible to do something similar for the Prisoner's Dilemma.

The answer is yes. Because the Prisoner's Dilemma reflects its disconnected parts, resolutions *must*, in some manner, create connections between the players. To show that this is the case, I describe two different approaches.

## 7.3.1 Again and again and ...

The incentives of the Prisoner's Dilemma game encourage the strategy of "screw thy neighbor;" it is to defect rather than cooperate. But if both players try to take advantage of their partner, they both suffer.

As the "parts" of this story are the individual strategies, a way to generate connections which encourage cooperation is to play the game again, and again, and .... The goal is to create something similar to what occurs in the gambling example described on page 115. Recall, risk accompanies a bet made with one person; if I bet for the Lakers, or for the Knicks, I could lose. But by merging the two parts, if I can find someone to take my bet on the Lakers and someone else to take my bet on the Knicks, new strategies emerge which eliminate the risk. In gambling, these new risk-free strategies ensure a profit no matter what happens in the game. By repeating the prisoner's dilemma game, new strategies arise which allow cooperation.

To explain these new strategies, recall the advice to "turn the other cheek" if a partner violates his or her trust by defecting. A competing philosophy is the political advice, "Don't get mad; get even." A repeated game provides opportunities to follow the latter advice. More specifically, my partner knows that if he defects on me, the next time we are in the same setting, I will get even; I will defect just to punish him. It is this "get even" version of "Do unto others as they did to you" which creates the connections between the two games and which helps to encourage cooperation.

This "tit-for tat" strategy is so natural that it was quickly discovered. As William Poundstone reports in his expository book describing the Prisoner's Dilemma and its history, in the early years of game theory, the strategists at Rand Corporation repeatedly played the game to discover what people would do in practice. For instance, to obtain a quick, short term profit, one player tried to take advantage of his opponent by defecting. His opponent decided that the best response was to teach him a lesson by playing "tit-for-tat." "You defect on me and I promise to defect on you the next round." Eventually a cooperate-cooperate strategy resulted.

Particular attention and excitement was created in the early 1980s with this "tit-for-tat" strategy when Robert Axelrod, a psychologist from the University of Michigan, challenged the academic community to design a computer program to compete in a repeated Prisoner's Dilemma competition. The winner of this competition was Anatol Rapoport who introduced the simple tit-for-tat strategy. The simplicity of tit-for-tat suggests that when some of the better minds are applied to this challenge, more creative examples can be found. But, no; "tit-for-tat" proved to be the superior approach. Indeed, in 1984 Axelrod wrote a delightful book describing this tit-for-tat effect and how it encourages cooperation.

The importance for us about "tit-for-tat" is that it has a strong "Do unto others" nature. This way of providing connections, then, is similar to our above recipe for avoiding the sour effects of Sen's result.

## 7.3.2   Learning from prostitution and drug sales

Most of us are appalled and confused with news accounts of prostitutes relying on greedy, abusive pimps, or the potential violence associated with the sales of illegal drugs. Why do these disturbing problems occur?

In a new book addressing the sources and potential remedies for crime, Katri Sieberg analyzes these so-called "victimless crimes." As she argues, drug sales are illegal; both the pusher and the buyer are committing a crime. In most parts of the world, prostitution is illegal; both the prostitute and the customer are committing a crime. It is the illegal nature of both partners which almost begs for a Prisoner's Dilemma explanation.

As Sieberg explains, if the prostitute and the customer both "cooperate," the prostitute earns money and the john receives the desired service. But the prostitute could defect without providing any services, or the customer could defect by refusing payment after enjoying the sexual favors. If they both defect, the customer leaves deprived of the desired pleasure and the prostitute is out the desired money. A similar story holds for drug sales.

For comparison sake, consider a legal business encounter involving, say, the sale of computers. A situation similar to the above occurs if a customer takes a new computer but does not pay for it. Or, the business can defect by taking the customer's money but refusing to supply a computer. Neither situation is hypothetical; reports of someone doing one or the other occasionally are reported in the evening news. The important point is that the wronged person can do something about it; he or she could contact the legal authorities for relief.

In the law abiding portion of the world, the Prisoner's Dilemma story has no relevance primarily because of the ability to appeal to legal institutions. But, the prostitute is not going to call the police to complain that a john failed to pay. If only to avoid the damaging publicity, a john probably would refuse to report a "payment without sex" encounter. Likewise, a drug dealer will not inform the local authorities that his client failed to pay; the client should be reluctant to report being cheated out of his drugs.

These are very real concerns faced by the underground economy. The problem, of course, reflects the lack of legal institutions. As Sieberg's argument develops, this hidden business world needs to create surrogate institutions to provide protection; they need some structure which allows an escape from the Prisoner's Dilemma nature of their environment. In these settings, the "tit-for-tat" game theory solutions may assume the "Rat-a-tat-tat" sound of gun fire; a friendly cop at the corner may be replaced with a pimp. While all of this is highly unsavory to most of us, it introduces a necessary layer of surrogate institutions for the illegal economy.

Remember, the Prisoner's Dilemma can be modelled in terms of Sen's result. In the result developed by Brunel and me, connections among the divorced parts were developed by creating a setting which prevents a decisive player making a decision which incurs a strong, negative externality on another player. Similarly, Sieberg's analysis of crime, gang wars, and other underground activity shows how, in a natural but undesired manner, connections are invented to gap the "divorced parts." Again, the resolution involves finding ways to reincorporate information and actions lost by divorcing a whole into separate parts.

## 7.4 Summary

What have we learned? For convenience, to ensure accuracy, to reduce complexity, a standard approach is to decompose a problem into parts. But, this approach imposes an unintended, heavy cost. By emphasizing disjoint parts and ignoring the coordinating information — which, quite frankly, we may not realize is needed — we run the real risk of jeopardizing our initial goals. This approach can introduce an information assassin.

All of the connecting information — the fabric which distinguishes the whole from the parts — must be included. While we explored in the last two chapters how to do this, the challenge continues. Yet, in a surprisingly natural manner, Arrow's, Sen's, and a variety of lesser known difficulties can be resolved. The approach is to modify the way in which binary comparisons are used; the modifications reintroduce the rationality assumption about the voters. For Arrow's result, this leads to the Borda Count; for Sen's it involves avoiding strong negative externalities that decisions can impose on the other agents. Most surely, there are many related assertions that have yet to be discovered.

# Chapter 8

# Glossary, Notes, and Technical Talk

To assist the reader, certain basic terms and results often used in the discussion are catalogued here. This is followed with brief notes and references to help the interested reader to further investigate these topics. Rather than providing a complete listing of relevant references, my intent is to suggest places to start. Finally, comments about axiomatics and a technical, geometric proof of Arrow's Theorem are given. This proof is designed to emphasize how binary independence loses information about voters and allows nonexistent irrational voters to influence the procedure's outcome.

## 8.1 Glossary

**Anscombe Paradox.** (Page 123.) A profile example showing that, by pairwise voting, a majority of the voters can be on the losing side on a majority of the issues.

**Arrow's Theorem.** (Page 43.) This assertion is responsible for inspiring much of the research activity about voting and decision processes over the last half century. It requires the voters to have strict (i.e., no indifference) transitive preferences; there are no restrictions on how each voter ranks the alternatives. The societal outcomes are to be transitive. The only restrictions imposed on the decision procedure is that it satisfies the Pareto and the Binary Independence Conditions. The conclusion is that with three or more alternatives, the only possible procedure is a dictatorship.

**Binary independence.** (Page 39.) Procedures satisfy this condition if the societal rankings they produce for each pair depends strictly on each voter's relative ranking of the pair; the procedure does not use any information about the other alternatives.

**Borda Count (BC).** (Page 43.) This is the positional voting procedure which assigns points to candidates in a manner resembling the "Four-point" grading system often used to rank students according to their grades. In voting, with three alternatives, two, one, and zero points are assigned, respectively, to a voter's top, second, and bottom ranked candidate. For ten candidates, the number assignment is $9, 8, \ldots, 1, 0$.

**Black's single peaked condition.** (Page 176.) The alternatives are placed along a line. Above each alternative, a dot is placed indicating the relative approval the voter has for this alternative where "higher is better." Next, connect the dots with straight line segments. Black's condition requires the graphs for all voters to have a single peak.

**Condorcet Triplet.** (Page 85.) The Condorcet triplet is illustrated with the special listing of the three rankings $A \succ B \succ C$, $B \succ C \succ A$, $C \succ A \succ B$. An alternative description is that it is a list of three transitive rankings where each candidate is listed in first, second, and third place once. The *Condorcet n-tuple* is defined similarly; it is a listing of $n$ transitive rankings for $n$ candidates where each alternative is in first, second, $\ldots$, last place precisely once.

**Compatibility Theorem.** (Page 52.) A consequence of Arrow's Theorem, this result essentially asserts that whenever any set of alternatives is analyzed via pairwise comparisons, the outcome can differ from ways in which the alternatives are analyzed as a full group.

**Gibbard-Satterthwaite Theorem.** (Page 136.) Should there be three or more candidates, then, all "reasonable" procedures (i.e., ignore dictatorships) admit settings where it is in the best interest of some voter to vote strategically.

**Intensity of Binary Independence (IBI).** (Page 189.) When determining the relative societal ranking of a pair of candidates, in addition to using each voter's relative ranking of the pair, the procedure also can use the information about the number of other candidates which separate the specified two in a voter's ranking.

**Minimal Liberalism (ML).** (Page 56.) In this condition, which is central to Sen's Theorem, at least two voters are permitted to make binding societal decisions about the ranking of their assigned pair of alternatives; each of these *decisive voters* is assigned at least one pair. In a real sense, these decisive voters are dictators over their assigned pairs of alternatives.

**Oligarchy.** (Page 162.) A select group of voters with near dictatorial powers. When all members in this group have an identical ranking of a pair, this common ranking is the societal ranking. However, should even one of the oligarchy members have a ranking different from others, then the societal ranking is a tie.

**Ostrogorski Paradox.** (Page 127.) This is an example where one party enjoys support because a majority of the voters prefers a majority of the party's stands, but a different party wins a majority of the majority votes over these issues. While closely related to the Anscombe Paradox, the difference is that the Ostrogorski Paradox emphasizes particular parties.

**Pareto.** (Page 38.) The Pareto condition, as used here, is an unanimity vote over a pair. Namely, if all voters have the same ranking of a particular pair of alternatives, then that common ranking is the pair's societal ranking.

**Positional voting method.** (Page 74.) This is a voting method where specified points are assigned to candidates in the manner they are *positioned* on a voter's ballot. The usual *plurality* vote is the positional method where one point is assigned to a voter's top candidate and zero points to all others. Another method is to vote for all but one candidate; here, one point is assigned to all candidates except a voter's bottom ranked candidate. As this method is the same as voting *against* the bottom ranked candidate, this "anti" voting procedure is called the *antiplurality* method. The Borda Count is another method.

**Prisoner's Dilemma.** (Page 63.) In this game, each player has incentives to refuse to cooperate with the other player. However, if both players fail to cooperate with the other, then what each receives is less than what they would have earned through cooperation.

**Profile.** (Page 36.) A listing of each voter's preference ranking of the candidates.

**Sen's Theorem.** (Page 56.) Sen's Theorem questions whether it is possible for individuals to have the right to decide what should happen with particularly assigned pairs of alternatives (minimal liberalism). In addition to requiring the voters to have unrestricted transitive preferences, it requires the Pareto condition. It states that if two or more individuals have the right to make decisions over pairs, then no procedure can prevent societal outcomes which include cycles.

**Transitive rankings.** (Page 35.) This is a condition imposed on rankings of alternatives which mimics how points on a line are ordered. Namely, if $A \succ B$ and $B \succ C$, then it must be that $A \succ C$.

**Unintrustive Liberalism.** (Page 200.) This condition modifies minimal liberalism by asserting that a voter can be decisive as long as his or her decision does not *strongly* annoy another voter.

**Unrestricted Domain.** (Page 36.) Each voter can have any (strict transitive) ranking of the alternatives as a personal preference.

**Weighted voting.** (Page 192.) Weights are assigned to voters; each voter's ballot is counted as though it were cast by the number of voters in the assigned weight.

## 8.2   Notes

Rather than providing complete notes and references, I offer starting conditions for the interested reader. Where a person responsible for a particular development is specified in the text, appropriate references can be found in the Bibliography. For instance, I like Allan Gibbard's description about conflict caused by the tee shirts worn by the anticonformist and conformist, so I refer to his result several times. The reference to this work is easily found under Gibbard.

### Preface.

The important works of Borda [11] and Condorcet [20] have been translated and reprinted in books authored by Ian McLean and his coauthors F. Hewitt and Arnold Urkin [40, 41]. An abbreviated history of Borda is in the introductory chapter of my book [57] *Basic Geometry of Voting*.

### Chapter 1.

The marching band analysis (page 3) was developed for my web page right after the Ventura election. It quickly was discovered by supporters of the Reform Party leading to several "interesting" email messages. The voting example on page 12 was developed and first used in an invited paper [64] for the *Proceedings of the National Academy of Sciences*.

George Hazelrigg's example [28], labeled "Voodoo Mathematics," appeared in the journal *Prism*.

My description about the opinion polls concerning the different options during the impeachment period for President Clinton emphasizes ABC News only because I watched that network that evening. All other networks reported the same polling behavior.

## Chapter 2.

Kenneth Arrow's seminal result is in his book *Social choice and Individual Values.*[2]. While it is impossible to do justice to the many different books and papers generated by Arrow's result, I suggest browsing through Jerry Kelly's web page

"www.maxwell.syr.edu/maxpages/faculty/jskelly/biblioho.htm."

Another starting place might be the work of John Weymark [25, 7] and his colleagues, and Jerry Kelly's book [33].

To find more about Sen's striking result, I suggest starting with his book *Collective Choice and Social Welfare* [78] or his paper [79] describing the impossibility of a paretian liberal. A place to start on Allan Gibbard's nice work is his paper [24].

Dana Mackenzie, a reporter who obtained an early draft of this book, was sufficiently intrigued by the Bobek-Bonaly-Kwan ice skating example (page 40) to use it in his feature article in the October, 2000, *SIAM News* describing Arrow's Theorem and recent advances in voting theory. The example was then adopted by other reporters in the days right around the 2000 Presidential elections.

The themes for Chapters 2 and 3 were partially explored in my book *Basic Geometry of Voting* [57] and in two papers; one in *Social Choice and Welfare* [62] and the other in *Mathematics Magazine* [61]. On pages 27, 51, comments are made about recent voting results showing how election rankings can vary radically; they were developed in (Saari [66, 67]). For a more complete description, which includes recent research results, let me suggest my book *Chaotic Elections! A Mathematician Looks at Voting* [70]. The comments stating that all non-Borda positional methods can have a ranking precisely the opposite of the pairwise rankings is only the tip of a very big iceberg. The interested reader might check the original reference [50, 53, 63] and the expository (for mathematicians) article [58].

## Chapter 3.

Salles's extension of Sen's censorship example, page 77, is in [75].

A persistent theme of this chapter is to understand why fundamental problems of choice theory are caused by the Condorcet triplet and $n$-tuples. This material — the ranking wheel description and its extensions to agendas (e.g., the material on page 91), tournaments, and so forth — are based on results from my papers [63, 66, 67]. The notion of "phantom irrational voters" was developed in my books [56, 57] and papers such as [61, 62, 63, 66]. For arguments demonstrating stability, a starting place might be papers by Nakamura [42] and by Le Breton and Salles [34]

**Chapter 4.**

Simpson [82] discovered his paradox by examining medical data, but Colin Blyth [10] deserves most of the credit for popularizing, describing, and analyzing this phenomenon. In my paper [49], and then using a different approach involving "chaos" as described in [58], I developed ways to connect Simpson's paradox with voting and other paradoxes from statistics and the social sciences and to extend the results. This issue is pursued in still a different way in a paper with Deanna Haunsperger [27]. This last paper shows how this phenomenon can arise even with Bayesian updating. Be assured, there are many other papers on this topic; e.g., Nurmi [37] explores political science consequences.

A convenient place to learn more about the Anscombe and Ostorgorski paradoxes is with Hannu Nurmi's recent book [37] *Voting Paradoxes and How to Deal with Them*. The explanation of these paradoxes given here comes from joint work with Sieberg [72]. Our interest in this topic was sparked by conjectures Sieberg developed while doing the statistical analysis for the paper [12] by Steven Brams and his colleagues; this paper provides examples of these voting paradoxes.

The fair division problem has a long history, but the reader interested in learning about it might start with the book *The Win-Win Solution* [13] by Steven Brams and Alan Taylor.

The National Academy of Science report mentioned in the section on apportionment problems is reference [9]. In my opinion, some of the best papers analyzing the apportionment problems are those penned by Huntington [29, 30] in the 1920s. Renewed interest in this topic is due to Balinski and Young's widely read paper [5] which was followed by their 1982 book [6] *Fair Representation*. In my books [56, 57], I developed a geometric approach to explain the source of many of these apportionment paradoxes as well as to generate as many examples and paradoxes as desired. In this book, for instance, I prove that many of the problems arise because the apportionment problem is closely connected with mathematical chaos.

The Gibbard [23] - Satterthwaite [76] Theorem has had a significant impact on economics and voting theory with a literature that continues to grow and grow. Rather than trying to describe it, check Kelly's's webpage. The geometric "directional" explanation used for this theorem appears in a more abstract form in [56, 57]; it was applied to characterize all ways to manipulate specified voting procedures in [69] and in papers with Vincent Merlin [38, 73].

Support for my prediction that the genome project will generate an enormous amount of litigation comes from many issues of the journal *Science* describing the conflict which already is emerging. For more information about legal cycles, reasonable places to start are with the references Osborne [45] and Tyree [85].

I recommend the Narens and Luce paper [44] to experts; I suspect their insight will lead to many other conclusions.

**Chapter 5**

Scarf's example [77] probably was the first to raise serious doubts about Adam Smith's story. A significant extension is the Sonnenshein [83, 84] -Mantel [36] -Debreu [22] conclusion.

This striking SMD result has a personal attachment. To explain, after Hugo Sonnenshein described his results [83, 84] to me, I accepted the mathematics as being correct, but found his assertion hard to accept. The mystery proved to be a powerful magnet which kept attracting me to this topic until I finally understood his conclusion as measured by conjecturing and proving the results [55, 59] about how dropping commodities allows anything to happen. The observation that SMD allows any form of chaotic dynamics appears to be first observed in [59]. My results describing how to avoid some of the sting of SMD and my extension were announced in [65] at a conference analyzing "The Theory of the Market" at the Academy of Sciences in Amsterdam.

Paul Samuelson was among the first to discuss the dangers of a traditional "cost-benefit analysis," and the Chipman and Moore work [17, 18, 19] is among the best descriptions of the difficulties.

The material where binary independence is replaced with a triplet independence (starting on page 150) is from my papers [63, 62, 66, 67]. The comment about statisics refers to Haunsperger's paper [26]. For more information about voting paradoxes, see my book *Chaotic Elections! A Mathematician Looks at Voting* [70].

**Chapter 6**

The pope selection process is described in my books [56, 57] and my paper [60]. I first learned about this election process from Richard Keickhefer, my former colleague at Northwestern University and the chair of its Department of the History of Religions. Also at Northwestern, Ehud Kalai sparked my interest in finding weak conditions to avoid Arrow's conclusions. Kalai was the principal author on a couple of nice papers [31, 32] advancing this topic. The sharpest result (to the best of my knowledge) is the "Erik the Dictator" procedure which is described less dramatically in [56, 57]. For other work, I recommend that of Weymark and his coauthors [25, 7].

R. Wilson [86] found the first "negative dictator" results — this is where the outcome always reverses an identified voter's preferences. The other described extensions of Arrow's theorem come from my article [51].

Sen [80] probably is among the first to appreciate that Condorcet's triplet causes some of the three alternative, pairwise voting difficulties. To the best of my knowledge, the understanding that only the Condorcet terms cause these problems for any number of alternatives is first described in [56, 57, 63, 66].

Duncan Black's observations and results are in his seminal book *The Theory of Committees and Elections* [8]. C. H. Coombs investigated some of these ideas around the same time. The discussion about how Black's conditions allow different election outcomes comes from papers with F. Valognes where the more relevant one is [71]. The comments about "recently found" and where "I characterize the lost information" refer to my papers [66, 67]. The results concerning ways to resolve Arrow's result through the use of IBI are first reported in my paper [54].

**Chapter 7**

The joint results with Brunel, Theorem 12 on page 200, are in Anne Brunel's Ph.D. thesis [14] from the Université de Caen and further developed in our paper [15]. Her thesis also introduces an inventive way to compare different philosophical descriptions of "individual rights." Sieberg's book [81] analyzes more than prostitution and drug sales to include gangs, prisons, etc., etc. Our conversations clarified how her results are related, at least in sprit, to Brunel's and my approach toward Sen's result.

## 8.3   Axioms

Some readers of an early draft of this book recommended adding a discussion about the unexpected explanation of Arrow's and Sen's classic results given here. To explain, it had been accepted that the building blocs of Arrow's axioms proved that only a dictatorship could be constructed. My explanation, however, emphasizes how some "axioms" negate other "axioms." What persuaded me to address this question was Duncan Luce's observation that comments are needed "since the message some might take away [from my argument] is that axiomatizations can be very dangerous approaches whereas anyone who knows mathematics knows that axiomatizations have historically been very useful."

### 8.3.1   The use and abuse of axioms

In high school geometry we learned how the building blocks of "axioms," such as points and lines, are so basic that they must serve as a starting point. These lessons from early in our education capture the sense of how axioms — statements that need no proof because their truth is self evident — are used.

Axioms are the building blocks, they are the "atoms" of mathematics. Just as atoms are combined to create molecules, and molecules combined to construct more complex structures, axioms are creatively combined to generate complex mathematical structures, which are further combined to create even more complex entities. Luce is correct; axiomatics have added power to mathematics by consolidating seemingly different developments, by raising new issues, problems, and concerns, and by creating new mathematics.

Thanks to axiomatics, mathematics has developed the strength to regularly transcend our personal experience. For instance, none of us — well, at least not me — has experienced a five or six dimensional world. But, even a first year graduate student in mathematics is comfortable dealing with a six, or a seven, or even an infinite dimensional space. Thanks to the axiomatic approach, there is acceptance about the structure of these spaces which, although we cannot experience them, provide powerful tools to explore and understand our real world. As Luce accurately observed, "axiomatizations have historically been very useful."

"Axioms" are intended to be fundamental and independent. If two or three axioms can be combined to form another "axiom," we reject the last one as being an "axiom." Instead, by being a consequence of the more fundamental building blocks, it is treated as a mathematical "molecule." Similarly, a couple of axioms cannot combine to negate or emasculate another. Yet, this negation effect happened in Arrow's Theorem. What went wrong?

One explanation uses my comparison of axioms with "atoms." In an earlier time, atoms were considered to be the fundamental building blocks; but not now. We now know about electrons and neutrons, and we know that even they are not sufficiently basic to always provide a proper starting point. So, when we encounter results such as those given by Arrow and Sen, where some axioms gang up to nullify another one, we should interpret the lack of independence as meaning that we have not started with a sufficiently fundamental set of building blocks — of axioms. As the earlier discussion suggests, for instance, "transitive preferences" is a "molecule;" it does not qualify as an atom leave alone an electron or neutron.

More basic than "transitive preferences" are the binary comparisons of a pair. In this setting, Arrow's result asserts that the sequencing property of combining these more fundamental units in a transitive manner is incompatible with other properties. If the emphasis had been placed on more appropriate units, explanations may have been found decades ago.

## 8.3.2   More fundamental complaints

I have a more fundamental complaint. While examples may exist, I cannot think of a single useful mathematical theory which was created in a vacuum; I cannot think of a theory which started when a mathematician arrived at work thinking "Today I will invent some axioms, put them together, and see what emerges." Mathematicians are far too pragmatic to ever consider doing anything like this. We would dismiss this approach as resembling the story of seating monkeys at typewriters and waiting for them to compose all of Shakespeare's works. It could happen, but it is more realistic to expect junk.

Instead, rather than using axiomatics at the start of a field, mathematicians typically wait until a topic has reached a sufficient level of maturity. Namely, axioms are devised and developed after there is a body of evidence and results, after the usefulness of certain directions have been established and a general direction of development is evident, after there is a need to consolidate conclusions and find more basic explanations. By working with this vision, with this direction, axiomatic development can be exciting!

Now consider the social sciences. For the most part, they are not academically mature disciplines. This is not a put down or criticism; it is an observation. Indeed, the fact that many of these areas are in early stages of development, where they need to explore new directions, to uncover and examine appropriate concepts rather than making technical advances, is precisely what makes them exciting and appealing — at least for me. But, this also means that, for the most part, it is premature to attempt an axiomatic development in the "fundamental building block" sense described above.

There are notable exceptions; two that immediately come to mind are Gerard Debreu's 1959 monograph *Theory of Value* from economics and Duncan Luce's 1959 book *Individual Choice Behavior* for psychology. Both books start with axioms; both books use these axioms in a mathematically correct way as building blocks to develop a surprisingly rich theory which addresses many different issues.

Do they explain everything in their relative disciplines? Of course not; that is impossible. As such, it is not difficult to find economic examples which fail to be subsumed by Debreu's work, and Debreu created an individual decision problem that is not covered by Luce's assumptions. These examples do not negate the works; they only mean that different assumptions, different axioms, are needed to create a more encompassing theory. For instance, maybe Luce's "atoms" need to be replaced with "electrons;" Amos Tversky proposed such an approach.

### Axioms? Or assumptions?

Some of the social sciences, in particular social choice and decision analysis, are almost obsessed with "axioms." However, I know axioms; I have worked with axioms for a long time; for the most part, what they use are not axioms. Proof comes from the goal of several of these scholars; they use their "axioms" to derive "impossibility" results. Just the nature of these conclusions suggests that their "axioms" are not independent.

Nevertheless, this literature can be useful by interpreting what they call "axioms" as "assumptions" or "hypothesis;" these kinds of constructs can be conflicting and contradictory. In this manner, the nomenclature difference becomes immaterial — unless someone really believes that he or she is dealing with "axioms." Let me explain.

A common argument supporting axiomatics is, "I want to know what I am getting." This can be expected from axioms, but only if the "axioms" truly are used as building blocks as in Luce's development. When a consequence from Luce's book is cited, be assured that it is a direct descendant of his "choice axioms." But, a gross and common misuse of "axioms" in the social science literatures are the so-called "axiomatic characterizations" of something. What a serious mistake and misnomer; rather than the implied image that we are dealing with consequences of "building blocks," we are merely dealing with a collection of isolated properties that, perhaps for certain quirky reasons, happened to be satisfied only by the specific object.

To explain with an analogy, suppose the American colleges and universities are to be "characterized" in terms of the IQ scores of its students. It is not unbelievable for the student with the highest IQ to be at an obscure school which gives mediocrity a bad name, call it UXUM (I hope no school has these initials!). This conclusion does not mean much about UXUM; it just means that an isolated trait happened to be satisfied only by UXUM. Indeed, it is entirely possible for UXUM to also have the student with the lowest IQ. Similarly, in several of the so-called "axiomatic characterizations," "axioms" should be replaced with the more accurate "particular properties." In other words, many of these "axiomatic characterizations" characterize nothing; they just identify some quirky consequences.

Indeed, with the traditional, incorrect use of "axioms," again,

> "for a price, give me any decision/election procedure you wish. Tell me whether you want it promoted or attacked. I will design an appropriate 'axiomatic characterization' of the procedure which will do the job."

If this can be done, and trust me, it can, then it is clear that these "characterizations" do not truly describe "what you are getting."

To accomplish this challenge, I just need to find either an isolated "positive" or "negative" property which is satisfied only by the specified procedure. But, before illustrating that this can be done, let me briefly digress by introducing a profile where ten million voters prefer $ABC$ and another ten million prefer $BCA$. It is reasonable to expect the societal ranking for this profile to have $C$ at the bottom; only she is bottom ranked by half and middle ranked by the other half of the voters. Next, compare $A$ and $B$. Each is top ranked by half of the voters. But as $B$ is second ranked by half while $A$ is bottom ranked by half, it is reasonable to expect that the societal ranking has $B$ comfortably ranked above $A$. In fact, it is arguable that the societal ranking $BAC$ should prevail even if a couple thousand more voters preferring $A$ arrived.

Back to "axiomatics." Suppose I am hired by one person to promote the plurality vote, and by another to bash it. No problem. To promote this procedure, I would advance some technical conditions — the purpose of these "axioms" is to narrow our attention to positional methods — and include the positive "axiom" that the procedure *always* elects a candidate who is supported by a majority of the voters. Only the plurality vote satisfies this condition; thus, this determines a "positive axiomatic characterization" of the plurality vote.

To be paid for my bashing job, I would use the same technical conditions and replace the above "positive axiom" with the "negative axiom" that with three candidates, the procedure can have a winner who is bottom-ranked by as close to two-thirds of the voters as desired. Again, only the plurality vote satisfies this "negative axiomatic characterization."

Does either "characterization" tell us what we are getting from this procedure? Of course not; just as with the two UXUM students, they only identify extreme, isolated properties that only this procedure happens to satisfy. The negative characterization emphasizes special types of profiles such as where 34 voters have the ABC ranking, 33 have BCA, and 33 have CBA. While more difficult to prove, the positive assertion must involve examples of the above 20 million-voter type with one more $A$ voter; the conclusion is true, but it now is arguable that the election result is the wrong one. Yes, axiomatics are powerful and useful — but when correctly used.

## 8.4 A proof of Arrow's Theorem

While I believe that a "correct" way to prove Arrow's result is with orbits of symmetry groups, this technical approach is not commonly known in this research area. To sidestep this difficulty, I introduce a less abstract geometric approach to capture the symmetries which cause these and many other social choice issues. This new geometric proof displays how binary independence allows a procedure to confuse the preferences of the actual rational voters with non-existent cyclic preferences.

### 8.4.1 Geometry of rankings

To geometrically represent the three pairwise rankings of $\{A, B, C\}$, start with one pair, say $\{A, B\}$. Represent its strict rankings by the two endpoints of an interval; one endpoint represents $A B$, the other designates $B A$, and the midpoint is the tie $A = B$. The symmetries either keep a specified ranking fixed, or interchange the identity of who is top-ranked. Let $\mathcal{I}$ denote the identity setting which keeps a ranking fixed and $\mathcal{F}$ the operation which flips the ranking. So, $\mathcal{I}(A B) = A B$ while $\mathcal{F}(A B) = B A$. Of course, $\mathcal{F}(A = B) = (B = A)$ imposes no practical difference.

Two pairs require two intervals; the rankings for each pair are represented by their endpoints. To emphasize their independence, position the line segments orthogonally. The four vertices from the resulting square (Figure 8.1a) designate the four possible strict rankings. Figure 8.1a's horizontal and vertical lines capture, respectively, the $\{B, C\}$ and $\{A, B\}$ rankings where the preferred candidate is indicated by the arrows. The labels of the vertices designate the following rankings.

| Vertex | Ranking | Vertex | Ranking |
|--------|---------|--------|---------|
| $I$    | $AB, BC$ | $III$ | $CB, BA$ |
| $II$   | $AB, CB$ | $IV$  | $CB, AB$ |

$(8.1)$

The geometry neatly captures the "flips" to use to convert any vertex into any other. Flips in the horizontal and vertical directions change, respectively, only $\{B, C\}$ and $\{A, B\}$ rankings while keeping the other ranking fixed. To find the flips needed to reach a target vertex, trace the edges from the starting to the ending vertex. For instance, to change vertex $I$, the rankings $\{AB, BC\}$, into $III$, the opposite pair $\{BA, CB\}$, one approach is to go upward from $I$ to $IV$ (moving along the $A$-$B$ edge; i.e., flip the $\{A, B\}$ ranking), and then to $III$ (i.e., flip the $\{B, C\}$ ranking).

$$(\mathcal{F}, \mathcal{I})(AB, BC) = (BA, BC),$$
$$(\mathcal{I}, \mathcal{F})(BA, BC) = (BA, CB).$$

With the allowed flips and identities, it is possible to start at any vertex — any pair of rankings — and reach any other vertex. This collection of possible outcomes is called the *orbit of the group action*.

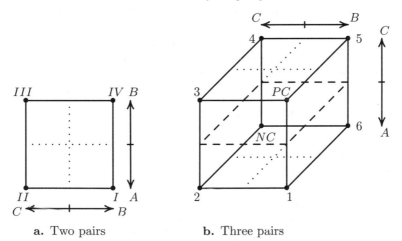

a. Two pairs                    b. Three pairs

**Figure 8.1.** Geometry of rankings

Similarly, to capture the $\{A, B\}$, $\{B, C\}$, $\{C, A\}$ rankings, represent each pair's strict rankings by the endpoints of a designated interval. Position the three intervals in orthogonal directions to define a cube. The Figure 8.1b cube extends the Figure 8.1a square outwards from the page; think of the $\{A, C\}$ interval as coming outwards from each vertex of the square. In Figure 8.1b, think of the square as in the horizontal plane (so the square is rotated backwards along its bottom edge) and then position the new $\{A, C\}$ interval in the vertical position.

This construction divides each Figure 8.1a vertex into two cube vertices in the vertical direction — one new vertex adds the $AC$ ranking to the two vertices from the square, while the other adds $CA$. Vertex $II$ from the square, for instance, generates the cube vertices 2 and 3 representing $(AB, CB, AC)$ and $(AB, CB, CA)$; they define, respectively, the transitive rankings $ACB$ and $CAB$.

While vertices $II$ and $IV$ define cube rankings compatible with transitivity, vertex $I$ creates the cube vertex 1 with the transitive ranking $ABC$ in the $AC$ direction, and what I call (to reflect the "positive" direction in Figure 8.1b) the *positive cycle* (PC) $AB, BC, CA$ in the $CA$ direction. Similarly, the $CA$ choice converts $III$ into the cube vertex 4 with the transitive ranking $CBA$ while $AC$ defines the vertex with a *negative cycle* (NC) $BA, CB, AC$. The eight vertices of the Figure 8.1b cube define following ranking sets. (When the pairwise rankings are transitive, the transitive ranking is used.)

| Number | Ranking | Number | Ranking | |
|:------:|:-------:|:------:|:-------:|---|
| 1 | $ABC$ | 4 | $CBA$ | |
| 2 | $ACB$ | 5 | $BCA$ | (8.2) |
| 3 | $CAB$ | 6 | $BAC$ | |
| $PC$ | $AB, BC, CA$ | $NC$ | $BA, CB, AC$ | |

Using usual coordinates to describe Figure 8.1b, $NC$ is at the origin while the $x$, $y$, $z$ coordinate directions represent, respectively, the $\{A, B\}$, $\{B, C\}$, $\{A, C\}$ pairs. To determine which flips change a specified vertex into another, trace the cube edges from an initial to the ending vertex to find a connecting route. As with the square, all eight sets of rankings can be generated by starting with any specified set and then successively applying appropriate flips — pairwise symmetries.

Each symmetry change is independent of the others (it captures the sense of binary independence), so the natural set of rankings for pairwise behavior are the *eight* triplets. But, two of them are cyclic rankings. Stated in another manner, the assumption about transitive preferences imposes a constraint which conflicts with the natural (binary independence) symmetries of the pairs. A source of social choice problems now can be identified from Figure 8.1b; on each of the six surfaces of the cube, three vertices define transitive rankings but the last is a cyclic ranking.

## 8.4.2   Moving about

I prove the following result which is more general than Arrow's Theorem.

**Theorem 13** *For three alternatives, suppose that all voters have transitive preferences with no restrictions on their strict ranking, that all outcomes are transitive, that the procedure satisfies binary independence and that the procedure has at least two outcomes for each pair of alternatives (namely, for each pair, two profiles can be found which give different rankings of the pair). If a procedure exists which satisfies these conditions, then its outcome always is determined by the preferences of a particular voter.*

To understand why this result is more general than Arrow's, notice that a procedure satisfying Arrow's Pareto condition automatically requires each pair to have at least two outcome; indeed, just select two unanimity profiles with different rankings of the particular pair. However, it is possible to have two outcomes for each pair without satisfying Pareto. For instance, a procedure may always reverse a voter's rankings. Or, consider the procedure with only the two societal outcomes $ABC$ and $CBA$; while this procedure cannot satisfy Pareto (if it did, it also would have, for instance, the societal ranking $BAC$), it does have two different rankings for each pair.

A dictator satisfies the above conditions, so it remains to prove that the only procedures satisfying these assumptions must be based on a single voter's preferences. The first step is to find all voters who can influence the societal ranking of each pair and under what circumstances.

### Who influences the outcome?

A given profile $\mathbf{p}_1$ defines an $\{A, B\}$ ranking. Change each voter's $\{A, B\}$ ranking, one at a time, until the societal ranking changes. Identify the voter causing the change, say Mikko, and remember all other voters' $\{A, B\}$ ranking which allowed Mikko to make an $\{A, B\}$ societal difference.

Do the same for all other starting positions and all possible orders of when a voter changes his ranking. For each approach, identify the voter whose $\{A, B\}$ preference change changed the societal ranking; i.e., identify the voter and label the associated rankings of all other voters in this setting.

For instance, with another way to change voter rankings, Torik's change in $\{A, B\}$ preferences might change the societal $\{A, B\}$ ranking.

Do the same for all three pairs. If the societal rankings change only when a one voter, say Mikko, changes his preferences, we are done as this makes Mikko the dictator. So, assume some procedure does not depend on only one voter's preferences. Namely, for some two pairs (without loss of generality, assume they are $\{A, B\}$ and $\{B, C\}$)

- there is a particular arrangement of voters' $\{A, B\}$ rankings so that the societal rankings changes when Mikko changes his $\{A, B\}$ ranking, and

- there is a particular arrangement of voters' $\{B, C\}$ rankings so that the societal rankings changes when Tyler changes his $\{B, C\}$ ranking.

### Selecting preferences

For each voter other than Mikko and Tyler, the above arrangement specifies his $\{A, B\}$ and $\{B, C\}$ ranking; choose his $\{A, C\}$ ranking to be compatible with transitivity. These preferences will remain fixed throughout the following argument. The rankings for Mikko and Tyler are selected next.

For Tyler to influence the societal $\{B, C\}$ ranking, Mikko might need to have a particular $\{B, C\}$ preference. If so, then select Mikko's preferences to always respect this requirement. So, for the rest of the argument, Mikko's preferences must come from either the $BC$ or the $CB$ face of the Figure 8.1b cube. Whichever face is required, one of the four vertices is a cyclic ranking.

As Mikko must be permitted to change his $\{A, B\}$ ranking, his rankings could come from either of two edges of this face. (This is where the proof distinguishes between rational and irrational voters.) Notice, one edge has Mikko varying his preferences between a transitive and a *cyclic* ranking — this between vertices $PC$ and 5 on the $BC$ face — while the other edge has Mikko's choices varying between transitive rankings — between vertices 1 and 6 on the $BC$ face.

Thanks to binary independence, as far as the procedure is concerned, it does not matter which edge is used. The procedure just registers the changes Mikko makes in his $\{A, B\}$ ranking. In other words, it is irrelevant to the procedure whether Mikko is rational or irrational. This freedom of choice for Mikko mimics the Chapter 3 construction of examples illustrating Sen's result where it does not matter whether the preferences are rational or irrational; the two kinds of preferences are indistinguishable. The only reason to select a choice which is rational is to illustrate that it is possible to have transitive preferences. But the rationality has no effect on the procedure. This "rational" choice is illustrated in Figure 8.2a when Mikko needs an $BC$ ranking for Tyler to influence the $\{B, C\}$ societal outcome; Mikko changes his preferences between types 1 and 6.

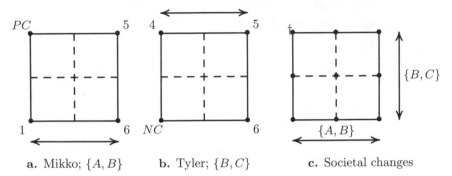

**a.** Mikko; $\{A, B\}$      **b.** Tyler; $\{B, C\}$      **c.** Societal changes

**Figure 8.2.** Proving Arrow's result

Similarly, for Mikko to influence the societal $\{A, B\}$ outcome, Tyler may need to have a specific $\{A, B\}$ preference. This restricts Tyler's preferences to flip between the two vertices on an edge of either the $AB$ or the $BA$ face. Whichever face is appropriate to satisfy Mikko's needs, one of the four vertices represents a cyclic outcome. Again, Tyler has to select one of two edges from this face; varying along one edge would classify him as an irrational voter, varying along the other would classify him as a rational voter. Again, thanks to binary independence, it is immaterial to the procedure which edge Tyler selects. For instance, to satisfy the transitivity condition, select the edge without this forbidden cyclic vertex. In the special case of Figure 8.2b where Tyler needs an $BA$ preference to accommodate Mikko, Tyler's preferences change between types 3 and 4.

As there are two choice of edges for Mikko and for Tyler, there are four possibilities; by satisfying binary independence, the procedure cannot distinguish among them. Three of these possibilities involve an irrational society (where one, or both voters select the irrational edge); only one choice involves the intended rational society. As with the pairwise voting example (e.g., page 86), we must expect the procedure to satisfy the "more likely" irrational society; we must anticipate cyclic outcomes.

### 8.4.3   Societal changes

The choices for changes in Mikko's and Tyler's preferences do the following:

1. Whenever Mikko or Tyler change their preferences, they always keep the same $\{A, C\}$ ranking.

2. Because Mikko keeps the same $\{B, C\}$ ranking, Tyler's changes in $\{B, C\}$ preferences change the societal ranking of this pair.

3. Because Tyler keeps the same $\{A, B\}$ ranking, Mikko's changes in $\{A, B\}$ preferences change the societal ranking of this pair.

Independent of what the other does, when Mikko and Tyler change preferences, so do the societal $\{A, B\}$ and $\{B, C\}$ rankings. Even more, their preferences are designed to ensure that no voter changes $\{A, C\}$ preferences. Consequently, binary independence ensures that the $\{A, C\}$ societal ranking remains fixed no matter what Mikko and Tyler do.

Geometrically, the fixed societal $\{A, C\}$ outcome corresponds to slicing the Figure 8.1b cube at the appropriate $\{A, C\}$ societal ranking. The $A = C$ societal outcome, for instance, slices the cube along the dashed lines in the middle of the cube to define a square. Otherwise, the societal outcomes are given by the rankings on the top face (the $C A$ societal ranking) or bottom face (the $A C$ societal ranking) of the cube.

So, the $\{A, C\}$ societal ranking corresponds to an appropriate square slice of the cube. Since all societal outcomes must remain in this square, the societal changes in the other two pairs caused by Mikko and/or Tyler actions are represented by changing points in the horizontal and vertical directions in the appropriate square as represented by Figure 8.2c. The nine points on the square, represented by the nine dots in a Figure 8.2c square, represent all ranking combinations of the remaining two pairs.

## Picnic spots

To understand the next step, suppose you and I are selecting a picnic spot. You can select any one of two north-south positions; I can select any one of two east-west positions. If our actions are independent of each other, the four possible picnic spots define the four vertices of a rectangle.

This rectangle comment identifies the needed geometry for both Mikko and Tyler to have a say in the societal outcome. If Mikko can determine two $\{A, B\}$ societal outcomes, this defines two points in the horizontal direction of the appropriate version of the Figure 8.2c square. Similarly and *independent* of what Mikko does, Tyler can determine two different $\{B, C\}$ outcomes; they are represented by two points in the horizontal direction of the Figure 8.2c square. As Mikko and Tyler change preferences in the allowed manner, four different societal outcomes can occur. Geometrically, these four points define the vertices of a rectangle. (So, the rectangle is a direct consequences of binary independence.)

To complete the proof, on each of the three squares (determined by the $\{A, C\}$ ranking), identify the non-transitive points. If it is impossible to create a rectangle out of the four remaining points, then it is impossible for both Mikko and Tyler to have an independent say in the rankings. Consequently, the procedure must depend upon the preferences of only one voter — a dictator.

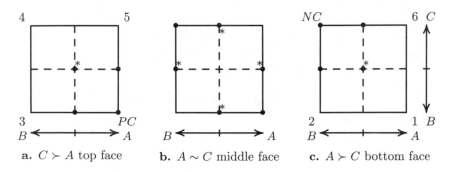

**a.** $C \succ A$ top face          **b.** $A \sim C$ middle face          **c.** $A \succ C$ bottom face

**Figure 8.3.** Societal rankings

Figure 8.3 has all three faces. Of the nine sets of rankings on each face, the ones which do *not* define a transitive ranking are denoted by a heavy dot. To check, recall that there are 13 transitive rankings; six are strict and the last seven involve ties. In Figure 8.3, these transitive rankings are the 13 points not covered by a heavy dot. To illustrate, the dot in the center of Figure 8.3a corresponds to $A = B, B = C$ but, instead of the transitive $A = C$, the third ranking is $C A$. Similarly, the dot on the bottom edge of the second square represents $A = B, A = C$, but, instead of the transitive $B = C$, the last ranking is $B C$. (As the second face is defined by $A = C$, the only transitive rankings are if $B$ is ranked above, with, or below $A = C$; these choices are the three uncovered points.) Finally, the midpoint on the left edge of the third square has $B A, A C$, but, instead of the transitive $B C$, we have $B = C$.

The proof follows because it is impossible to draw a rectangle on any of the three squares without involving a dot. I leave it to the reader to play with these rankings and the geometry of the cube to show that the only procedures are those which, "in some manner" are dictatorships, or reverse dictatorships. The "in some manner" restriction reflects the fact that instead of being a full dictator, the procedure may require the societal outcome to be $A = B$ rather than the dictator's $A B$ ranking. (For hints on how to prove this and other results, such as those below, see Saari [51].)

## Extensions

Nothing in the proof required the societal $\{A, B\}$ outcome to be based on the voters' $\{A, B\}$ preferences. So, imagine that Torik's views of $\{A, B\}$, Heili's views of $\{B, C\}$, and Jason's views of $\{A, C\}$ determine the societal $\{A, B\}$ outcome with a similar mixture of voter preferences applied to the other pairs. Again, with binary independence and the assumption that "there are at least two outcomes for each pair" replacing Pareto, it follows that if a procedure exists, it is based on the views of one, and only one, of the voters. Here, of course, something much different than a dictator arises. For instance, it could be that Heili the dictator's views of $\{B, C\}$ determine the $\{A, B\}$ outcome, her views of $\{C, A\}$ determine the $\{B, C\}$ ranking, and her $\{A, B\}$ preferences determine the $\{C, A\}$ outcome.

This flexibility accurately suggests that these results extend to settings other than those requiring rankings of the type described here. This is illustrated in (Saari [51]) where it is shown how these results extend to settings of probability, game theory, where the rankings of voters are given by "utility functions", and other higher dimensional settings. To extend assertions from three to any number of alternatives, just use a higher dimensional cube. The key fact, which is easy to show, is that the many non-transitive points on each face forbid rectangles to be formed.

## Quasitransitive outcomes

The final step in the above proof reduced to one of those child games where the goal is to try to draw a rectangle with the points allowed in the Figure 8.3 squares. Since this is impossible, change the game to make it possible. Just allow enough more points to be used in each square so that rectangles can be drawn.

For instance, by making the heavy dots accompanied with a star $(*)$ admissible, rectangles and squares can be drawn in each of the three faces. This means that a positive assertion is hidden in this geometry. To extract it, notice that all six points have two pairs ranked as indifferent while the third ranking is strict. As these points are the quasitransitive rankings (page 162), we now can suggest why the theorem which asserts that relaxing the assumption of transitive outcomes changes Arrow's conclusion from a dictatorship to an oligarchy (page 163) is true. Recall (page 162), an oligarchy is where a specified group of voters decide the societal outcomes. If they disagree on a pair, the societal outcome is indifference.

An oligarchy satisfies the conditions because if every oligarchy member agrees on the ranking of each pair, then that ranking is the societal outcome. Now assume there is a disagreement over $\{A, C\}$. As the rules of disagreement force a $A = C$ societal ranking, the societal outcomes involve seven of the nine points of Figure 8.3b. All we need to show is that the outcomes represented by the two dots without a star cannot occur. But one of the inadmissible points represents settings such as $AB, BC$ with $A = C$. But, if all *transitive* voters in the oligarchy have $AB, BC$ preferences, then they also have $AC$ preferences. Thus, these two points are avoided.

The argument showing why only an oligarchy suffices with these conditions differs only slightly from the above proof. A complete technical argument involves using the "moving" argument to find minimal sets of voters. These are the smallest subsets of voters for each pair whereby when they are in agreement about a strict ranking, then that is the societal ranking. The goal is to find what are the societal rankings when these voters change preferences, and that the same group decides for each pair.

While I omit technical details (which are similar to the above), the essence of the proof is the rectangle argument. Again, we just need to show that having different groups decide over different pairs forces the societal outcome to land on a forbidden dot.

If $\{Bob, Carl\}$ decide the $\{A, B\}$ ranking while David decides the $\{B, C\}$ outcome, where both strict outcomes can occur for either pair, then mimic the proof of Arrow's theorem to find settings where the societal outcome is a cycle. (Just have Bob and Carl move in the same way Mikko moved; have David move as Tyler did.) Indeed, *when disjoint groups can decide over different pairs and the outcomes can be strict, then societal cycles can arise.*

Now suppose that not all voters from these groups are in all of the groups. The goal is to show that a forbidden societal outcome of the $BA, AC$, but $B = C$ type can arise. To indicate the approach, suppose $\{Bob, Carl\}$ and $\{Carl, David\}$ determine, respectively, the $\{A, B\}$ and $\{B, C\}$ outcomes and all voters have the same $AC$ ranking. (By Pareto, this common $AC$ preference is the societal outcome.) Suppose Bob and Carl share the same $BA$ opinion — forcing the societal $BA$ outcome.

Transitivity of voter preferences and the above assumptions peg Bob's and Carl's preferences as $BAC$. David's preferences, however, remain free to be selected. So, should David prefer $CB$, his $\{B, C\}$ conflict with Carl forces the forbidden $B = C$ societal outcome.

While the sketch of a proof uses Pareto (to ensure the societal outcome agrees with the voters' opinions), this is not necessary. As with the earlier extensions of Arrow's result, all we need is that the voters' beliefs about a pair determine that pair's societal outcome. Even this condition can be relaxed to allow the societal outcome of each pair to be determined by the voters' opinions about *certain* specified pairs — not necessarily the same ones. As long as the admissible outcomes are quasi-transitive rankings, some select group determines the societal rankings. Again, as with Sen's and Arrow's theorems, the geometry of the cube and its "edges" show why binary independence allows irrational voters in this setting.

Hopefully, the reader is curious about what happens if the admissible societal outcomes include all points except the two cyclic ones. As this extension allows even more rectangles to be drawn, we must anticipate more procedures to emerge. They do; now an assigned group decides a pair's societal ranking. If everyone agrees, that is the societal ranking. If they disagree, a societal tie occurs. The membership of these groups can differ with the pairs. To avoid cycles, at least one person must belong to all groups. The reader may wish to experiment with the geometry to discover other conclusions.

# Bibliography

[1] Anscombe, G.E.M., On the frustration of the majority by fulfillment of the majority's will, *Analysis* **36** (1976), 161-168.

[2] Arrow, K.J. *Social Choice and Individual Values*, 2nd ed., Wiley, New York, 1963.

[3] Austen-Smith, D., Restricted Pareto and rights, *Journal of Economic Theory*, **26** (1982), 89-99

[4] Axelrod, R., *The Evolution of Cooperation*, Basic Books, 1984.

[5] Balinski, M., and H.P. Young (1975) *Amer. Math. Monthly* **82** (1975), 701-730.

[6] Balinski, M., and H.P. Young, *Fair Representation*, Yale University Press, New Haven, 1982.

[7] Blackorby, C., D. Donaldson, and J. Weymark, A welfarist proof of Arrow's Theorem, *Recherches Économiques de Louvain* **54** (1990), 259-286.

[8] Black, D., *The Theory of Committees and Elections*, Cambridge University Press, London, 1958.

[9] Bliss, G., Brown, E.W., Eisenhart, L.P, and Pearl, R. (1929) *Report to the President of the Nat. Acad. Sci.*

[10] Blyth, C., On Simpson' paradox and the sure-thing principle, *Jour. American Stat. Association* **67** (1972), 364-366.

[11] Borda, J.C., *Mémoire sur les élections au scrutin.* Histoire de l'Académie Royale des Sciences, Paris, 1781.

[12] Brams, S., D. Kilgour, and W. Zwicker, The paradox of multiple elections, *Social Choice & Welfare* **15** (1998), 211-236.

[13] Brams, S., and A. D. Taylor, *The Win-Win Solution: Guaranteeing Fair Shares to Everybody,* W. W. Norton, New York, 1999.

[14] Brunel, A., *Contribution à lánalyse des droits en théorie du choix social,* Ph.D. Thesis, Université de Caen, December, 1998.

[15] Brunel, A., and D. G. Saari, *Sen's theorem revisited,* NU and Université de Caen preprints, 1998.

[16] Brunel, A., and M. Salles, Interpretative, semantic and formal difficulties of the social choice approach to rights, pp 101-111 in *Freedom in Economics: New Perspectives in Normative Analysis,* ed. Laslier, J.F., Fleurbaey, M., Gravel, N., and Trannoy, A., Routledge, London, 1998.

[17] Chipman, J., and J. Moore, Compensating variation, consumer surplus, and welfare, *American Economic Review* **70** (1980), 933-949.

[18] Chipman, J., and J. Moore, The scope of the consumer's surplus argument, In *Evolution, Welfare and Time in Economics: Essays in Honor of Nicholas Georgescu-Roegen,* ed., A. Tang, F. Westfield, and J. Worley, D.C. Heath, Lexington, MA, 1976.

[19] Chipman, J., and J. Moore, Acceptable indicators of welfare change, In *Preferences, Uncertainty, & Optimality,* ed., Chipman, J., D. McFadden, C.M. Richter, Westview Press, San Francisco, 1990.

[20] Condorcet, M., *Éssai sur l'application de l'analyse à la probabilité des décisions rendues à la pluralité des voix.* Paris, 1785.

[21] Debreu, G., *Theory of Value,* Yale University Press, 1959.

[22] Debreu, G., Excess demand functions, *Journal of Mathematical Economics* **1** (1974), 15-21.

[23] Gibbard, A., Manipulation of Voting Schemes: a general result, *Econometrica* **41** (1973), 587-601.

[24] Gibbard, A., A Pareto-Consistent Libertarian Claim, *Journal of Economic Theory* **7** (1974), 388-410.

[25] Gibbard, A., A. Hylland, and J. Weymark, Arrow's Theorem with a fixed feasible alternative, *Social Choice & Welfare* **46** (1988), 291-308.

[26] Haunsperger, D., Dictionaries of paradoxes for statistical tests on $k$-samples, *Jour. Amer. Statistical Assoc.* **87** (1992), 249-272.

[27] Haunsperger, D., and D. G. Saari, The lack of consistency for statistical decision procedures, *American Statistician* **45** (1991), 252-255.

[28] Hazelrigg, G., Lies, damned lies, and questionnaires, *Prism*, Feb. 1999, p. 14 (Also, see Hazelrigg's example which the editors titled "Voodoo Mathematics at Work.")

[29] Huntington, E., The mathematical theory of the apportionment of representatives, *Proceedings of the National Academy of Sciences* **7** (1921), 123-127.

[30] Huntington, E., The apportionment of representatives in Congress, *Trans. American Math Society* **30** (1928), 85-110.

[31] Kalai, E., and E. Muller, Characterization of domains admitting nondictatorial social welfare functions and nonmanipulable voting procedures, *Journal of Economic Theory* **16** (1977), 457-469.

[32] Kalai, E., and Z. Ritz, Characterizations of the private alternatives domains admitting Arrow social welfare functions, *Journal of Economic Theory* **22** (1980), 22-36.

[33] Kelly, J., *Arrow Impossibility Theorems*, Academic Press, New York, 1978.

[34] Le Breton, M., and M. Salles, The stability of voting games, *International Journal of Game Theory* **19** 1990.

[35] Luce, R. D., *Individual Choice Behavior*, Greenwood, New York, 1959.

[36] Mantel, R., On the characterization of aggregate excess demand, *Journal of Economic Theory* **7** (1974), 348-353.

[37] Nurmi, H., *Voting Paradoxes and How to Deal with Them*, Springer-Verlag, NY, 1999.

[38] Merlin, V. and D. G. Saari, Copeland method II: manipulation, monotonicity, and paradoxes, *Journal of Economic Theory* **72** (1997), 148-172.

[39] McKelvey, R., General conditions for global intranstitivies in formal voting models, *Econometrica* **47** (1979), 1085-1112.

[40] McLean, I., The first golden age of social choice, 1783-1803, in *Social Choice, Welfare, and Ethics,* ed. Barnett, W., Moulin, H., Salles, M., and N. Schofield, Cambridge University Press, 1995.

[41] McLean, I., and F. Hewitt, *Condorcet: Foundations of Social Choice and Political Theory* Edward Elgar, 1994.

[42] Nakamura, K., The core of a simple game with ordinal preferences, *International Journal of Game Theory* **4**, 95-104.

[43] Nanson, E.J., Methods of election, *Trans Proc Roy Society Victoria* **18** (1882), 197-240.

[44] Narens, L., and D. Luce, How we may have been misled into believing in the interpersonal comparability of utility, *Theory and Decision* **15** (1983), 247-260.

[45] Osborne, G. E., *Handbook on the Law of Morgages,* West Publishing Co., St. Paul, Minn., 1951.

[46] Ostrogorski, M., *Democracy and the Organization of Political Parties,* Vol. I, II, Haskell House, New York, 1970.

[47] Poundstone, W., *Prisoner's Dilemma: John von Neumann, Game Theory, and the Puzzle of the Bomb,* Doubleday, 1992.

[48] Saari, D. G. Methods of apportionment and the House of Representatives, *American Mathematical Monthly* **85** (1978), 792-802.

[49] Saari, D. G. The source of some paradoxes from social choice and statistics, *Jour. Econ. Theory* **41** (1987), 1–22.

[50] Saari, D. G., A dictionary for voting paradoxes, *Journal of Economic Theory* **48** (1989), 443-475.

[51] Saari, D. G., Calculus and extensions of Arrow's Theorem, *Journal of Mathematical Economics* **20** (1991), 271-306.

[52] Saari, D. G., Doing the right thing, *Framtider* **2** (1992), 44-50.

[53] Saari, D. G., Millions of election rankings from a single profile, *Soc. Choice & Welfare* **9** (1992), 277-306.

[54] Saari, D. G., Inner consistency or not inner consistency, pp 187-212 in *Social Choice, Welfare, and Ethics*, ed. Barnett, W., Moulin, H., Salles, M., and N. Schofield, Cambridge University Press, Cambridge, 1995.

[55] Saari, D. G., The aggregate excess demand function and other aggregation procedures. *Economic Theory* **2** (1992), 359-388.

[56] Saari, D. G., *Geometry of Voting*, Springer-Verlag, New York, 1994.

[57] Saari, D. G., *Basic Geometry of Voting*, Springer-Verlag, New York, 1995.

[58] Saari, D. G., A chaotic exploration of aggregation paradoxes, *SIAM Review* **37** (1995), 37-52.

[59] Saari, D. G., The mathematical complexity of simple economics, *Notices of the American Mathematical Society* **42** (1995), No. 2: 222-230.

[60] Saari, D. G., The generic existence of a core for q-rules, *Economic Theory* **9** (1997), 219-260.

[61] Saari, D. G., Are individual rights possible? *Mathematics Magazine* **70** (1997), 83-92.

[62] Saari, D. G., Connecting and resolving Sen's and Arrow's Theorems, *Social Choice & Welfare* **15** (1998), 239-261.

[63] Saari, D. G., Explaining all three-alternative voting outcomes, *Journal of Economic Theory* **87** (1999), 313-335.

[64] Saari, D. G., More chaos, but in voting and apportionments? *Procecdings of the National Academy of Sciences* **96** (Sept. 14, 1999), 10568-10571.

[65] Saari, D. G., Do we model the correct market information? pp. 83-108 in *The Theory of Markets*, ed. P.J.J. Herings, A.J.J. Talman, G. van der Lann, North Holland, Amsterdam, 1999

[66] Saari, D. G., Mathematical structure of voting paradoxes I: pairwise vote, *Economic Theory* **15** (2000), 1-53.

[67] Saari, D. G., Mathematical structure of voting paradoxes II: positional voting, *Economic Theory* **15** (2000), 55-101.

[68] Saari, D. G., Bad decisions; experimental error or faulty decision procedures? Northwestern University preprint, Jan. 2000

[69] Saari, D. G., Suppose you want to vote strategically, *Math Horizons* (Nov. 2000), 5-10.

[70] Saari, D. G., *Chaotic Elections! A Mathematician Looks at Voting*, American Mathematical Society, Providence, RI, 2001.

[71] Saari, D. G., and F. Valognes, The geometry of Black's single peakedness and related conditions. *Journal of Mathematical Economics* **32** (1999), 429-456.

[72] Saari, D. G., and K. K. Sieberg, The sum of the parts can violate the whole, Northwestern University Preprint, December, 1999.

[73] Saari, D. G., and V. Merlin, Changes that cause changes, *Social Choice & Welfare*, August 2000

[74] Saari, D. G., and Katri K. Sieberg, Some surprising properties of power indices, *Games and Economic Behavior*, 2001.

[75] Salles, M., Rights, permission, obligation, in *Social Choice Re-examined*, ed. K. Arrow, A. Sen, K. Suzumura, Macmillan, London, 1997.

[76] Satterthwaite, M., Strategyproofness and Arrow's conditions, *Journal of Economic Theory* **10** (1975), 187-217.

[77] Scarf, H., Some examples of global instability of the competitive equilibrium, *International Economic Review* **1** (1960), 157-172.

[78] Sen, A., *Collective Choice and Social Welfare* Holden-Day, San Francisco, 1970.

[79] Sen, Λ., The impossibility of a paretian liberal, *Jour. of Political Economy* **78** (1970), 152-157.

[80] Sen, A., A possibility theorem on majority decisions, *Econometrica* **34** (1966), 491-499.

[81] Sieberg, K., *Criminal Dilemmas*, Springer-Verlag, New York, 2001.

[82] Simpson, E.H., The interpretation of interaction in contingency tables, *Jour. of the Royal Statistical Society,* Series B, **13** (1951), 238-241.

[83] Sonnenschein, H. "Market excess demand functions." *Econometrica* **40** (1972), 649-663.

[84] Sonnenschein, H., Do Walras identity and continuity characerize the class of community excess demand functions? *Journal of Economic Theory* **6** (1973), 345-354.

[85] Tyree, A. L., Circular priorities in secured transactions, *American Mathematical Monthly* **87** (1980), 186-193.

[86] Wilson, R., Social choice theory without the Pareto principle, *Journal of Economic Theory* **5** (1972), 478-486.

# Index